KU-624-665

LIVERPOOL JMU LIBRARY

3 1111 01496 6863

TABLE OF CONTENTS

Chapter Three: The Fearsome Seas: Fact and Fiction

Chapter Four: Maritime Historiographies

Chapter Five: From Representation to Reality

ACKNOWLEDGEMENTS

To the Caribbean Chapter of the College English Association, for funding and supporting our endeavours. We are also grateful to the University of Puerto Rico Sea Grant, for supporting the first edition of this book and the conference on which it was based.

To our respective institutions: to the University of California-Riverside for providing Vartan Messier with library materials and the opportunity to conduct independent research, and to the University of Puerto Rico-Mayagüez for granting Nandita Batra released time to complete the project.

Our thanks to Adhip Barua, Monisha Mullick, Pria Chatterjee and especially to Ruth and Vickram Crishna for their detective work in unravelling the puzzle of the altered Bombay skyline.

We greatly appreciate the kind help and support provided by José Jiménez and Stéphane Pillet in producing and promoting our projects.

Last but by no means least: to Pablo Bartholomew and Peggy Hinaekian for their generosity in permitting us to use their photographs and paintings, we owe an immense debt of gratitude.

—Vartan P. Messier and Nandita Batra

INTRODUCTION

THE MULTITUDINOUS SEAS: MATTER AND METAPHOR

NANDITA BATRA AND VARTAN P. MESSIER

> Will all great Neptune's ocean wash this blood
> Clean from my hand? No, this my hand will rather
> The multitudinous seas incarnadine,
> Making the green one red.
> —*Macbeth* II.ii.

> She sang beyond the genius of the sea.
> The water never formed to mind or voice,
> Like a body wholly body, fluttering
> Its empty sleeves; and yet its mimic motion
> Made constant cry, caused constantly a cry,
> That was not ours although we understood,
> Inhuman, of the veritable ocean.
> —Wallace Stevens, "The Idea of Order at Key West"

The sea has been part of our world for almost 4 billion years, for far longer than the human mind. That its reality precedes its representation is a given. Yet it also seems a given to say that our watery world exists in our minds as well as in matter, in fiction as well as in fact. Nevertheless, a sharp and persistent Cartesian opposition turns these apparent truisms into a bone of contention and diminishes the multiplicity of the bonds that humans have with the sea—metaphoric as well as material, representational as well as real.

In the social sciences, the dominant debate about our views of nature today is also the dominant debate about the sea: between those who emphasize the material issues of nature and the environment (known as the "realists") and those who emphasize the need to examine the social construction and origin of these issues (the "constructionists"). As Peter Dickens noted, "insofar as academia is capable of having a stand-up row, it is over this issue" (72). The realists accuse the constructionists of ignoring the "'reality' and independent existence of nature" (Burningham and Cooper 297) while the constructionists argue that the values of nature *are* constructed socially and cannot be taken as absolutes. In his book *The Social Construction of the Ocean*, Philip E. Steinberg notes that the "uses, regulations, and representations" of the sea by humans depend on the ways in which we have constructed it (i), delineating that "Three perspectives form the basis for most studies of human-marine interactions: the ocean as resource provider, the ocean as transport surface, and the ocean as battleground or 'force-field'" (11).

To begin with the so-called 'real' world, the world of matter: the sea, as any compendium of facts will tell us, was formed close to 4 billion years ago as a result of the escape of hydrogen from the earth's surface. Combining with oxygen, the hydrogen became rain, which filled all low-lying parts of the earth and now covers 71 % of its surface. Home to most plant and animal life on earth, it has been reputed to be the source of all life including human, but is nonetheless constructed as the "terra infirma" in opposition to the "terra firma" of land which humans made their home, with even the names of most oceans and seas of the world following those of their adjacent continents of land.

In contrast to this imposing array of physical detail, water and the sea are often connotative of nothingness. As W.H. Auden notes, "The sea, or the great waters, are a symbol for the primal undifferentiated flux, the substance which became created nature only by having form imposed upon or wedded to it" (6).[1] This motif—of life emerging out of the nothingness of water—appears in numerous cosmogonies. For instance, the Koran links the source of all life to water: "We made from water every living thing" (The Prophets, Sura XXI, verse 30); "And God has created every animal from water" (Light, Sura XXIV, verse 45). In Genesis, the earth has no form until the spirit or breath of God moves on the waters and sets into motion the divine creation of life over the next six days: "In the beginning God created the heaven and the earth./ And the earth was without form, and void; and darkness *was* upon the face of the deep. And the Spirit of God moved upon the face of the waters" (Genesis 1:2). The

---

[1] Auden's observation, from his book *The Enchafèd Flood: or, The Romantic Iconography of the Sea*, is based on his reading of Judeo-Christian and Hellenic cosmogonies.

Song of Creation in the Hindu Rig-Veda describes a primordial ocean of chaos before time:

> Then there was neither Aught nor Nought, no air nor sky beyond.
> What covered all? Where rested all? In watery gulf profound?
> Nor death was then, nor deathlessness, nor change of night and day.
> That One breathed calmly, self-sustained; nought else beyond it lay.

> Gloom hid in gloom existed first - one sea, eluding view.
> That One, a void in chaos wrapt, by inward fervour grew.
> Within it first arose desire, the primal germ of mind,
> Which nothing with existence links, as sages searching find.

> (Book 10 Hymn 129)

The Satapatha Brahmana repeats this motif when it describes life emerging from a cosmic egg that rose from the primordial ocean, which existed before the earth, air, sky—or even the gods—came into being:

> Verily, in the beginning this [universe] was water, nothing but a sea of water. The waters desired, "how can we be reproduced?" They toiled and performed fervid devotions [or, and became heated]; when they were becoming heated, a golden egg was produced. The year, indeed, was not then in existence; this golden egg floated about for as long as the space of a year. In a year's time a man, this Prajāpati, was produced therefrom. . . .He broke open this golden egg. There was then, indeed, no resting place, only this golden egg. At the end of a year he tried to speak. He said "bhuh"; this [word] became this earth—"bhuvah": this became the air—"svah": this became yonder sky. (XI.1.6.1-3.)

In Hellenic cosmogony, however, it is not the first Man but the goddess Aphrodite who is born from the sea, or more specifically, from sea-foam. Hesiod's *Theogony* describes Kronos' castration of his father Ouranus, whose severed genitals were thrown into the sea, becoming foam from which a female figure was formed. Passing the island of Kytherea, she then reached Cyprus where she emerged as Aphrodite on dry shores:

> And so soon as he had cut off the members with flint and cast them from the land into the surging sea, they were swept away over the main a long time: and a white foam spread around them from the immortal flesh, and in it there grew a maiden. First she drew near holy Cythera, and from there, afterwards, she came to sea-girt Cyprus, and came forth an awful and lovely goddess, and grass grew up about her beneath her shapely feet. Her gods and men call Aphrodite, and the foam-born goddess and rich-crowned Cytherea, because she grew amid the foam, and Cytherea because she reached Cythera, and Cyprogenes because she was born in billowy Cyprus.

In spite of his well-known aversion to religion, even Freud associated a feeling of eternity with the wet element, labelling it "the oceanic feeling," a term he derived from a letter from his friend Romain Rolland, which he summarized thus in *Civilization and Its Discontents*: "It is a feeling which he [Rolland] would like to call a sensation of 'eternity,' a feeling as of something limitless, unbounded—as it were, 'oceanic'" (11). Yet while Romain Rolland had placed this oceanic feeling in entirely a mystical sense, ultimately for Freud our connection with the universe around us could be traced back to our own ego (12). Even for an empirical scientist like Charles Lyell, the sea held a symbolic value. Noting that Lyell's view of evolution "leaves us with a vision of unending, cyclical change that leads to the disappearance, but not to the evolution, of species and cultures" (379), Lawrence Frank draws attention to Lyell's affinity with Byron's description of the eternity of the sea.[2]

Small wonder then that Roland Barthes claimed that the sea "bears no message," not merely because of its power to reflect rather than contain a gamut of different meanings but because of its seeming absence of evidence. In his discussion of semiology as a science that examines the messages contained in the signs shaping our socio-cultural landscape, he finds the sea to be void of a signifying field.

> In a single day, how many really non-signifying fields do we cross? Very few, sometimes none. Here I am before the sea; it is true that it bears no message. But on the beach, what material for semiology! Flags, slogans, signals, sign-boards, clothes, suntan even, which are so many messages for me! (*Mythologies* 112, fn2)

Barthes seems to suggest that the sea denotes nothingness not only because it seems a reflection of the individual psyche but because it bears no material manifestation of human passage or cultural history in contrast to the land, which seems to bear much more evidence of human actions.

The apparent signlessness of the sea notwithstanding, water for Gaston Bachelard is equated with introspection, not merely as metaphor but materially as well: it is "substantive nothingness." The matter of water is the same matter from which dreams and reveries are derived, and thus to meditate on water becomes a meditation on the self as in a mirror. But it

---

[2]   "Unchangeable, save to thy wild waves' play:
        Time writes no wrinkle on thine azure brow,
        Such as creation's dawn beheld, thou rollest now."
        —Byron, *Childe Harold*, Canto IV.

is the depth of the mirror that draws in the viewer, like Narcissus, to gaze upon and into oneself, seeing terror as well as transcendence. And so it seems that to some extent the sea's reflection of our own sense of being is echoed in Jacques Lacan's second consideration of his "mirror stage" as that which institutes a libidinal relationship with our own image. In this purely constructionist view, the sea does not have its own distinct ontology; it is rather a reflection of our own, its existential relevance bound to human experience.

While the land/water opposition was taken up by Barthes as we have seen earlier, Bachelard extends the antithetical relationship not merely to that between water and land, but to fresh water/sea water as well. Bachelard distinguishes between the human response to fresh water and sea water: "La mer donne des contes avant de donner des rêves" (206) [the sea generates stories before generating dreams (translation ours)], noting that the first experience of the sea is in the shape of a story: "la première expérience de la mer est de l'ordre du *récit*" (emphasis his, 206). Bachelard's observation suggests that the timelessness and signlessness that humans have seen in the sea have produced the desire to order and temporize it, and thus to establish a sense of order and sequence. In an extended sense, he sees this desire borne out of the ways in which our understanding of human existence is mediated by narrative as it systemizes and orders our experiences of the world both spatially and temporally.

Juxtaposed against the sea's vast cultural void, the advent of seafaring produced not only new territories but an entire culture, claimed Michel Foucault, one exemplified by "heterotopia," which "juxtapos[e] in a single real place several spaces, several sites that are themselves incompatible." Heterotopias are not utopias but "real emplacements" that "simultaneously represent, contest and reverse...all the other real emplacements in their environment," and for him "the ship is the heterotopia par excellence" (178-81). Meanwhile, W.H Auden suggests that domination of the sea marks not merely the beginning of biological life but the beginning of civilization, observing that "the sea, in fact, is that state of barbaric vagueness and disorder out of which civilization emerged" (6). Domination of the sea thus encapsulates the ordering of nature by humans and, as Philip de Souza points out, was "crucial to both the best and the worst aspects of civilisation" (cover blurb). Although the first boats were probably created for rivers and lakes rather than for the sea (de Souza 7), seafaring has produced the world as we now know it through the "discovery and exploitation of new territories, new peoples and new ideas," which led the way to the expansion of the world's history, its cultures and religions, and to economic globalization as we now have it. In addition, as Bernhard Klein has shown, it is the early modern era that produced "permanent maritime links and trade routes across vast oceanic spaces" in contrast to earlier "great seafaring empires" (such as the Roman, Carthaginian, Viking and Ming), which lacked the "technical means" to effect a permanent expansion of their borders on other shores. In contrast, the history-making voyages of Vasco da Gama, Magellan and Columbus, among others, paved the way for imperialism. Klein therefore places the imperial project of the sixteenth century as marking the "true beginning of globalisation" (Klein, "Historicizing"). Nevertheless while these fifteenth- and sixteenth-century oceanic voyages might have changed history, the most famous theoretic argument for the Free Sea was produced in the early years of the seventeenth century in Hugo Grotius' 1604 *Mare Liberum* (or Freedom of the Sea), which argued (on behalf of the Dutch East India Company) for freedom of not only the oceans and coastal waters but of seafaring, trade and fishing on the grounds that the law of the land (private property) could not be applied to the boundless sea. Initially, it was opposed by the British: John Selden's 1635 *Mare Clausum* argued that the sea *could* indeed be possessed. Eventually *Mare Liberum* was superceded by Cornelius Bunkeshoek's *De domino maris* (1702), which set cannon range as the limit of maritime control and was eventually adopted at the 'three-mile limit.'

The tension between this human imposition of a limit on the apparent limitlessness of the sea echoes the idea mentioned above of the human desire to order the sea along spatio-temporal coordinates and hence, for Hegel, ocean-going activated Western history. The geographical opportunity for ocean exploration was the condition of possibility for Western Europe's entry into world history:

> The sea gives us the idea of the indefinite, the unlimited, and the infinite; and in feeling his own infinite in that Infinite, man is stimulated and emboldened to stretch beyond the limited: the sea invites man to conquest, and to piratical plunder, but also to honest gain and to commerce. The land, the mere valley-plain attaches him to the soil; it involves him in an infinite multitude of dependencies, but the sea carries him out beyond these limited circles of thought and action. (90)

Without a doubt, the broader human outlook on the sea seems to have changed in the past few centuries with the advent of seafaring technology that permitted long-range exploration, commerce, conquest, and colonization, particularly by Western European and Euro-American civilizations.[3] This change of attitude runs parallel to historical shifts in the cultural trends of the so-called "old continent" and the coming of age of "humanism"; Enlightenment ideas transformed European society and in the modern era the development of empiricism in the sciences was perceived as a means to attain absolute knowledge about what constitutes human existence. In parallel, dominion of the sea was asserted by similar advances in the field of technology and the increased opportunity for transoceanic voyages, which in turn gave way to a reconsideration of the relationship between humans and the sea. This reconsideration towards the sea has been attributed to largely material causes by Alain Corbin in his informative book *The Lure of the Sea: The Discovery of the Seaside in the Western World 1750-1840*. Once considered a sinister, threatening power that was home to monsters, the sea has shifted its cultural signification in the West since the eighteenth century. He shows how attitudes to the sea altered with the Enlightenment and concurrent changes in art and literature, so that bathing in the sea became viewed as therapeutic and regenerative rather than unhealthy. This change became reflected at all levels, from the political in the exploration that resulted from an increased interest in travel, to the economic in the rise of sea towns, and to the cultural level in artistic and literary production.

It is therefore not hard to see why sea voyage literature reached its apogee in European and American literature in the nineteenth century. In fact, according to Margaret Cohen, maritime fiction (also known as "nautical fiction" or "*le roman maritime*") was crucial to the cultural construction of nation-building. Positing that "it was invented by James Fenimore Cooper with *The Pilot*" (1823), she draws attention to the ways in which "Cooper took the codes of historical fiction, pioneered by Walter Scott, to map the boundaries and identity of the nation, and translated them to the supranational space of the open sea" (483). In a wider cultural context, sea crossing encapsulates not merely the construction of national and cultural identity but their dissolution as well. The infamous Middle Passage from Africa to the New World and the *jahaji bhai* or "ship brotherhood" of the caste-prohibited "Kala Pani" (literally "Black Water") sea-crossing that transported indentured workers from India to South Africa and to the Caribbean are illustrations of this dissolution.

---

[3] Hegel distinguishes between colonization and conquest with regard to the ways in which Western Europeans settled in the so-called "New World"; "A wider distinction is presented in the fact that South America was conquered; but North America colonized" (84).

This brief attempt to retrace an archaeology of marine discourse—albeit its emphasis on the *"petits récits"* rather than the "grand narrative"—seems to reinforce a constructionist view of this watery world, a view that raises several questions. If the sea is, then, a construction, how has it been constructed? If it is valued so ubiquitously as a cleansing and purifying agent, why have humans wreaked such havoc on what was and perhaps still is considered the source of life? Perhaps, as Kimberley Patton has noted, it is the notion of the sea as infinity that has led to its pollution. Contemporary ecological perspectives might be an indication that we still view the human relationship with the sea as one of dominance, but that our view has shifted from Human as Dominator of the sea to Human as Steward of the Sea.[4] This recognition has nonetheless come at a price. While civilization has often been seen as the process of dominating the sea and other forces of nature, recent natural disasters—such as Hurricane Katrina in 2005 and the Asian Tsunami of 2004—have reminded us that our domination of the sea is, at best, fragile, at worst, illusionary.

The frontispiece photograph, "Bombay and the Sea" by Pablo Bartholomew, depicts the skyline of Bandra Seaface, Bombay's most upmarket suburb, framed by a stormy monsoon sea and sky. Situated on the Arabian Sea, which was a thriving commercial hub prior to the arrival of the Europeans, Bombay was composed of an archipelago of seven swampy islands inhabited by Koli fishermen whose goddess, Mumbadevi, is the origin of the city's present name, "Mumbai." Named *Bom bahia* (or "Good Bay") by the Portuguese, who appropriated it in the early 16th century, it then passed on to the British as part of Catherine of Braganza's dowry upon her marriage to Charles II. Upon being leased to the British East India Company, it became the first port in British India and a thriving maritime hub that lured many commercial interests. For many Westerners besides Whitman, the 1869 opening of the Suez Canal was indeed a "Passage to India." Bombay owes its best and worst assets to the sea. The areas separating the various islands have since been reclaimed, with long stretches of the seawall retained by concrete tetrapods. Officially renamed

---

[4] This shift in perspective has striking resonances with the predication of a Judeo-Christian Ecology by scholars such as J. Patrick Dobel. While many ecocritics blame the Judeo-Christian tradition for the ecological crisis by pointing to passages from Genesis as justifying human attitudes of domination, contempt, and disregard vis-à-vis nature, Dobel responds by referring to scriptures in both the Old and New Testaments that insist on an ecological ethic of stewardship, respect, and conservation of the earth's resources for future generations.

"Mumbai" in 1995 as a rejection of its colonially given name, the city has become a vast globalized metropolis of over 15 million, whose population continues to grow by the hundreds each week, leading not only to the destruction of greenery and mangroves that protected the island from flooding and tidal waves, but destroying the livelihood of local fishermen as well. Bartholomew's photograph highlights the fragility of the balance between Nature and "civilization" with dark monsoon clouds hanging ominously over the sea and the skyline of the city, which is constantly prone to flooding.[5] The Danda fishing village has been obscured by high-rise apartment buildings and luxury hotels, which are in turn dwarfed by the tallest feature of the skyline, the 985-foot Doordarshan television tower in Worli. The tallest structure in India (at present), it appears diminutive against the repressive density of the dark clouds and surging turbulent sea closing in on the cityscape. And so, in this representation of urbanization as a mark of the human impulse to control space, the menacing appearance of the sky and sea evoke a potential return to chaos and undermine the idea of Man as the dominator of nature.

§

This collection of essays is based on a conference of the same name and hopes to combine both the material and the metaphoric views of the sea. It was located in Mayagüez, a town on the west coast of Puerto Rico that has drawn its material existence—the town was almost destroyed by a tsunami in 1918—as well as its historic and cultural impact from the sea: for a long time it drew its livelihood from the tuna-packing plants that are now defunct. The conference was organized by the Caribbean Chapter of the College English Association and partly funded by the Sea Grant foundation. It drew together papers from writers who have both material and metaphoric relations with the sea: activists, divers, environmentalists and humanistic scholars. This collection is inspired by that conference, and more fully represents the topic by including essays by marine biologists and images by artists, photographers, and biologists.

The first chapter "The Sea as Metaphor" addresses our earlier observation that the sea has been seen as a symbol of chaos, flux, and alienation. Foucault associated rationality with the land and not the sea, a topic explored in Ian Copestake's paper, which, drawing attention to the fact that "water and madness have long been linked in the dreams of

---

[5] The most disastrous recorded incident of flooding in Mumbai occurred on 26 July 2005, with over 37 inches of rainfall (more than double the amount that fell over New Orleans during Hurricane Katrina a few weeks later).

European man," proceeds to trace "some of the reasons why this association between water and dejected mental states, in particular melancholia, has been especially prevalent in the American literary imagination." In the next essay, David Prescott-Steed examines some of the metaphors that the sea has produced, particularly those that have arisen from its unknowable quality. He traces the attribution of monstrosity of the deep sea and its creatures to its quality of being unknown. Thus the abyss has become a "culturally constructed metaphor for the seemingly unfathomable, the indistinguishable, the unknown." He analyses *The Abyss*, a BBC television series filmed around North America, and points out that "the efforts of the divers...demonstrate their attempts to socialise the abyss, to fathom its seeming endlessness, knowing full well that it must have an end and that it may only be a matter of time before humankind can achieve it." Using evocative visuals during her presentation, Jeffner Allen focuses on marine representation through images in an essay that is part of a larger work called *Diving Planetarity*, which "moves between futural histories of land and reef on the limestone island of Bonaire, in the Netherlands Antilles." As she points out, "The water worlds of this small island, among the many ever so small islands bypassed or localized to the point of apparent insignificance in the rush to comprehend globalization and ecological crisis, elicit generations of resonance that effectively shift representation of humanity, sea, time and space."

The next chapter takes a closer look at oceanic encounters and the multiplicity of relationships between humans and the sea. In "Safely Ashore," Bruce Robinson examines the "ambivalent relationship" to water portrayed in the world of Marcel Pagnol's films. Focusing on Pagnol's Marseille trilogy—*Marius, Fanny*, and *César*—Robinson examines the trilogy particularly in terms of its "tidal interplay of attraction and repulsion: a landlocked group of characters who often feed off the sea, but are adamant about remaining on shore." Among the many ambivalent and shifting metaphoric associations with the sea is its gender. Frequently seen as a mighty mother, the sea is explicitly gendered by Luce Irigaray and Jules Michelet as feminine, while for Bachelard water is feminine but the sea is masculine. For Hemingway, however, the sea was masculine *and* feminine. Mary Beth Gallagher's essay notes this distinction, reminding the reader of the narrator's observation in *The Old Man and the Sea* that "those who use cold and calculating modern fishing advancements describe the sea as male calling it 'el mar' while those like Santiago who 'love her' call her 'la mar.'" She suggests that the "sea as a feminine being becomes an infinite source of possibility" because as the source of life, it could also be the source of "mutation" and therefore new life.   Hence, the appropriateness of the sea as a background for Hemingway's short story "Sea Change" in which the hitherto heterosexual female protagonist decides to begin a lesbian relationship.   Mark Ott raises the issue of ecology by exploring Hemingway's "evolving ecological perspective" vis-à-vis the Caribbean Gulf Stream frontier. From a "no man's land" in *To Have and Have Not* (1937) in which the Gulf Stream is a "contested space where violence settles disputes in the midst of an indifferent natural world" it evolves to "an aquatic Eden filled with the mysteries of life, a harmonious, organic whole in *The Old Man and the Sea* (1953).   To examine the "pervasiveness" of Tennyson in Melville's "poetic consciousness" Karen Lentz Madison posits that both Melville's *John Marr and Other Sailors* and Tennyson's *Enoch Arden* "utilize the language of isolation, with its recognition of both a sailor's need for interaction and dependency and the loneliness incurred by its absence." Madison goes on to argue that the influence of the latter on the former can be assessed if one takes a closer look at the background and philosophy that inform both texts.

In the following   chapter "The Fearsome Seas: Fact and Fiction," Kathryn Ferguson and Graham Benton analyze the ways in which sharks have been portrayed in popular culture and the media as the most feared of all aquatic creatures.   In her examination of shark documentaries vis-à-vis the "contemporaneous positioning" of documentary film, Kathryn Ferguson points out: "In thinking of 'the environment,' we too often neglect the vast submerged eco-systems that make up a huge portion of our world. This may be due in part to the fact that we tend to translate 'the environment' to 'our environment' which is, for the most part, limited to land; we are terrestrial creatures."   Her paper specifically examines Richard Fitzpatrick's documentary films about sharks, arguing that "rather than demonstrating how vulnerable humans are to sharks, we begin to see how vulnerable sharks, and concomitantly the ecologies of the underwater world, are to us." Continuing the analysis of shark films, Graham Benton proceeds to "reverse the poles of this binary to look not at the fiction-alization of the shark documentary but at the documentarianization of shark fiction." His essay examines *Jaws* and *Open Water* to suggest that the two shift between fact and fiction. As he puts it, "*Jaws* and *Open Water* oscillate between these two positions: they articulate our fears and instill terror precisely because they cannot so easily be interpreted, categorized, and finally de-fused. As divergent yet important variations on the shark tale, they are focal points on a screen that charts our anxiety about comprehending that which resides under the sea and our inability to fully capture that which lies beneath the surface of the text."

Several historians (such as Bernhard Klein and Gesa Mackenthun) have felt the need to defend the sea from the accusation that it is "history-less," claiming that the best defence comes from poet Derek Walcott, in his poem "The Sea is History": "Where are your monuments, your battles, martyrs? / Where is your tribal memory? Sirs,/ in that gray vault. The sea. The sea / has locked them up. The sea is History." In the first essay of the chapter "Maritime Historiographies: The Sea is History," Maeve Tynan examines this view of the history-filled sea as "medium for the passage operates as an interstitial site that both conjoins and separates colonizer and colonized." She sees the trope of the voyage encapsulating "the uprooting effect of Imperialism" particularly in the poetry of Derek Walcott. As she puts it, "Walcott's Odyssean travellers opt to voyage through history, a dynamic quest into the future that repudiates the past and grounds his poetics in the here and now." Tom Leskiw's paper also addresses the topic of untold history, by examining the mutualism between humans and sea creatures, and the ways in which natural and human histories have intertwined. As he points out, "long before recorded history, humans have observed the comings and goings of other animals." Noting that seas have been a "barrier to travel since time immemorial and crossing them has often entailed the crossing of a frontier," his essay examines the most isolated archipelago in the world—the Hawaiian islands—in order to show how Polynesian mariners' "intimacy with the sea" gave them the ability to use "subtle clues for navigation," clues provided by not only the colour, taste and patterns of the sea but by fish, plants and seabirds as well. He focuses especially on the mutualism between humans and the kolea, or Pacific golden-plover, to show how the sea-bird's migratory patterns served as a guide to Polynesian explorers. "Sea" birds exemplify a liminal status between land and sea. Breeding ashore (as Robert Madison reminds us) they are nevertheless generally encountered at a distance from the land. Madison's paper continues the examination of tropical sea birds, but those that straddle fact and fiction in Melville's imagination. This prompts Madison to demonstrate how knowledgeable the author of *Moby-Dick* was about natural history by retracing the genesis of his œuvre through the research of various renowned Melville scholars such as Mary K. Bercaw Edwards.

Most papers presented at the conference, as well as those included in this volume, have explored the representation of the sea, which, given the literary/cultural nature of the College English Association is not surprising.   Yet, in an attempt to address both the material and the metaphoric dimensions of the sea, the last chapter of the collection moves from "Representation to Reality." Jessica Behm's essay, "Mare Memoriae," examines the desire to find an aquatic source for human life that dominates not only imaginative responses to the sea but scientific discourse as well. In doing so, she discusses the philosophies of Aristotle and Bergson, as well as the glass artwork of contemporary Swedish artist Bertil Vallien to assert that "matter is always mediated by water." The next two essays turn specifically to the material sea, and in particular to the Caribbean, to examine the ways in which humans have attempted to restore the aquatic and coral environment that they have damaged. One, by marine biologists Sean Griffin and Michael Nemeth, suggests long-term plans for Natural Resource agencies.   The other, by activist Steve Tamar, recounts the creation of a Marine Reserve at the grassroots level. Griffin and Nemeth examine the ways in which "Natural resource agencies respond to ship groundings on coral reefs in order to assess damages, take emergency action to mitigate impacts and provide for restoration to avoid the loss of natural resources." They recommend a "careful, systematic assessment and documentation of the injury along with a detailed restoration plan" that is "based on an understanding of how the ecological processes on a coral reef influence the recovery of the system to insure an effective restoration of the community." Tamar describes the creation of a Marine Reserve at Tres Palmas Beach in Rincón, Puerto Rico, the venture, in response to a petition drive, evolving into a collaborative non-hierarchically organized project initiated by the Surfrider Foundation in tandem with Natural Resource and Government agencies.

§

These last two essays have focused on the material rather than the metaphoric sea, with both essays outlining the ways in which human domination of the sea has taken the form of abuse by disregarding its fragile yet essential ecosystem. While they differ in the steps that they propose, both are an illustration of a shift in the nature of the relationship between humans and the sea noted earlier: from humans as colonizers/abusers of the sea to humans as stewards/preservers of the sea. This shift is associated with the changing ways in which we humans have come to understand our individual being as well as the collective existential condition that we share with others of the same planet. Such is the paradigm shift initiated by the post-war interdisciplinary discourses in cultural studies, critical theory, and continental philosophy. To understand these implications, it seems relevant for us to retrace the cultural discourse that has mapped the ways in which the modern paradigm advocated the separation between humans and nature before we outline some of the epistemological and ontological currents of thought that have enabled this paradigm shift.

In his seminal book *The Order of Things*, Foucault lays the foundation for a critique of modernity, which was later expanded in his subsequent works, by tracing the cultural conditions of knowledge that gave birth to the human sciences making "Man" an exclusive subject of study and empirical enquiry at the beginning of the eighteenth century as a historically determined being.   Situating the separation of words/signs from the things they represented at the end of the sixteenth century, he outlines the ways in which the progression of the emerging scientific/empirical endeavour to identify, name, distinguish, list and classify things, according to specific criteria which defined them, drew out distinct categories of beings and living species, subjects and objects. Whereas the human sciences studied Man in his living, labouring, and speaking capacities, "human nature" and "nature" were configured as complementary yet oppositional functions, and in the order of things, humans were placed at the top of the hierarchy, "*à la place du roi*." Under these conditions of knowledge—conditions that Foucault dubs the "modern *epistémè*"—one is able to comprehend the attitude of humans towards others; by carefully mapping out the constitutions of beings and things with the tools that were made available by a scientific or empiric body of knowledge, humans assumed a certain type of proprietorship, which in turn allowed them to use and abuse other beings and things for their own purposes.   And so Foucault proposes that it is perhaps the disappearance of "man" that would allow for the birth of a new era:

> If those arrangements [of knowledge that invented man] were to disappear as they appeared, if some event which we can at the moment do no more than sense the possibility—without knowing either what its form will be or what it promises—were to cause them to crumble, as the ground of Classical thought did, at the end of the eighteenth century, then one can certainly wager that man would be erased, like a face drawn in sand at the edge of the sea. (387)

Likewise, Gilles Deleuze and Félix Guattari examine the hierarchical structures that have defined modernity and capitalism to propose a radical departure. In the introductory chapter of *A Thousand Plateaus*, Deleuze and Guattari explain that to reach this objective we need to get rid of arborescent systems of thought which hold things together within established power structures and patterns: "Arborescent systems are hierarchical systems with centers of significance and subjectification" (16). Therefore, they propose the model of the rhizome, a structural model of thought which, in its nodal configuration, undermines hierarchical thinking. Rhizomatic structures do not follow established linear and genealogical patterns, as each node is self-sufficient yet interrelated with the one of which it is an off-shoot, indicating both a rupture and a connection, and thus emphasizing multiplicity and heterogeneity.

Although their methods differ, all three thinkers aim for the same objective. All three endeavour to criticize the modernist and essentialist notion of a centralized, universal and rational subject in favour of a decentralized epistemology of dispersed bodies and multiple subjectivities.

We might ask whether the rhizome can adequately knit together the rift that seems to have characterized human relationships with the Sea in particular and Nature in general. Or is this too little too late, with the only option being the "disappearance of man" that Foucault envisages? Alternatively, in visualizing a posthuman world, we might follow Donna Haraway's futuristic model of a "cyborg," a creature in whom nature and culture are fused. Discarding the Gaia and "back-to-Nature" approaches, her Cyborg Manifesto concomitantly denies the myth of a "natural" Eden destroyed by the "culture" of humans. The Cyborg for her is this inseparability of Nature and Technology, and, as she puts it, "I'd rather be a cyborg than a goddess" (*Simians* 181). In addition to goddesses, she also steers clear of the Scylla and Charybdis of constructed nature and "real" nature: "My crude characterization does not end up with an 'objective world' or 'nature' but it certainly does insist on the world. This world must always be articulated, from people's points of view, through 'situated knowledges'" (Promises 313). Rejecting "representation" in favour of "articulation," she pinpoints some of the problems with a purely con-structivist approach:

> Some science studies scholars have been terrified to criticize their constructivist formulations because the only alternative seems to be some retrograde kind of "going back" to nature and to philosophical realism. But above all people, these scholars should know that "nature" and "realism" are precisely the consequences of representational practices. Where we need to move is not "back" to nature, but elsewhere, through and within an artifactual social nature, which these very scholars have helped to make expressable in current Western scholarly practice. (Promises 313)

In Haraway's view nature will always be mediated, as this unmediated nature will never be accessible to us: even attempts to purge nature of its constructions are in themselves a human construct.

Along similar lines to the postconstructivist, posthumanist approach of Haraway, Bruno Latour would lead us to believe that his work contains the strategic "materiality," the ground for political action, that the likes of Foucault, Deleuze and Guattari have been criticized for lacking. Nonetheless, his critique of modernity runs along similar lines to theirs. In his book *We Have Never Been Modern*, Latour notes that with their "purifying practice"—which Foucault refers to as "disciplinarization"—the moderns have separated nature from culture, and ultimately, humans from non-humans. In contrast to Foucault, however, Latour does not see the disappearance of Man, but merely his redistribution, a reconfiguration of his constitution. The Moderns distinguished between Nature's trans-cendent dimension and society's immanent dimension in contrast to the premodern perspective that there was a continuous connection between the two and that any change in either would reflect itself across the board. Unwilling to return to the premodern paradigm of the total nonseparability of Nature and Society, Latour recognizes that amidst their many shortcomings the moderns' "major innovation" is "the separability of a nature that no one has constructed—transcendence—and the freedom of manœuvre of a society that is of our own making—immanence" (140). He insists that it is the work of mediation and not purification that allows the existential conditions of their interconnected ontology: "Nature and Society are not two distinct poles, but one and the same production of successive states of societies-natures, of collectives" (139).

In purging the modern *épistémè* (to use Foucault's word) of its "purifying practice" Latour recognizes that consequently, the nonmoderns become the direct heirs of the Enlightenment. For him, the failure of the Enlightenment resides in the fact that it lacked the anthropological knowledge to account for the interconnectedness between Nature and Society. Politically, Latour claims that the transparency of these "hybrid networks"[6]—a concept that to some extent parallels Deleuze and Guattari's rhizome[7]—will let us "combine associations freely without ever

---

[6] For Latour these networks not only interconnect subjects and objects, but also what he dubs "quasi-objects"; things which do not solely and squarely fit in either of the nature and society categories: "quasi-objects are much more social, much more fabricated, much more collective than the 'hard' parts of nature, but they are in no way the arbitrary receptacles of a full-fledged society" (55).

[7] Latour draws the parallel himself by using the terms "network" and "rhizome" interchangeably in certain instances, but as Martin Fuglsang and Bent Meier Sorensen suggest in *Deleuze and the Social* (Edinburgh: Edinburgh UP, 2006), Deleuze and Guattari's notion of the rhizome implies a hybrid construction that transforms itself continuously, and so Latour's concept of a hybrid network "would

confronting the choice between archaism and modernization, the local and the global, the cultural and the universal, the natural and the social" (141). Latour argues for a true democracy where things and beings, humans and nonhumans, are all given a voice through chosen representatives: "Half of our politics is constructed in science and technology. The other half of Nature is constructed in societies. Let us patch the two back together, and the political task can begin again" (144).

We might well ask whether the sea receives this status of a being, or whether, always a thing, its chosen representative must forever be human, thus obviating any possibility of dialogue and ultimately reinforcing the division between sentient beings and non-sentient things. Perhaps this perception is one that is conditioned by the modern worldview inherent to our sense of cultural history and it might be appropriate to ask whether the word "and" in our title "Humans and the Sea" is ultimately a cop-out, encapsulating the enduring binary that separates humans from the sea, beings from things, culture from nature. Did our ancestors straddle this binary in their "primitive" animistic view of the world? Is this binary an inescapable feature of modernity and human "progress"?

Current cultural theory has promoted the shift from humanism to post-humanism with the aim of bringing about a more ethical decentralized neo-humanism for the global era, and it is to be hoped that this decentralization will also aim to consider the viability of a thalasso-ethical world as well. It is beyond the scope of this essay either to promote—or even envision—a "thalassocentrism" as a "post" to replace our inescapable land biases and anthropocentrism, or to provide a solution—or even answers—to the questions raised above. Instead, perhaps the variety of essays contained in this volume will encapsulate the convergence and divergence of the undeniably situated barriers that have brought together and separated humans and the sea.

---

therefore seem to be too focused on ordering mechanisms and their functioning" (240).

Works Cited and Consulted

Auden, W.H. *The Enchafèd Flood, or, The Romantic Iconography of the Sea*. Charlottesville, VA: University Press of Virginia, 1979.

Bachelard, Gaston. *L'Eau et les rêves; essai sur l'imagination de la matière*. Paris: J. Corti, 1963.

Barthes, Roland. *Mythologies*. Trans. Jonathan Cape. New York: Hill and Wang, 1972.

Burningham, Kate and Geoff Cooper. "Being Constructive: Social Constructionism and the Environment." *Sociology* 33.2 (1999): 297-316.

Carlson, Patricia Ann, Ed. *Literature and Lore of the Sea*. Amsterdam: Rodopi, 1986.

Cohen, Margaret. "Traveling Genres." *New Literary History* 34 (2003): 481–499.

Connery, Christopher. "*There was No More Sea*: the Supersession of the Ocean, from the Bible to Cyberspace." *Journal of Historical Geography* 32 (2006): 494-511.

Corbin, Alain. *The Lure of the Sea: The Discovery of the Seaside in the Western World 1750-1840*. Trans. Jocelyn Phelps. Middlesex: Penguin, 1995.

De Souza, Philip. *Seafaring and Civilization: Maritime Perspectives on World History*. London, Profile Books, 2001.

Deleuze, Gilles and Félix Guattari. *A Thousand Plateaus: Capitalism and Schizophrenia*. Trans. Brian Massumi. Minneapolis: University of Minnesota Press, 1987.

Dickens, Peter. *Reconstructing Nature: Alienation, Emancipation and the Division of Labor*. London and New York: Routledge, 1996.

Dobel, J. Patrick. "Stewards of the Earth's Resources: A Christian Response to Ecology." *Christian Century* 94.2 (1977): 906-909.

Foucault, Michel. "Different Spaces." *Aesthetics, Method, and Epistemology*. Ed. James D. Faubion. Trans. Robert Hurley. New York: The New Press. 1998. 175-185.

—. *The Order of Things: An Archaeology of Human Sciences*. New York: Vintage, 1994.

Foulke, Robert. *The Sea Voyage Narrative*. London: Routledge, 2003.

Frank, Lawrence. "Reading the Gravel Page: Lyell, Darwin, and Conan Doyle." *Nineteenth-Century Literature* 44.3 (1989): 364-387.

Freud, Sigmund. *Civilization and Its Discontents*. Trans. and Ed. James Strachey. 1st American ed., New York: W. W. Norton, 1962.

Hansen, William. "Foam-Born Aphrodite and the Mythology of

Transformation." *The American Journal of Philology* 121.1 (2000): 1-19.

Haraway, Donna. "The Promises of Monsters: A Regenerative Politics for Inappropriate/d Others." *Cultural Studies* Ed. Lawrence Grossberg, Cary Nelson, Paula A. Treichler. New York; Routledge, 1992. 295-337.

—. *Simians, Cyborgs and Women: The Reinvention of Nature*. New York: Routledge, 1991.

Hegel, G.W. F. *The Philosophy of History*. Trans. J. Sibree. New York: Prometheus Books, 1991.

Klein, Bernhard. *Fictions of the Sea: Critical Perspectives on the Ocean in British Literature and Culture*. Aldershot: Ashgate, 2003.

—. "Historicizing the Early Modern Ocean." 14 April 2008. <http://privatewww.essex.ac.uk/~bklein/Research.htm#Current%20Pro ject>

Klein, Bernhard and Gesa Mackenthun. *Sea Changes: Historicizing the Ocean*. New York: Routledge, 2004.

Latour, Bruno. *We Have Never Been Modern*. Trans. Catherine Porter. Cambridge, MA: Harvard University Press, 2007.

Patton, Kimberley. *The Sea Can Wash Away All Evils: Modern Marine Pollution and the Ancient Cathartic Ocean*. New York: Columbia Univ. Press, 2006.

Penner, Hans. "Cosmogony as Myth in the Vishnu Purāna." *History of Religions* 5.2. (1966): 283-299.

Steinberg, Philip. *The Social Construction of the Ocean*. Cambridge: Cambridge University Press, 2001.

CHAPTER ONE:

THE SEA AS METAPHOR

MADNESS AND THE SEA IN THE AMERICAN LITERARY IMAGINATION

IAN D. COPESTAKE

From the settlement of the New World to the writing of *Moby-Dick*, the sea has played a distinct role in the formation of America's consciousness of itself as both an idealised place and a place in which ideals can be tested out.[1] This relatively short period of history also marks a transition, indeed a reversal, in attitudes to the sea that is reflected in the use made of it as a literary motif. What is of interest here is the increasing use made of that motif in America's literary output to specifically critique the ideals projected onto the land.

In the twenty-first century it is far easier for us to relate to the idea that the spectacle of the sea revives us in some way. We travel to it, walk along its beaches, breathe in its air and take the appetites it awakes in us back to our inland lives. I recall a sharp sense of the sea's restorative potential when visiting San Francisco and staying for several weeks in a hostel in the Tenderloin district of the city. The poverty of the area was initially overwhelming, while the contrast in wealth and the apparent indifference of what appeared to be a completely different city only a few blocks away was also difficult to stomach. The (to a European eye at least) enormous pickup trucks and SUVs housing only a single person seemed indicative not only of enormous inequities of wealth and opportunity but of the layers of insulation which protected much of the city from the sort of realities I would walk through once I left my hostel. After only a few days of these contrasts and contradictions the sight of the Pacific provided an immense release. Its simplicity, power and rhythm made a mockery of the confusions inherent in the human life of the city. By looking at the sea one perceived an immensity of space and a widening

---

[1] Parts of this essay first appeared in another version in the following publication: Ian D. Copestake, "'Off the Deep End Again': Sea-Consciousness and Insanity in *The Crying of Lot 49* and *Mason & Dixon*." In *American Postmodernity: Essays on the Recent Fiction of Thomas Pynchon*. Oxford: Peter Lang, 2003. 193–215.

of perspective which was simple yet stunning because the physical fact of the sea was so radically different from the fact of the city. The very real relief it offered was in this case not related to an experience of the sublime but more akin to what Robinson Jeffers termed the "inhuman," whereby the fact of the complete difference between the observer and the ocean reflected a division between man and nature which should be acknowledged and accepted rather than bridged.

What is less easy to relate to is the complete reversal of perception which the prevalent notion of the sea as redemptive, had undergone. Despite its obvious dangers, neither the modern shore-dweller nor the seafarer view the sea as a fearful realm to be shunned whenever possible. But as both W. H. Auden and Kathleen Grange have noted, the historical changes of perspective which have occurred follow a movement away from the fear and hostility which dominated Stoical and Classical perceptions of the oceans. Auden notes that the sea was

> the symbol for the primal undifferentiated flux, the substance which became created nature only by having form imposed upon or wedded to it. The sea, in fact, is that state of barbaric vagueness and disorder out of which civilization has emerged, and into which, unless saved by the efforts of Gods and men, it is always liable to relapse. (18–19)

Historically the sea was viewed both literally and metaphorically as anathema to mankind due to its hostility and inhabitability and also because symbolically it embodied chaotic emotions that man should strive to define himself in opposition to:

> Since tranquillity was the state most desired, it was better to quench rather than indulge emotion. Such a viewpoint was directly contrary to Aristotle's theory that the emotions were useful spurs to action. The debate which ensued between the followers of the Stoics and the Aristotelians was to be a chief issue in moral philosophy from ancient times to the eighteenth century. (Grange 514)

In *Mountain Gloom and Mountain Glory*, Marjorie Hope Nicolson traces the same shift in sensibility by focusing on changing attitudes in English writing expressed towards mountains rather than oceans, and acknowledges that "[i]nsofar as 'ocean' attitudes can be isolated, there are parallels, though the English—an island people and a seafaring race— never seem to feel the same distaste for the sea as for the 'hook-shouldered hills'" (xii). As Alain Corbin has explained, prior to the "irresistible awakening of a collective desire for the shore" (53) epitomised by the Romantic sensibility and notions of the Sublime, the "first steps towards admiration" (19) were made possible by the impact throughout Europe of ideas derived from advocates of natural theology:

> This pious interpretation of the spectacle of nature and the harmonious image of the Earth after the Flood must be taken into account in order to understand the new way of appreciating the sea and its shores that was taking shape at the dawn of the eighteenth century. Natural theology was contributing successfully to erasing the original repulsive images. (26)

A foundation was thus laid for the Romantic and modern view of the sea which completed the reversal in attitude.

What is interesting in terms of literary treatments of the sea is that once the sense of the sea as "repulsive" had been undermined it gained increasing attention as an object of aesthetic contemplation (rather than being ignored) and became the recipient of a whole range of projected human emotions and desires. As Roger Stein has noted,

> [L]ike his English contemporaries, rarely does the American writer of fiction devote long sections of his book to the sea experience. The lodestone of the eighteenth century and the novel is society; and the sea seems to work against that, to be disruptive of social order. It is to be endured and not, for the most part, to be enjoyed for itself. (17)

Whether expressive of chaos, passion, freedom, danger, experience, death or life, the sea came alive as a recipient of projected human anxieties and hopes once the predominantly Stoic fear of the sea, and the unreasoned emotions it had long represented, had been overcome.

The timescale of these perceptual changes runs parallel to changes in attitudes towards insanity, and, furthermore, sees their respective paths intersect. Foucault argues that the Classical perception of the sea as a metaphor for the sufferer of insanity's own chaotic and violent impulses—reflecting the "ceaseless unrest" (9) of the "great turbulent plain" (10)—helped to sanction changes in perceptions of the insane and definitions of insanity itself, ushering in a new era of control and treatment of the mad. The revival of ancient associations between forms of madness and the sea during the Enlightenment period eased the transition into medical fact of equally neglected ancient practices for the treatment of insanity through the use of sea travel. It had been deemed an effective means of stimulation by which to alter a patient's physical constitution, improve digestion, and provide distraction from morbid or obsessive preoccupations. However as Corbin (57–59) notes the affecting of a melancholy temperament was deemed fashionable among the English ruling classes during the sixteenth and the start of the seventeenth centuries, but waned under the impact of Robert Burton's 1621 *Anatomy of Melancholy* who classified and analysed this temperament as a disease. What was once fashionable soon became an ailment in need of treatment, a fact which Corbin argues "served . . . to assuage the new anxieties that were looming up one after another throughout the eighteenth century among the ruling classes" (57). The bringing together again of melancholia and the sea through the revival of ancient therapeutic practices thus can be seen to reflect a range of anxieties, from insecurities over social status to epistemological uncertainty, rather than actual illness. Such treatments had originally gained currency due to their response to long standing humoral theories of the body, which were based on the belief that vapours from the spleen or contaminated blood resulted in black bile which upset the natural balance of the body's fluids and contributed to the onset of dejected states. However, it is the codification of anxiety as illness which is anticipated and satirized by Ben Jonson in *Volpone* (1606), when the shallow Lady Would-Be disappears from the play following her own and her husband's failed scheming, and is reported to have adopted the guise of the melancholic and taken advantage of the escape its treatment affords: "My lady's come most melancholic home. / And says, sir, she will straight to sea, for physic" (Act V, Sc. 4, 1206).

Madness shares with the sea the fact that it is a realm of experience which defies man's ability to know it completely. Invariably such resistance to knowledge does not prevent man from taking advantage of the impasse in certainty. Insanity and water have thus, as Foucault suggests, "been long linked in the minds of European man" (9) because it is only in the realm of dreams that man could ever claim complete knowledge of either the vastness of the ocean or the causes of madness. Man's relationship to both realms, therefore, becomes an index of unknowability as well as an index of man's arrogant refusal to accept such limits.

Melville sets out to confront the implications of this approach to knowledge in *Moby-Dick*. At the outset Ishmael contemplates his recurrent melancholy by stating his intention of taking to sea and cites the by now long defunct humoral theories to support his decision. In doing so he foregrounds the merging of fantasy and reality, medical fact and speculative fictions, which has characterised the perceived nature and treatment of melancholia from Aristotle onwards:

> It is a way I have of driving off the spleen, and regulating the circulation. Whenever I find myself growing grim about the mouth; whenever it is a

damp, drizzly November in my soul; whenever I find myself involuntarily passing before coffin warehouses, and bringing up the rear of every funeral I meet; and especially, whenever my hypos get such an upper hand of me that it requires a strong moral principle to prevent me from methodically knocking people's hats off – then, I account it high time to get to sea as soon as I can. (12)

Ishmael's subsequent confrontation with the monomania of Ahab confirms Melville's awareness that America's historical relationship to the sea had been anything but a harmonious wedding of meditation and water. In Charles Olson's words, what concerned Melville, and what continues to resonate with American writers who bring these motifs together, is the fear that "it [is] not the will to be free but to overwhelm nature that lies at the bottom of us as individuals and a people" (12).

The confuting of fantasy as medical fact in enlisting the sea as an aid for the treatment of melancholic states reflects the larger problem of the imposition of will on "facts" which elude definition and which in the context of American's relationship to the sea has an interesting history. The seventeenth-century sea deliverance narratives of America's first settlers reflected the predominant classical and Stoic perception of the sea as a fearful realm of hidden dangers which man should under normal circumstances shun completely. The belief in Providence common to all writers of such narratives, be they Puritan or fiercely anti-Puritan, informed the value of these dramatic accounts of deliverance from the horrors of death at sea. These accounts also showed the prevalence and power of a typological view of the world, in which such escapes could be seen to confirm the presence of God's blessing on individual settlers' calls to faithfulness. In this context an intersection between the topics of madness and the sea occurs in the attacks made in the late seventeenth century by English critics of the Providential designs of the Puritans, such as Thomas More, who made use of a growing number of medical tracts investigating the nature of religious enthusiasm and pointed to melancholic vapours as providing the aberrant source of that enthusiasm. Meric Casaubon's 1655 "Treatise Concerning Enthusiasm" helped support the views of critics and satirists who deemed that delusion rather than divine blessing was at the heart of their Providential schemes.

The Puritans might have been, according to their enemies, mentally unwell, but the influence of their visionary heritage on what Sacvan Bercovitch calls the "sacred drama of American nationhood" (132) continues to this day. For Bercovitch, the Great Migration and the War of Independence are linked by evolved perceptions of Providence influenced by the growth and power of scientific rationalism. For as long as the Divine Order remained reflected in the laws of nature which scientific enquiry brought to light, a revised cultural framework facilitated the emergence of an American national self-identity which outgrew its origins in the outmoded typology of Providence. The development of America's national self-perception thus preserved in adapted form a cultural authority which endorsed the myth of America's manifest destiny.

There seems to be a common thread in terms of what is at stake for American writers or their fictional characters, when they confront the sea or other bodies of water. What draws Thoreau to Walden Pond, and gives added significance to the final sight of the sea at the close of *The Great Gatsby*, is the repeated need to find an answer to the question of how fine the line between idealism and delusion is, and whether it is possible for a society to cohere outside the ideals which have historically consolidated its identity. If informing myths are seen to reflect nothing more than the imposition of will upon nature then can one make do with the value of things outside of ideals? For a modernist poet like William Carlos Williams writing in the 1920s, the need to provide an affirmative answer to that question is one reason that

so much depends
upon

a red wheel
barrow

glazed with rain
water

beside the white
chickens (224)

The "unpoetic" but sensuous details of mundane existence must be enough to provide a platform for value, not ideas which colour a perception of those bare facts. In Williams's poem the facts described remain resistant to interpretation, allowing them to stand as both things and words unencumbered by metaphoric meaning. In contrast, the details of the whaling industry which absorb the attention of Melville's Ishmael provide a platform for the plumbing of profound depths, while the spectre of Ahab's monomania warns of the delusions which may befall the believer.

To return, finally, to San Francisco. Through its many echoes of *Moby-Dick*, Jack Kerouac's *On the Road* suggests the issues at stake when motifs of madness and the sea intermingle. The reason for Sal Paradise's desire for the trip he embarks upon with Dean Moriarty, is to aid his own recovery from depression:

> I first met Dean not long after my wife and I split up. I had just gotten over a serious illness that I won't bother to talk about, except that it had something to do with the miserable weary split-up and my feeling that everything was dead. With the coming of Dean Moriarty began the part of my life you could call my life on the road. (3)

The aim of the trip is not stated and so the journey itself is its own reward informed by Sal's desire from the outset to reach the Pacific. When that destination is reached road-trip and sea-voyage converge as they finally make San Francisco:

> "There she blows!" yelled Dean. "Wow! Made it! Just enough gas! Give me water! No more land! We can't go any further 'cause there ain't no more land!" ... When we staggered out of the car on O'Farrell Street and sniffed and stretched, it was like getting on shore after a long voyage at sea. (170)

However this does not mark the end of the novel, for Kerouac's tale, like *Moby-Dick* which it echoes, offers a quest for value in tension with an acceptance of its possible absence, and soon enough the road beckons once more.

What such works posit through the interaction of motifs of madness and the sea is, at the very least, the question of whether life can be lived by an individual or a community, without an idealism to support it. If the answer must be affirmative, in order to avoid delusions, then new sources of value must be found which sustain life when the journeys out to sea or on the road finally come to an end. This it seems to me is the challenge which American writers in particular take on, and which brings their fictions repeatedly to the shore.

Works Cited

Auden, W. H. *The Enchafèd Flood: or, The Romantic Iconography of the Sea.* London: Faber & Faber, 1951.

Bercovitch, Sacvan. *The American Jeremiad.* Madison: U of Wisconsin P, 1978.

Corbin, Alain. *The Lure of the Sea: The Discovery of the Seaside in the Western World, 1750–1840.* Trans. Jocelyn Phelps. Berkeley: U of California P, 1994.

Foucault, Michel. *Madness and Civilization: A History of Insanity in the Age of Reason*. 1961. Trans. Richard Howard. London: Tavistock, 1967.

Grange, Kathleen M. "The Ship Symbol as a Key to Former Theories of the Emotions." *Bulletin of the History of Medicine* 36 (1962): 512–23.

Jonson, Ben. "Volpone." Ed. M. H. Abrams. *Norton Anthology of English Literature: Sixth Edition, volume 1*. New York: W. W. Norton, 1993.

Kerouac, Jack. *On the Road*. London: Penguin Books, 1976.

Melville, Herman. *Moby-Dick*. 1851. New York: W.W. Norton, 1967.

Nicolson, Marjorie Hope. *Mountain Gloom and Mountain Glory: The Development of the Aesthetics of the Infinite.* 1959. New York: Norton, 1963.

Olson, Charles. *Call Me Ishmael*. 1947. Baltimore: Johns Hopkins UP, 1997.

Stein, Roger B. "Pulled Out of the Bay: American Fiction in the Eighteenth Century." *Studies in American Fiction* 2 (1974): 13–36.

Williams, William Carlos. *The Collected Poems of William Carlos Williams: Volume I, 1909–1939*. Ed. A. Walton Litz and Christopher MacGowan. New York: New Directions, 1991.

Contemporary Mass Media Representations of the Abyssal Zone

David J. Prescott-Steed

In 1903, marine biologist Carl Chun first discovered, described, and named the *Vampyroteuthis Infernalis* (quite literally, *Vampire Squid from Hell*) (Wood, par. 1). Chun's discovery made a valuable contribution to oceanography but his choice of terminology also saw him contribute to a broader tradition of bestialising the deep-sea and its inhabitants, of interpreting the unknown as monstrous and, with it, of inferring scientific grounds for a xenophobic sub-text.

More than a century later this *modus operandi* of bestialising deep-sea creatures has persisted, having found a firm place in the entertainment industry. Chun's bestially connotative classification now seems to belie the "classic" ethos of scientific activity which includes the qualities of being "impersonal and objective," where the researcher "maintains a distance from what they are studying and … remain cold and rational" (Sjøberg, par. 8). For, in as much as hell "is in the human mind" (Cavendish 111), interpretations of the abyss are inherently subjective. Chun's interpretation, and others like it, find themselves unwitting underscores for the deep-sea rhetoric found in mass media contexts such as when the BBC's 'Natural World' series episode *The Abyss* (Fisher et al.) transmits images of deep-sea "beasties" to millions of viewers, and when the U.S. drama series *Surface* (Pate et al.) represents the ocean depths as a lava filled pit inhabited by prehistoric monsters.

Most people will never have the opportunity to experience abyssal flora or fauna *in situ*, a condition arguably critical to the formulation of an independent interpretation of specimens, and so assumptions about the deep-sea remain at least partially reliant on the information provided by nature documentaries. Deep-sea exploration remains beyond the limits of commonly lived experience, while the rhetoric through which these programs construct mediated 'made for television' descriptions of the deep-sea and its inhabitants is easily transmitted into the homes of distant viewers.

On the other hand, although the deep-sea functions as a stage upon which approaches toward the unknown can be played out encounters with the unknown are not restricted to deep-sea probes. Potentially, the 'unknown' surfaces every time a new question is raised and with each opportunity for novel experience. By way of questions of context or of self, day to day to day life sees the individual continuing to face their own unknown and sensations of indeterminacy, their own abyss—these "risks of self-growth" (Wegscheider-Cruse, qtd. in Giddens 78). It seems reasonable to suggest that bestialising the unknown, through representing the deep-sea as monstrous, also means putting the ongoing formation of cultural selves at stake.

In this essay I provide a brief introduction to the abyssal-zone in general and abyssal fauna in particular, in each case identifying the way that interpretations of the abyss are used to make sense of the seemingly unfathomable depths. With this groundwork in place, the attention is turned to the program *The Abyss*, taking it as a paradigm of the deep-sea documentary as a tele-visual format. At this point, the ethical framework that *The Abyss* offers the viewer for negotiating the unknown is examined with comments regarding the implications of applying their model to broader cultural contexts concluding this discussion.

The Abyssal Zone

Oceanography refers to the deep-sea as the abyssal zone, which consists of abyssal flora and fauna, abyssal sediment, and an abyssal plain. Peter Batson notes that the "abyssal plain is, for all intents and purposes, completely flat—a vast realm that covers 40 percent of the world's sea floor" (28). He makes the point that most

> of the living space on earth has never been bathed in light. There are submerged mountains ... whose summits have remained in darkness throughout their entire history ... The great abyssal plains sprawling across much of the globe have never seen a glimmer of sunlight and until the expanding sun boils the oceans away into space in several billion years time, they never will. (49)

It is important to note, as do Paula Keener-Chavis and Paula Coble, that the oceans depths "have historically and inextricably been linked with 'exploration' and 'discovery'...–explorers driven by the human spirit of discovery and a fundamental need to know" (1). Deep-sea exploration subjects nature to the control of culture, but it also illuminates a desire to resolve the indeterminacy that the unknown provokes. In addition, Corbin notes that historically, "discovering the abyss ... [became] a compulsory stage in a voyage experienced as an initiatory rite ... [V]isitors laughed at how slight the danger actually was, while at the same time relishing their memories of child-like fright" (13).

How is this resolution to sufficiently take place in light of Peter Snow's claim that, even today, only one percent of the abyss has been explored? Which cultural reference points become active in the drive for knowledge of an abyssal zone, when what becomes clear in the face of it is our own ignorance? (qtd. in Fischer et al.)

To a large extent, the answer to my question of the abyssal zone lies in interpretations of its namesake. The abyss is a culturally constructed metaphor for the seemingly unfathomable, the indistinguishable, the unknown. Formally, it is defined as "1. The great deep believed in the old cosmogony to lie beneath the earth; the primal chaos; the bowels of the earth; the infernal pit, hell. 2. A bottomless chasm; any unfathomable cavity or void space. Freq. *fig.*" (Brown 11).

These definitions present some contrasting characteristics. On the one hand, the abyss is framed as a vast body of water (the Biblical chaos, seemingly infinite creative potential) and on the other hand it is framed as a demon filled pit of fire (hell, seemingly infinite destructive potential), thus lending itself to an almost "universal" belief in hell (Van Scott i). For not only the task of deep-sea fauna classification, but a range of opportunities to make sense of deep-sea environment, interpretations of the abyss as a cultural metaphor provide the explorer with key models of deep-sea interpretation. What results are readings in which objective scientific data is elucidated by aspects of culturally constructed subjective notions of the abyss, and where vast aquatic masses are described as

> black, pitch black. Sunlight penetrates only the very uppermost layers of the water column: the bright blue veneer of the epipelagic zone; and the twilight blue realm below it, the mesopelagic zone ... Red light is the first to be absorbed, reaching only below the upper few metres [of the ocean water] before it is all but gone. ... As a result, the faces of passengers descending in an unlit submersible take on a grisly hue as the red tones are strained out. Everyone turns a revolting zombie-like shade of green. (Batson 49-50)

Beasts of the Abyss?

To attempt to fathom the mysteries of the ocean bordered on sacrilege, like an attempt to penetrate the impenetrable nature of God ... Consequently, the ocean inspired a deep sense of repulsion … marine species, hidden in the mysterious darkness of the deep, could not be named by man. (Corbin 2)

Far from living up to the story of Genesis, which in Tyndale's Old Testament the abyss was "void and empty, and darkness was upon the deep" (15), the abyssal zone accommodates a myriad of undecideable organisms, their characteristics only further obscured by the lightlessness of the zone.

Snow has observed that, while "many people thought" the abyss was a life-less void, they have recently discovered that "it's actually teaming with life" (qtd in Fischer et al.). Global estimates of the number of marine species inhabiting it range from 500,000 to 10,000,000, though there is currently "no inventory of the fauna of even a single ocean basin, [and so] extrapolation of total species numbers of the global abyssal fauna is impossible or at best very speculative" (Arbizu and Smith, par. 1). But because the deep-sea remains largely unknown the naming of its various features and creatures, while resulting from particular interpretations of the abyss, also plays an integral role in its ongoing interpretation.

As with the previous example, names of abyssal fauna disclose science's reliance on cultural subjectivity. Of the newly discovered species, some now bear names such as Triplewart Seadevil (*Cryptopsaras couesi*), Ogrefish (*Anoplogaster cornuta*), Common Black Devil (*Melanocetus Johnsoni*) Rat/Rabbit Fish (*Chimaera Monstrosa*) and, of course, the Vampire Squid from Hell (*Vampyroteuthis Infernalis*). It is not uncommon, through an investigation of the visual and behavioural characteristics of these kinds of creatures, to find that the titles can be significantly disproportionate to the creatures themselves. In particular, the size of creatures often belies the image that their name pre-supposes. For example "for all its ferocious aspect, the 'common black-devil', as this species is known, reaches a maximum length of five inches" (Tyson, par. 4). The Ogrefish, while this is a name that plays into notions of a monstrous deep, is approximately 12 cm long (5 inches) (Oregon Dept. of Fish & Wildlife). In another example, the scientific name *Chimaera monstrosa* alludes to a hideous beast. The word *Chimaera* (the same as *Chimera*) means "a fire breathing monster with a lion's head, a goat's body, and a serpent's tail [as found in Greek mythology]. A grotesque monster represented in painting etc." (Brown 387). Needless to say, this fish possesses none of the physical characteristics of a lion, a goat, or a serpent. Names like *Chimaera monstrosa* and *Vampyroteuthis Infernalis* seem particularly excessive.

In the case of the Anglerfish, and though it has been identified, scientists are yet to determine its species or family. The Oregon Department of Fish and Wildlife refer to both the Genus/species and Order/family of the Anglerfish as yet "to be determined" (with these circumstances lending it to notions of the abyss as an origin in chaos).

The fish is one of many in the category of 'undecidable.' However, Collins and Mayblin argue that "[u]ndecidables are threatening [because] they poison the comforting sense that we inhabit a world governed by decidable categories" (19). Here, the impetus for applying pre-established assumptions about the abyss to deep-sea discoveries is disclosed. The so-called 'beasts' stand as a testament to the preservation of a sense of cultural coherence and control over the natural world—to the demonisation of the unfamiliar as a means to affirming cultural norms.

In as much as "[m]any people fear complex indeterminacy," the task of attributing identities to deep-sea creatures becomes one whereby oceanography refers back to pre-established assumptions about the abyss, i.e. taking

> refuge in some ready-made cultural shell that provides them with convenient guidelines … and a feeling of security in a [deep-sea] world that would otherwise appear to be a mass of "humming and buzzing confusion." (Bramann, par. 6)

Plumbing the Depths

In order to make sense of the ocean depths, appealing to notions of a hellish abyss is a standard practice in popular mass-cultural contexts. While science fiction productions are adept at constructing a frightful deep-sea 'other' nature documentaries, in their presentation as non-fiction and as scientifically grounded, are a more fitting focus for this discussion.[1] In particular, the BBC's Natural World series episode *The Abyss* (Fisher et al.) is one such program that appeals to notions of a demonic and monstrous abyss, i.e. where different assumptions about the abyss can be seen to be played. In keeping with Nietzsche's premise that "if thou gaze

---

[1] Aired on Australian television early 2005, the U.S. drama series *Surface* is one such example that centres on the appearance of mysterious sea creature in the deep ocean and is one example of "entertainment for all ages in the tradition of 'E.T.' and 'Close Encounters'" (Pate et al., 2005a, 2005b). James Cameron's film *The Abyss* (1989) is also a classic example of translating deep-sea knowledge into a science fiction narrative.

long into an abyss, the abyss will also gaze into thee" (97), in what way is the rhetoric used in *The Abyss* telling of Western cultural attitudes to the deep-sea or, even, to the unknown itself?

It is worth acknowledging, as a preface to this case study, that *The Abyss* employs devices that are characteristic of natural science documentaries as a tele-visual format. One such device is the staging of events and an instance of this is identified. However, it seems just as important to remember that the specificities (and ideologies) of the natural science documentary as a genre contribute to the overall portrayal of their subject matter (in this case, the abyss) and that it is this portrayal that inevitably reaches the homes of a mass viewing public. Arundhati Roy has made the following observation:

> The danger of today's genre of wildlife programs is that they falsely reassure audiences with an appearance of plenty, while an entire generation is created with a confrontational view of nature based on human dominance over animals. Victims of the tyranny of formula, popular programs would have us believe the animal kingdom is … [a]n endless stream of ultimate, ruthless, fanged and fearsome killers on the dangerous battlefields of nature! Really it is us who are feasting on what little remains with a self-imposed entitlement to capture, wrestle, wrangle, throttle, eat, prod, harass, dominate and manipulate our animal subjects at will. (par. 7)

The Abyss comprises of footage taken during deep-sea explorations at three sites around America. The sections of footage have been woven into each other during the editing process to create the sense of a simultaneous, and therefore unified, fathoming of the abyss. It is a British programme that employs British media figures and it has been made for an English speaking audience. Narrated mainly by Peter Snow (stationed on the *Western Flyer* research ship in Monterey Bay just off the Californian West Coast), it also contains footage of Kate Humble (stationed by the Cayman Wall in the heart of the Caribbean) and Alastair Fothergill (stationed by the mid-Atlantic Ridge).

If the abyss represents the most unknown part of nature, an active distancing of the viewer from a site of the abyss can be a reminder to the individual that they are well (maybe safely so) within the boundaries of civilisation. In this way, it is not only a reminder but also a form of reassurance in the knowledge that the unknown is a long way away. This act of Othering the abyss alienates the notion of the unknown and, in turn, frames the notion of indeterminacy as something that occurs. If this act of distancing the individual from the abyss is addressed as a means to identifying a way that indeterminacy is negotiated, then it can be suggested that this act stands as less of a negotiation of the limits and more as a means to their affirmation.

Viewing a programme such as *The Abyss*, the viewer observes a series of navigations through what arguably are the most extreme of natural environments. The limits of the individual's understanding of the abyssal environment are constructed in line with the information that is being transmitted to them via the television set or the internet. The show begins with an allusion to the action that is yet to be seen, and it uses the abyss to organise and contextual this information. The abyss is then used to resolve the viewer's indeterminacy as to what lives down in the depths of the abyss, to putting a demonic slant on what lies in wait in the unknown, or even in depth itself. The spectator can perceive themselves to be gaining a sense of the abyss, however mediated and second hand this sensation is, without having to move from the site of the television set. The limits of this mediated experience are pre-determined. By the time the viewer receives the broadcast, its parameters have already been set. The individual's understanding of the abyss is shaped by the information provided in this context, in a limited space and time. The program is finite and so any contribution to the information it contains must be located outside of the boundaries it possesses.

The initial monologue of *The Abyss* provided by Snow, and the rhetoric contained within this passage, supports my interpretation that the aquatic abyss takes on the role of a celebrity. The viewer is enticed by the promise of excitement and immediacy. Snow proclaims the show to be a "broadcasting first," noting that the crews have spent the day observing volcanic activity under the Atlantic, deep-sea sharks in the Caribbean, and deep-sea creatures in the Bay of Monterey. The introduction concludes with Snow's claim that some of the creatures have "hardly ever seen before," and with him informing the viewer that "now is your chance to catch up with some of the action that we've seen today from the abyss."

Berlyne believes "curiosity is a motivational prerequisite for exploratory behaviour … [noting that] Exploration refers to all activities concerned with gathering information about the environment" (qtd. in Edelman, par. 2). Berlyne points out that this has the following implications:

> the conflict and question of whether exploratory behaviour should be defined in terms of the movements that an animal or human performs while exploring or in terms of the goal or purpose of the behaviour observed. A clear distinction between these two may not always be possible. (qtd. in Edelman, par. 2)

Here, Berlyne addresses what it is that motivates exploratory behaviour. In terms of the viewing audience of *The Abyss*, a sense of curiosity in the unknown is encouraged by Snow's introduction. A degree of trust, at this point, is placed in anticipation that the following events will satisfy this curiosity in some way, to put an end to whatever indeterminacy Snow has been successful in provoking.

Commenting on Monterey Bay's underwater landscape during the first minutes of *The Abyss*, Snow notes that "there is something unique about this place" and notes that it has "an extraordinary under sea canyon, deeper than the Grand Canyon." Snow uses this famous feature of the American landscape, a popular tourist destination, as a means to inform the viewer as to the scale of this particular under water landscape, one that is not inhabitable by human beings. Working to further inform the viewers understanding of this geographical context, he draws on the viewer's knowledge of their own geographical context. Snow states that this canyon "begins just off shore and, within a few miles, reaches depths of well over a mile. If we were in Britain, to find waters this deep we'd have to be hundreds of miles out into the heart of the Atlantic." This comparison supports the understanding that this wild aspect of nature, and particularly this vast provocateur of human uncertainty, is at a safe distance from the viewer.

Accompanied in the monitor filled control room by Bruce Robison and Mike de Gruy, Snow extends his commentary with a reference to a submersible Tiburon. A key piece of technology, in the deep-sea search for self-satisfaction, is the Tiburon noted by Snow to be "one of the most advanced unmanned subs in the world. It's covered in cameras and it's going to be our eyes on the alien world below us." Yet, from the perspective of potentially 10,000,000 deep-sea creatures, it is the explorers that are the aliens. In as much as a human presence expresses a will to self-assert in the depths, maybe it is the individual that is the monster. What is conceivably more out of harmony, the gaping mouth of an Anglerfish or the sight of a human being meandering around in pitch darkness in an environment with a pressure fifty times that experienced on the ocean's surface?

Anthony Giddens discusses how "human intervention in the natural world has been so profound, and so encompassing, that today we can speak of the 'end of nature'" (136-7). He argues McKibben's point that "socialised nature" is partly characterised by its failure to offer any of the "consolations" of old nature such as "the retreat from the human world, a sense of permanence, or even of eternity" (137). The efforts of the divers, in *The Abyss*, demonstrate their attempts to socialise the abyss, to fathom its seeming endlessness knowing full well that it must have an end and that it may only be a matter of time before human kind can achieve it. In historical terms, the abyss alludes to a sense of eternity and infinity. By theoretically positioning the end of the abyss at a point beyond present-day determination, the spectacle of any ground gained in the abyss is heightened. The sensation of the abyss is capitalised upon as is industrial culture's sense of mastery over nature.

Nature provides the stage for deep-sea exploration though the *The Abyss* dictates one way that the viewer should observe and interpret this stage. The answers to the viewer's questions as to how the abyss is to be interpreted have been pre-determined and catered for through the dialogue that is offered during the programme. What does it mean to be abyssal, to be unfathomable, to be pitch black? The viewer who asks such a question does not need to sense indeterminacy for too long, nor do they need to venture further than the television set for their negotiation of this sensation.

Each of the three explorers articulates their feelings with regard to the forthcoming descent. Referring to the ocean in Monterey Bay, Snow provides a preliminary answer to the abyss in his suggestion that "there is something unique about this place." He continues by observing that "[i]t has an extraordinary under sea canyon, deeper than the Grand Canyon, that begins just off-shore and, within a few miles reaches depths of well over a mile."

The word 'extraordinary' is used on numerous occasions, throughout this programme, to express something that is "[o]ut of the usual or regular course of order [or the] kind of thing usually met with" (Brown 897). Through repeated use of this word, connoting the exceptional and the unseen or unexpected, it becomes almost a rhetorical anchor for communicating impressions of the abyss and each time, also, exposing a limit of language.

The initial presentations offered by Kate Humble and Alastair Fothergill, in the programme *The Abyss*, seem to anticipate the individual's precariousness in the watery abyss. What this means is that the explorers' navigation of the abyss, and the commentary they provide, can be interpreted as demonstrative of an imposition upon the creatures of the abyss and, in this way, upon the abyss itself. Just as artists who depicted the abyss were forced to draw on their powers of imagination in order to determine the indeterminable, so too do the interpretations and observations of these explorers seem to be shaped by their cultural context. An example of each of these two presenters shall now be provided.

At the surface Humble expresses her indeterminacy by saying "I have no idea how deep it is down there and, more importantly, I have no idea of what lives down there ... probably more people have been to space than they have been to the depths of the ocean."[2] This statement can be thought to echo the establishing shot in a sitcom, an initial point of insight that serves to contextualise the events that are to follow. Therefore, the sensation of indeterminacy takes on the role of the establishing shot. While waiting to descend into the abyss, Fothergill also takes the opportunity to articulate his feelings. He explains, "At the moment I'm feeling a wonderful mixture of complete excitement and total terror ... It's totally dark. It's very, very cold down there."

Fothergill tells the viewer that, in view of his descent into an abyss, his imagination is running wild. He is also suggestive of the impact of his exploration, sharing his understanding that "[t]here's absolutely no light whatsoever down there from the surface and we're illuminating it, and I have to say that if there's any wildlife down there they're going to get one hell of a shock." With these comments, Fothergill presupposes a negotiation with the abyss that is guided by historical paradigms.

In *The Abyss*, one of Snow's companions detects a Humbold Squid on a monitor and offers some information about it. Robison comments that "these things are giant. They're two, three sometimes four feet long." The length of the squid on the monitor is not identified. The viewer is simply told of a possibility of the squid's length which could, in this instance, be as little as two feet and only sometimes could such a squid grow up to four feet. This allusion to length, and the insistence that a four foot squid should be considered a giant, contributes to a sensationalising of the identified animal, making it seem bigger than it possibly actually is. This aspect of an abyssal environment is subject to the embellishment of the interpreter. It cannot be determined what the cameras will capture in their lenses during the dive and so it is the presenters' task to make the most of what is seen in view of the possibility that it will make it through the final

---

[2] This sense of journeying into the unknown was addressed by Jean-Michel Cousteau when he said, "The people who were putting up millions of dollars were asking my father, 'So, Captain, what do you expect to find?' and his answer to those people who were about to make major commitments was, 'If I knew, I wouldn't go'" (108).

edit. On the experience of navigating the abyssal plains, Lawrence remarks:

> the ocean floor was as flat and boring as the plains of West Texas are to a long-haul trucker. The depth measurements changed little for indeterminably long periods of time, leaving the scientist on watch little to do but mark down times on the recording strip in military style. (163)

Far from reflecting an abyssal chaos, for example, the abyssal zone can be thought of as somewhat uneventful, with the handful of discoveries that are made making up for the gaps in between. Snow's asks Robison: "How possible is it to discover something quite new?" Robison replies that it "happens frequently, far more often than you might expect." He suggests that the "deeper we go the more frequently we find new animals and the deep sea is so poorly explored, we know so little about it, that almost every dive brings us something new."

The following conversation from *The Abyss* about abyssal fauna is telling. Snow asks Robison what the most exciting thing that he has ever captured is. Robison replies, "I think, without question, the most exciting animal that we've ever captured is Vampyroteuthis." De Gruy goes on to offer an anecdote concerning the Vampire Squid to Snow and Robison, who are accompanying him in the *Western Flyer* control room. He (Fischer et al.) notes that the foot long creature is "absolutely magic," recalling a past experience of observing one in front of cameras:

> They brought this up, put it into a tank, and suddenly it started performing. [Snow can be heard laughing in the background] We just gave it a little light, gave it an opportunity and look at what this thing does. It just goes on and on, spinning inside out, exposing these wild 'cirri' [fleshy spines] underneath. It just kept going and going.

Here, the abyss is quite literally placed on show, as it were, as a source of entertainment and of novel experiences. However, this is not a show that the Vampire Squid puts on. It is a defence mechanism that it employs in an attempt to ward off possible threats. The squid was probably frightened. It was removed from its natural environment, put in a tank in front of film cameras and, inevitably, in front of lights, and it was simply trying to protect itself. Yet this goes unmentioned and, instead, the viewer is encouraged to overlook this also for the sake of entertainment. Here, the spectacle of the strange is entertaining, maybe in the same way that a circus might display the world's smallest man or a bearded lady. The publicly broadcast treatment of Vampire Squid is a prime example of the abyss becoming more a means to human entertainment than a place of scientific inquiry and illuminates Berylne's concern that "[a] clear distinction between these two may not always be possible" (qtd. in Edelman, par 2).

Once well into the depths of the Caribbean, having descended down the side of the Cayman Wall, Humble makes the announcement that a depth of "300 metres" has been reached and she starts to inform the viewer of her intentions. Humble says that Gary, who is in the submersible also, and she have brought a "65 pound yellow finned tuna" with them down into the abyss. They have done this so that they can lay it on the ocean floor and use it at bait for the abyssal fauna that may be nearby. Humble does not claim to know exactly what the tuna will attract though does disclose some presumptions when saying that "we hopefully will be able to attract in all these fantastic deep sea beasties and we will get a prime view from where we are." Here, the abyss is again put on show, demonstrating Kilborn's point that the "various kinds of dramatic interaction between representatives of 'homo sapiens' and members of the animal kingdom" have emerged over the last few years to accommodate "contemporary television's requirement for action sequences and dramatic confrontations." Kilborn also adds that, while "traditional wildlife film making has quite often resorted to the staging of events, the demands of contemporary television have meant that some form of dramatic enactment is now almost *de rigueur*" (par. 20).[3]

As time passes, during which little seems to be happening in the abyss, Humble expresses her annoyance at the absence of the underwater 'show' that she had hoped for (implying that the viewer is also waiting in vain). "Really frustratingly," she says, "we think we just spotted a shark right on the edge of our lights." The shark has detected the scent of the tuna but this "isn't good enough" for Humble and her co-explorer, not satisfied at dragging a dead fish into the abyss just to see something sniff it. Humble wants the shark "to come in and get a great big bite of it." She suggests that the light being emitted by the submersible is preventing the shark from getting too close, announcing a revised plan to "turn all the lights off, sit here in the dark and, obviously, as we see something come in we'll slam our lights on and see if we can get any pictures."

---

[3] The French idiom *de rigueur* suggests that something is "[r]equired by custom or etiquette" (Brown 641). This means that, in as much as "television increasingly dictates the terms for representing wildlife" (Kilborn), the style of representation to which the abyss befits a particular position with regard to what is considered fashionable in the context of the natural science genre.

All of a sudden, shouting can be heard as Humble commands the sub's operator to put the lights on. Humble can be heard. However, the moment the lights are put on the shark disappears out of sight. Humble considers the possibility that the lights are causing a problem and communicates a revised plan of action. The submersible has red lights mounted on it and these cannot be seen by the deep-sea creatures. Humble points out that this is the "great thing about" them. She adds that the operator and herself are "gonna make some clever adjustments to our camera." This way, if there are any deep-sea creatures in the vicinity, "we'll fool them and will see what else comes in."

Whereas depictions of hell have been used historically as a means for social control through the threat of an eternity of punishment, the invention of the camera has enabled an individual such as Humble to go down into the abyss to construct a disciplined view of the unfamiliar in the guise of seeing what it 'really' looks like. The conception of beasts in the abyss work to validate previously held notions of the character of the abyss as well as attributing a sense of authority to the negotiation of the abyssal plains. Humble's efforts to fathom an abyss work as a powerful metaphor for industrial culture's attempts to rationalise the natural environment. The use of photography offers a "means of establishing and maintaining power … with the images produced through it becoming additional means of control" (Foucault, qtd. in Pultz 9).

In as much as she is being filmed, Humble's illumination of the aquatic abyss shows the viewer her current environmental context whilst confirming her inevitable and insurmountable separation from it. Humble demonstrates an attempt to gradually dismantle the human ignorance that is pervasive in this mostly unchartered environment and as the same time, trying to keep the creatures in ignorance of her presence by pretending that she is somehow not there. This course of action makes little sense in an environment where most of the known creatures are blind. The light that her submersible emits can only penetrate a few metres into the darkness of the abyss and is dwarfed by the blackness of the space surrounding her.

Footage of Humble finds her playing games with the so-called 'beasties' thus conveying to the viewer that the unknown is a toy, as if it were a pre-occupation of children rather than one of the determination of adults. Humble's actions present the abyss as subject to the individual, rather than the other way around. Behind this understanding of the abyss is the power of industry and yet, in as much as deep-sea exploration relies on it, industry illuminates its own limitations.

Meanwhile, Fothergill observes the hydrothermal vents that continue to fill the water with acidic hydrogen sulphide rich gas which normally is poisonous to all life forms (qtd in Fisher et al). Drawing a parallel between the abyssal landscape and Biblical creation, he mentions that "[o]ne of the most remarkable things of all about these vents is the conditions we've found here, the horrific conditions that we've found here."[4] Fothergill speculates on whether the "enormous pressure, the total absence of light, and high temperatures may just be exactly the same conditions that prevailed when life on earth first began."

The closing comments, provided by Snow, and the accompanying footage, are designed to affect a sense of textual closure to *The Abyss*. However, the messages that have been communicated by this production leave a lasting impression.

There is a scene in which a submersible can be seen moving slowly past an underwater rock formation. The camera position is lower than that of the submersible and so emphasises a sense of technological 'height' in the abyss. The moving water distorts the viewers' impression of the lights of the submersible, as they disappear quite suddenly into the darkness of the water. Snow confirms that research into the abyss has led to a drastic shift in knowledge, that although "many people thought" the abyss was lifeless they have recently discovered that "it's actually teaming with life." In informing the viewer that the abyss is still an unknown realm, saying that "we've only explored one percent of it," Snow confirms that depth of ignorance with which the deep-sea has been encountered in the first place.

In View of an Abyss

The pre-established models of the abyss outlined at the beginning of this discussion, watery chaos and hell, denote a seemingly unfathomable realm. With little more than these pre-conceptions to draw from, their role in the interpretation of deep-sea environments continues to be a significant one. In the context of *The Abyss*, the deep-sea is presented not so much in terms of the real threat surrounding culture's descent into the depths of the natural world, but of an opportunity to entertain a mass audience. Here,

---

[4] According to Fothergill, "some scientists even speculate that the first building blocks of life were not found in the primordial soup of shallow lakes near the surface, but were first constructed right down here at the bottom of the ocean. It seems that we may be looking at the very birth of life on earth right from here, in the very depth of the abyss" (qtd. Fisher et al. 14)

entertainment has been cloaked in the assumptions of objectivity afforded to science. In addition, it seems that this program uses the abyss as an opportunity to reinforce cultural assumptions rather than to challenge or debunk them. This latter option is arguably more conducive to the task of advancing knowledge than to further solidifying its limitations as appears here to be the case.

I cannot help think that the model of negotiating the unknown offered by *The Abyss*, one that lends itself more to a cartoon than to a critical survey, denies the broader cultural sphere an opportunity for serious insight into what precisely it is that exists beyond our highly categorised and domesticated cultural contexts. Maybe it is when mass cultural products that support this opportunity enter our lounge room that voyages into the darkness of the deep-sea will show the contemporary Western world in a more favourable light.

Works Cited

The Abyss. Dir. James Cameron. Perf. Ed Harris, Mary Elizabeth Mastrantonio, Michael Biehn. 1989. Videocassette. Twentieth Century Fox, 1993.

Arbizu, Pedro Martinez, and Craig Smith. "The Deep Unknown." 2006. Census of Diversity of Abyssal Marine Life (CeDAMar). 4 Jan. 2007. <http://www.coml.org/descrip/cedamar.htm>.

Batson, Peter. *Deep New Zealand: Blue Water, Black Abyss*. Christchurch: Canterbury University Press, 2003.

Bramann, Jorn. "Multiculturalism and Personal Identity." 2005. Frostburg State University. 17 Oct. 2005.<http://faculty.frostburg.edu/phil/forum/Multicult.htm>.

Cavendish, Richard. *Visions of Heaven and Hell*. New York: General Publishing Company Limited, 1977.

Collins, Jeff, and Bill Mayblin. *Introducing Derrida*. Cambridge: Icon Books, 2000.

Corbin, Alain. *The Lure of the Sea: The Discovery of the Seaside in the Western World 1750 - 1840*. Berkeley: University of California Press, 1994.

Cousteau, Jean-Michel. *Ocean Futures.* Paper presented at the Risk and Exploration: Earth, Sea and the Stars, NASA Administrator's Symposium, Naval Postgraduate School Monterey, California, 2004.

Edelman, Susan. "Curiosity and Exploration." 1997. California State University. 1 Nov. 2005. <http://www.csun.edu/~vcpsy00h/students/explore.htm>.

Fisher, Peter, Peter Brownlee, Elizabeth Farkas, Daniel Blackman, & Matt Cooper (Writer). The Abyss [Television broadcast]. In Simon Nash (Producer), *Natural World*. Bristol: British Broadcasting Corporation (BBC), 2002.

Giddens, Anthony. *Modernity and Self-Identity: Self and Society in the Late Modern Age*. Cambridge: Polity Press, 1991.

Keener-Chavis, Paula, and Paula G. Coble. Exploration and Discovery: Essential Elements in Earth and Space Science Literacy. *Marine Technology Society Journal, 39*(4), 14, 2005/06.

Kilborn, Richard. "A Walk on the Wild Side: the changing face of TV wildlife documentary." *Jump Cut: A Review of Contemporary Media*. 48. 26 Jul. 2006. <http://www.ejumpcut.org/currentissue/AnimalTV/text.html>.

Lawrence, David M. *Upheaval from the abyss: ocean floor mapping and the Earth science revolution*. New Brunswick: Rutgers University Press, 2002.

The New Shorter Oxford English Dictionary. (4th ed.). 2 vols. Oxford: Oxford University Press, 1993.

Nietzsche, Friedrich. *Beyond Good and Evil: Prelude to a Philosophy of the Future* (H. Zimmern, Trans. 3rd ed. Vol. 12). London: T. N. Foulis, 1911.

Oregon Department of Fish & Wildlife. "Anglerfish." 1 Nov. 2005. <http://hmsc.oregonstate.edu/odfw/finfish/fom/fish1001.html>.

Pate, Jonas et al. "Surface: About the Show." 9 Dec. 2005. <http://www.nbc.com/Surface/about/about/>.

Pultz, John. *Photography and the Body*. London: Everyman Art Library, 1995.

Roy, Arundhati. (2005). "Wildlife Television: The Future." Retrieved July 26, 2006. <http://www.21paradigm.com/wild_tv.php>

Sjøberg, Svein. "The Disenchantment with Science." 2000. University of Oslo. 26 Jul. 2006. <http://folk.uio.no/sveinsj/The%20disenchantment%20with%20scienceExp.htm>.

Surface. Dir. Jonas Pate, and Josh Pate. Perf. Lake Bell, Carter Jenkins, Jay R. Ferguson, Rade Sherbedgia, Leighton Meester. 2005. DVD. Universal Home Entertainment.

Tyndale's Old Testament. William Tyndale, trans. London: Yale University Press, 1992.

Tyson, Peter. "Deep-Sea Bestiary." Oct. 2005. Public Broadcasting Service (PBS). 1 Nov. 2005. <http://www.pbs.org/wgbh/nova/abyss/life /bestiary.html>.

Van Scott, Miriam. *Encyclopedia of Hell.* New York: St Martin's Press, 1998.

Wood, James. "Introducing Vampyroteuthis Infernalis: The vampire squid from hell." 1999. 12 Dec. 2006. <http://www.thecephalopodpage. org/vsfh.php>.

DIVING PLANETARITY

JEFFNER ALLEN

Touch waves with fingertips   Dark sky with moon   night rests
heavily on the surface   blue green vapor trails flash fish through
water   Roll back   slip in   And down   a smooth space   infinite
succession of linkages   precise direction discerned by glimpses of rising
bubbles shadowed by stars of thick night   passages in which yesterday
is today and tomorrow
                                             Long time   dissolves and
coalesces   stillness of motion   you   flickering in and out of realms
Brief moment in which to dive multiple generations of resonance   the
necessity of sufficient air   while drifting   less than a day   less than a few
days   a flickering nothing

A poetic sounding with images, "Diving Planetarity" moves between
futural histories of land and reef on the limestone island of Bonaire, in the
Netherlands Antilles. The water worlds of this small island, among the
many ever so small islands bypassed or localized to the point of apparent
insignificance in the rush to comprehend globalization and ecological
crisis, elicit generations of resonance that effectively shift representation
of humanity, sea, time and space.
    Simadan, harvest songs from the inland town of Rincon, Bari, songs of
sorrow and the year's hardships, Tumba, replete with satire, banter, gossip,
Wals, merengue, calypso, reggae, salsa, jazz, recent compositions inspired
by Sunday music and dance at Lac—shape the island vibrations, tensions
between young and old, economic decisions to leave or to stay. The
moment of acoustic cosmogenesis for Diving Planetarity, though, is sound
in water, which for humans, is non-directional. Underwater voicings dive
Waf di Salina, pier for shipping salt, Kas di Katibu, huts inhabited by the
enslaved who worked the salt pans, and Cai heaped with conch shells, cay
that encircles the mangroves before slipping into the bay. Sponges,
crinoids, reefs and sand, drop deep into bottomless sea.
    Flitting shadows, music of zumbi, ghosts, played at night in the
countryside around oil candles, become waterbourn before the silence of

fishers who at dawn fold nets on the shore, before flamingos that fly hundreds of miles and return the same day at the green flash of sunset.

Flickering in the indirect light of a night dive during coral spawning, the brief moment of this reflection draws from local and global discourses of coral reef communities of Bonaire. Spring planting of coral in the fields of the kunuku, global warming, and Baranka Mama, Bonairean mother of all things, pierce earth's navel, where already, before, even, the arrival of the Spanish and of the African enslaved, it is said, "All who have died live on Bonaire." Silver Iguana, Guaca di Yuwaboina, of the living-dead Bonaire reef, is a figure that articulates, with these words, a voluminous timespace. Land arises from the sea, yet is not land, reef? Neither apart, nor one, dead coral sustains crops; living coral rebalances, balances, the memorial bones of ancestors.

i.

Branching coral shattered massive columns toppled boulders
overturned   intervals fill with rubble   Dislodged colonies pack
together loosely in matrix of encrusting algae and remain nearby   or are
carried vast distances   some stay in place
                    Luminous slow   thin tissues of coral cover limestone
skeletons beaked parrotfish break the commotion of silence   bite grind
chunks of dead coral that pass through as mud sand   sponges urchins
  worms mollusks bore into limestone while searching food   excavate
galleries for shelter   generate silt which may protect or suffocate coral
When air is limited   where to pause while diving the reef?

Hurricanes   storms   metamorphic oscillations   these modern reefs not
successive generations growing orderly atop one another   no solid frame
or preserved fabric   Obliteration of surface detail   abrasion of coral
texture   Overgrowths of coralline algae bind together fragment
                    Magnification   minimalization ceaseless imagination
a towering skeleton   twelve feet high   of star corals may be six
hundred years   Growing half an inch each year   brain coral three feet in
diameter may endure three hundred years and if healthy   continues to
unfold

Darwinian evolutionary theory   competition driven economics of
  checks and balances   Coral reefs a pristine process? the more
complex the more stable more tightly integrated   regulated

interdependence of individuals and species   "the rigidity of coral enables
a reef to withstand waves and 'rise' above its surroundings"   Systematic
regulated diversity   lofty zone of "mutual" benefit
                              Valuable real estate secured by snapshot image?
reef: a continually shifting composition   the more components and
greater the complexity   the less stable   intermediate disturbances   long
term oscillations   reefs without corals   coral without reefs
   disequilibrium

Struggles for years over food   light   space   tentacles enmesh   with
stinging spines or sticky mucous threads   plankton in their nightly
migration rising from the deep   At the junction between coral heads
extrusion of filaments to defend or attack   release of toxic chemicals
   shading of neighbors   smothering of mounds by mucous

excessive mucous blooms bacteria   kills corals by oxygen depletion
accumulation of poisons   if insufficient   mucous enables bacteria to
attack directly   yet   mucous can fend off a bacterial attack   repair
wounds   regenerate lost tissue   Once thought by European botanists to
be plants   not until 1725 did the French naturalist Peyssonnel show
that coral are animals

Transparent mucous covered membrane connects thousands of polyps
   that touch   communicate   share distribution of nutrients   continuous
living tissue that secrets externally a skeleton   if there is one   of calcium
carbonate limestone   Where sinuous valleys are separated by intervening
ridges   individuals within a single valley share
common living tissue and have rows of closely associated mouths
fission of connecting tissues between polyps   budding of polyps   increase
in size coral plates   mounds   ropes   whips   rods   fans   If broken off
pieces of coral may contain cryptic tissue   remnants of surviving life that
might regrow

Broken coral   washed ashore   worn smooth from surf and wind   *Bury
this stone under your fields at spring planting   all earth will flourish
there will be enough to eat and hunger need never be feared* speaks the
Silver Iguana, Guana di Yuwaboina
                 Women talk together while walking across fields

planting the kunuku   surrounded by sea cliffs cactus green hills
scattering seeds and coral pieces for harvest

A trembling of the images   release enables motion   suspension while
stretched out in the water column   At the faintest movement feel bones
in process of floating in a sort of sack   awareness given delicately by
undulatory movement

ii.

Effulgent emptiness   blue shadow   multiple compositions of aging and
beginnings from so brief a moment of coral spawning   nearly
synchronous release into water of pink orange green yellow globules
   which soar toward surface
                                        Gliding here there drift over edge
planktonic glass fish swarm nipping cheeks   sea lilies open tentacles
magnificent translucent   red brittle stars drape arms expectantly over
rims of pink tube sponges   barracuda hover mouths agape
   water dense with debris from schools of circling fish   await   intent

Round bulging eggs press open   protrude coral polyp mouths   egg
clusters swirl up from the depths   burst of rising clouds of gamete
bundles   expectant silver tarpon arrive just in time congregating
overhead   gregarious excess now more shallow   chemical signals
release

                                        Conch shell promenades
as hermit crab with turquoise eyes rides atop   corkscrew anemones
extend pink-tipped arms to catch white dots   yellow black white
   butterfly fish feed in pairs   claws of lavender stripped transparent
shrimp scoop bountiful piles of eggs   an energetic frenzy   banquet

Freedom of the seas   prerogative to catch as much as one can   surfaces in
tropical zones by beginning of the eighteenth century   at which time most
coral reefs were subjected to colonial administration
                Ships navigated in fog by following loud cries of migrating
green sea turtles   turtle migrations vast aggregations could impede
ships   decline and near extinction of the sixteen to thirty-five million

adult turtles once in western Atlantic seas occurs when sea turtles are
caught for more than a century as food for the enslaved   Runoff that
begins with deforestation of Barbados from sugarcane cultivation in the
seventeenth century induces decline by nineteenth century of hard corals
in shallow waters of the Caribbean despite abundant strands of acropora
coral on Barbados during the previous half million years[1]
               at just the moment that one image is replaced by another
there appear effects and combinations of formlessness and color

Population explosion? plague? biological nightmare?
               Crown of thorns   mother-in-law's cushion   fire carrier
acanthaster planci   gray green seastra   wraps itself around braches of
blue staghorn coral   momentarily everts stomach through mouth at center
of one dozen two dozen arms each a foot long or more covered with
poisonous spines   spreading stomach grasps staghorn polyps and seals
tight   Juices pour from star's voluminous digestive membrane   coral
polyps liquefy into slime   stomach retracts leaving bare skeleton
   soon covered with filamentous algae   A female star produces one
hundred million eggs in a breeding season

Programs of vilification and eradication   led by international scientific
and economic bodies   declare war on the killer star[2] Dislodged with steel
spike   arms retract   sharp spines flatten   body collapses from dehydration
star dies in thirty minutes   injected with copper sulfate   two divers
working for thirty-five days kill 25850 or 115 per hour
   held in contained zones and left to starve   dead within six months
Yet if even a piece breaks off   seastar regenerates
                         Oceans of worlds   doing by non-doing
tickling seastar feet   harlequin shrimp probe with antennae   feet retract
star remains still for hours   pair of painted shrimp crawls onto star's
back   pierces tough outer skin   star moves off coral shrimp
   shrimp mount star   excise skin segments   remove gonads

---

[1] Karen A. Byorndal and Alan B. Bolton, "Green Turtles at Conception Island
Creek, Bahamas," *Proceedings of a Workshop on Assessing Abundance and
Trends for In-Water Sea Turtle Populations*, ed. Bjorndal, et al. (Miami: NOAA,
2000)

[2] Jan Sapp, *What is Natural? Coral Reefs in Crisis* (Oxford: Oxford University
Press, 1999).

How far the umbilical cord winds   coral boulder of Baranka Mama
Matimati di Mushidari   coral cavern passage   place of traditional justice
of the ancestors   into the sea of the navel of the earth
        Perhaps it does not surprise that Bonaire painter Winfred Dania
himself deaf and mute describes his work with reference to his
   painting "Baranka Mama" as a place in which he experiences
dimensions that only those who are deaf or blind can experience
dimensions of darkness and silence

Alluring ambiguities of tropicalist logics   of planetary time and human
action entice   climatologies of global warming foretell   northward
movement of tropical heat   melting of polar ice cap   imminent demise of
human world   death of coral reef coming of the deluge
   ethnoclimatologists decry intense resource use "driven" by poverty of
tropical countries   rapid population growth in tropical regions and
migration to coastal areas   technological innovations for reef
exploitation
            Coral reef degradation depletion linked to tropicals that do
not stay in place   to counter the "setting back" of development by
   countries mandated to become "developing" globalization policy sets
forth to "alleviate" tropical poverty that relies on fishing for food by
monitoring and quarantine of reefs   supplanting traditional fishery
and local practices that preserve reef resources   with oil-gas-mineral
industries   tourism

*Five legged brittle stars crawl onto reef catch balls on waving arms   lay
on backs to gather more packages to eat egg drifts stick to Velcro bodies
in thick layers*
        *Large brittle star jumps atop smaller star   both covered with
 floating stuff   stand high on tips of toes bodies arch oral discs
elevated   until dancing slide roll and roll one over the other draped
with eggs   roll down and off coral slope*

Tropical currents may not always be harmful to corals   zooxanthellae
   single cell plants living in tissues of some corals   often 30000
zooxanthellae to a single polyp energize saturate polyps with oxygen for
respiration remove metabolic waste may participate in
calcification   When ocean temperatures are unusually high

some zooxanthellae lose ability to convert light into utilizable food and
energy and evacuate coral mound
            Coral tissue bleaching   white pox   yellow blotch   white plague
yet some zooxanthellae live independently of their coral host   and are
reincorporated when warming decreases   polyps vacated by one algae
species are sometimes repopulated by another or by several algae species
Corals flexible   may modulate their use of nutrients   stretch extend
their skeletons in response to global conditions

Bloom mutation toxicity and the sublime   iceberg currents may overturn
tropicalist prophesies   contrary to speculation concerning
   global warming highs   warmth of the medieval warm period from 800
to 1300 was greater than that of the twenty-first century and was followed
by the little ice age 1300-1900   Earth still within an interglacial period
is forecast in relation to cycles of the sun's orbital motion to experience
a cool climate of long duration with its coldest phase around 2030   and
another around 2200 accompanied by severe cooling

reef disintegrates into discontinuous rows of disparate images
   submarine trace   an almost impossible montage

Floating with fins crossed   your my hands reach out   orange mucous
covered balls slip away   Clouds of matter thick upward rain   soft coral
plumes stream fine flakes   Sea a murky oil broth   eggs coat underside of
waves   Latecomers linger   satiety   sleep of reef scattered with debris of
packets eggs

iii.

Planktonic for days weeks planulae enter westward flow of surface
*   water pushed by trade winds   move across Caribbean enter Gulf Stream*
travel a thousand one hundred miles from Bermuda to little Bahama bank
in seventeen days   Rafting recruits hold to floating debris from eastern
Pacific tropical Indo-Pacific
*   Orange cup coral transport into Caribbean*
attached to ship hull   planulae swim upward toward light hundreds of
cilia propel tumble in currents flip somersault   Despite antimicrobial
protection predator deterrent compounds most
are eaten within a few hours of their release or disintegrate in ocean

Whole larvae ingested and regurgitated rapidly by pufferfish swim away
undamaged after release from pufferfish mouth

Swimming downward planulae creep over reef bottom   travel several
millimeters one centimeter each day   resume swimming for small
distances   grasp substrate with tentacles   shift away from planulae
settling at the same time   search for crevices cracks   protection from
smothering by sediment or being scraped off by grazing fish
* planula attaches and within hours becomes a polyp*
                            Continuous superimposition multiple exposures
loss of contours   slow tectonic events   eclipse interval   gap in time
breakup of Pangae   formation of Gondwana continent of South America
Africa Madagascar India Antarctica Australia
   seafloor spreads breaking up suturing   over six hundred million years
succession of reef ecosystems emerges and disappears in tropical oceans

Crystal lattices of coral skeletons   hard corals   latecomers first appear
in shallow waters of Bavarian Austria Italian Alps   Indo-China
   followed by mass extinctions   a fourteen million year interval during
which corals are "missing"   Darwinian spirit of evolutionary
development   twinned with nostalgic yearning for a past that never
was postulates inexplicable crisis to explain gaps[3]   cannot think corals
devoid of customary hard cover "natural" clade   as bare naked exposed
                  Naked   each renders asunder the relations it is
   multifarious soft bodied coral ancestors   translucent pliant
relational rather than evolutionary cycles of aging   metabolic
innovation at critical points in earth history enables survival   anemone-
like ancestors   flexible transform back and forth
between calcified and soft bodied forms

The everyday stories of Guaca di Yuwaboina   Silver Iguana   tales with
several drifts and Afrocentric-indigenous-colonial-missionary-Latino-
Papiamentu-Caribbean hyphenations bring reminders of cosmogenic
powers and slivers of innovation   Snared in the meshes of long time

---

[3] George D. Stanley Jr., "The Evolution of Modern Corals and Their Early
History," *Earth Science Reviews* 60 (2003): 195-225. See also, Nancy Knowlton
and Jeremy B.C. Jackson, "The Ecology of Coral Reefs," *Marine Community
Ecology*, ed. Mark Bertness, et al. (Massachusetts: Sinauer Associates, 2001)

the Iguana said   already before even the arrival of the Spanish and of
the African enslaved *tur cu a muri taki tur otro tambe   lo bini aki*
   all who have died are here   all others too   they are coming here   to
this small island-reef

Between blue gray sky hills ocean waves of Bonaire and a sea below the
sea sea of the navel of the earth   Winfred Dania's "Alle zielen wonen op
Bonaire" paints faces of all who have died themselves within the waters
and coral cavern of the Bonaire reef
   Feather sea pen muscular foot under sand extends tentacled polyps as
particles float by in the current

Coralline illusion an intensification of attraction   profusion of
lavender-tipped giant anemones vast plains of elkhorn staghorn great
star lettuce coral in which what would not be almost is

   boulder star coral mountainous star coral gray brown yellow plates
sheets knobby   brain coral symmetrical brain coral whorls bowls
fleshy artichoke coral solitary green disc coral brilliant sea fingers fire
coral stony coral yellow wire coral soft coral pink creamy tissues dotted
with polyps feather plumes purple sea fans   Sea whip spins away
from reef and into open water long stalks bright orange orange red

A physics of multiple dimensions   membranous universes that cannot
perceive yet lie next to   a single particle wave motion invokes infinite
worlds contingencies indeterminacies   that collide distort ripple
possibilities of energetic transfer transient
peripheral motion between   ephemeric shifting of bodies   coral

                                                Nip of damselfish
as drift across sand sea grasses garden of eel chases away stars   in five
years human bodies do not exist all atoms having been replaced   living
bone too is pliant
   three spot damsel fish guards algal matted garden grazing and weeding
algae on small patches of dead coral

CHAPTER TWO:

OCEANIC ENCOUNTERS: AMBIVALENCE, CHANGE, AND CROSS-FERTILIZATION

SAFELY ASHORE: MARCEL PAGNOL'S ATTITUDES TOWARD THE SEA

BRUCE ROBINSON

Despite its intimate connection with the Mediterranean, the world of Marcel Pagnol's films and plays has an ambivalent relationship with water; contradictory longings and aversions, even among those characters whose life is most strongly connected with the sea, impel much of the dramatic conflict. This tension is naturally most evident in those works whose action unfurls on the cusp of the Mediterranean, most notably around the harbor of Marseille. Marius' obsession with seafaring drives the drama of one play (and its subsequent filmed version), his seafaring is responsible for the emotional situation of a second, and yet it is his categorical rejection of that obsession that creates the convenient rapprochements of the third of what is often referred to as Pagnol's Marseille trilogy: *Marius*, *Fanny*, and *César*.

Small boats in Pagnol's films often prove untrustworthy; ironic counterpoints to the romantic ideal of "*voyages lointains*"; though hardly in the same context, think Rimbaud, and "Le bateau ivre."[1] A seafarer, or at least a character who spends much of his time on the water, such as the ferryboat captain, Escartefigue, refuses to venture past the *transbordeur*, and one character whose business it is to furnish supplies and sails to mariners is accused of being accessory to the drownings of those who go to sea but do not return.

All, of course, presented in a comic mode, but nonetheless, one can see in Pagnol's work a tidal interplay of attraction and repulsion: a landlocked group of characters who often feed off the sea, but are adamant about remaining on shore. And remaining at home too, for the two themes are allied, as Pagnol at once gently mocks and yet clearly participates in a

---

[1] Rimbaud's *bateau ivre* is no travelogue, but it certainly plays off the fascination with exotic elsewheres. Though it is hardly comparable on a symbolic level, I am relating Pagnol's wobbly, i.e., drunken, boats and Marius' romantic dream to Rimbaud's description of an unsteady voyage to the "*incroyables Florides*."

Marseillais insularity that reveals itself both as pride of place and as inability, or refusal, to conceive of the value of an "other" or an "else-where." Despite the grand opening shot of Pagnol's Marius, in which the grand billowing sails of a three-masted sailing ship become the screen on which we read the opening credits, it is the *transbordeur*, Marseille's iconic bridge, destroyed by the Germans in World War II that more accurately represents Pagnol's attitude: connected to the sea, but above it, a mechanism by which to avoid the water, or accommodate oneself to it.

For Pagnol, water remains a largely landlocked element, despite the abundant evidence to the contrary: the almost-inland sea of the Mediterranean often in the background in the films of *Fanny*, *Marius*, and *César*, as well as in his later *Naïs*. His characters will dig for it, successfully in *La fille du puisatier*, and with fatal results in *Jean de Florette*, stop it up and withhold it, in *Manon des sources* as well as in *Jean de Florette* (i.e, the two parts of *L'Eau des collines*) but rarely will they venture upon it, and often when they do, only trepidaciously, as in *La femme du boulanger* (The Baker's Wife) as the priest, keeping his cassock relatively dry by riding piggyback on the shoulders of the village schoolmaster, church and state in concert, is taken through the shallows to the island upon which the baker's wife is trysting with a servant of the marquis. Major characters in two other works, both, incidentally, taken from fictions by Jean Giono, as was *La femme du boulanger*, come close to drowning—but far from the sea, one during a rainstorm, one in a stream.

Pagnol's film career begins with the opening shots of *Marius*, a film made with fairly thorough fidelity from his successful stage play. Immediately, though, the titles superimposed upon the large sails of a three-masted schooner acknowledge the new process—and this was a new process, talking pictures—something Pagnol had gone to London to see for himself in an extraordinary, for him, voyage outside of France: Pagnol might have written of people voyaging, but he was not a traveler himself. The camera pans around the ship, but we see primarily masts and sails, for the practical reason that we are reading the dark titles against the light canvas. And, while absent of any sense of intention, the modern spectator can note the visual ancestry of this early sound film in some early (1896) Lumière films, such as *Départ d'un transatlantique* and *Marseille, vieux port*.

We see Marseille then, its iconic bridge, ships of varying dimensions, its harbor that appears to be the sea insinuating itself into the city. Walter Benjamin, writing almost contemporaneously, describes it in a much more picturesque, or accurate, manner, as "the yellow-studded maw of a seal with salt water running out between the teeth, [exhaling] a stink of oil, urine, and printer's ink." We don't get that sense in Pagnol's films that are centered in Marseille, although elsewhere, in films such as *Angèle*, taken from a Jean Giono novel, the city does become that den of iniquity that Benjamin's language suggests, and that is sensationalized by several other French films made during the thirties, such as, Maurice Tourneur's *Justin de Marseille* (1934/5), Pagnol's own *Angèle* (1934), Edmund Greville's *Port du désir* (1955), and the more recent *French Connection II*, (John Frankenheimer, 1975), Jacques Deray's set-in-1930s France *Borsalino* (1970), and the made-for-TV series, "Fabio Montale," (2001) directed by José Pinheiro and based on the Marseille crime novels of Jean-Claude Izzo.

Once past the long shot of Marseille, the opening shots of Marius gaze at the sailmaker's shop, Le voilier Panisse, then at the Bar de la Marine, César's establishment, and at Marius himself, inside the bar but looking out at the ships in the harbor. The opposition is clear enough, but if we needed more, Marius can tell by its note the horn of the Saigon, the whistle coming from the Yara. The ship's tones quickly meet their comic counterpart in the coffee percolator, whose whistle wakes, in the middle of the morning, the napping César, and this comic counterpoint continues through the film: the deep whistles of the outbound vessels, and the shrill responses of coffeepot and harbor-bound ferryboat.

We, of course, are looking at Marius, one hand at his hip, the other resting on a chair, and we must also be looking at Fanny off to the left, but we are also looking at Marius regarding the sailing vessels in the harbor, inchoate voyages and voyagers, themselves set against a backdrop of imperturbable Marseille across the harbor: we thus see Marius both placed, and speculatively placing, or re-placing, himself.

One of the vessels swaying in port—Pagnol's insistence upon real locations would become legendary, although he perhaps mistrusted the artifice of film as much as he valued the integrity of physical settings–is the ferryboat, set against the backdrop of the transbordeur, the modernistic stark iron bridge spanning the harbor. "Admiral" Escartefigue notes that he has made the 206-meter voyage every day for 30 years, and the ironic admiral who suffers from seasickness remarks of the ships departing the harbor, rather than merely traversing, that, yes, "*ils vont loin*," but that "*d'autrefois, ils vont trop profond*".[2]

---

[2] "they go far," "in other instances, they go too deep."

Ginette Vincendeau remarks that "within the film's paradigm of sea voyages, the ferryboat ... functions metonymically as part of the Marseillais familiar scene. It also works metaphorically, both as a sign of a doomed folklore (its existence is threatened by the ... bridge) and as a representative of the small-scale, routine existence Marius wants to leave behind ..." (80). Modern history has changed this perspective: the Germans demolished the bridge, and the success of Pagnol's films may have ensured the lovability if not the necessity of the antiquated ferry, now a tourist attraction in Marseille.

Escartefigue, the nautical but none-too-seaworthy ferryboat captain, is in fact one of only two characters in *Marius* (the other is his stoker, although we'll see some others in *César)* whom we actually see afloat. Marius might go to sea, but we do not see him on board or under sail. His bedroom features framed illustrations of sailing vessel and steamship, as well as a portrait of Fantomas, and it's clear that to Marius, the sea represents escape, evasion, the lure of the exotic—all that, for him, Marseille is not. The sea is promise, potential, and the land is a future in which Marius helps his father by tending bar and cleaning tables at the ironically named Bar de la Marine, although, conversely, his father César describes this longing as "la folie de la mer. Il voulait naviguer."[3] And to Fanny, the eponymous heroine of the middle title in Pagnol's Marseille trilogy, the sea is in fact that rival that she has suspected elsewhere, in the guise of another woman.

Marius's "*envie,*" as he calls it, is "*partir n'importe où, mais très loin.*"[4] The unbounded sea beyond the port becomes then the unknown but knowable, all that is kept from him and that he sees others keeping from themselves, on the border of experience, making sails, crossing the harbor, serving sailors in the bar, or, in Fanny's case, selling shellfish from a street stand, but never venturing beyond to "les îles sous le vent," French Polynesia most directly, but, more generally, anywhere beyond the visual border of the *pont transbordeur*. Fanny's only impulse toward the sea is hardly life-affirming: if Marius leaves her (he leaves not knowing that he's left her pregnant) she threatens that she'll throw herself into the sea.

Not all small boats in Pagnol's stories meet an untimely end—the "Fanny," the launch we see in the final volume of the trilogy, is merely renamed "Le Pescadou" as part of Césariot's ruse to visit Marius incognito, and the harbor ferryboat sails without mishap—but M. Brun's

---

[3] "The folly of the sea. They wanted to sail."
[4] "desire," "to leave for wherever, but far away."

newly purchased "Pittalugue" wallows comically—and I believe we can hear the barely suppressed chortles of the film crew in that scene—before capsizing, and the "Naïs," wickedly referred to as easily capsizable just after we have seen Naïs herself seduced by Frédéric, in Pagnol's adaptation of a Zola novella, *Naïs Micoulin*, does indeed capsize in what is clearly suggested as the first of Micoulin's several attempts to secure the death of his daughter's lover.

Following his success with the Marseille films, Pagnol moved inland: Angèle barely escapes drowning while locked in her father's basement during a downpour, and Panturle almost drowns in a stream in *Regain*. We go back to sea, briefly, in *Naïs*, but it is only in *L'Eau des collines* (Water of the Hills) most popularly represented by the films *Manon des sources* and *Jean de Florette*, that water, albeit the nonsalty variety, resumes a substantive role. These works exist as a novel, as two films Pagnol himself produced and directed in the fifties, and, most popularly, as two films remade by Claude Berri, trading liberally between the two ur-fictions. Nowhere in these stories do we see the sea, but water, and the control of water, is central to the plot.

From Ugolin whistling as he waters his first plantings, we are never far from the issue of access to water. In order to ensure the failure of Jean de Florette's farm, César Soubeyran and his nephew, Ugolin, dam the spring which could have ensured the farm's success. Jean de Florette dead, his death caused most immediately by his attempt to use dynamite to see deep within the earth for a water source, and the Soubeyrans the new owners of the property, the waters of the spring are unblocked by those who blocked it. The subsequent revenge taken by Manon, Jean's daugher, in damming the source of the town's water, leads to the acerbic comedy of the religious procession to pray for the return of water to the town, just as Jean de Florette had earlier prayed for rain ("faites qu'il pleuve").

It may not be at all accurate, nor just, for Pagnol to be thought of primarily in terms of the Marseille trilogy, and of man's longing to sail the sea; Pagnol simply makes use of that folkloric trope as a way to embark on his own mythmaking. And yet Marseille, its port, and the Malaisie, the ship upon which Marius sails, nonetheless retain a core position in our popular—and therefore critical—conception of Pagnol. I think it would delight Pagnol still, as it did delight Pagnol, to see himself so connected in the popular imagination with Marseille and the sea, when his more crucial attention was directed elsewhere, geographically and thematically.

Works cited

"Marseilles," Edmund Jephcott, trans., in *Walter Benjamin, Selected Writings*, vol. 2: 1927-1934, Michael W. Jennings, ed.. Cambridge: Belknap Press, 1999.

Ginette Vincendeau, "In the name of the father: Pagnol's 'trilogy.'" *French Film: Texts and Contexts*, Susan Hayward and Ginette Vincendeau, eds. London and New York: Routledge, 1990. 67-82.

A SEA OF POSSIBILITIES: ERNEST HEMINGWAY'S "THE SEA CHANGE"

MARY BETH GALLAGHER

The sea as a background for Ernest Hemingway's short story, "The Sea Change," is integral to the meaning and enhances the woman's compulsion to embark on a lesbian affair. In Jungian terms, the archetypal image of the sea is equated with the female symbolizing the unconscious, mystery, infinity, possibility, and fertility. Hemingway is not unfamiliar with this idea of a gendered sea. In *The Old Man and the Sea* (1952), Hemingway differentiates between the masculine and feminine view of the ocean. Those who use cold and calculating modern fishing advancements describe the sea as male calling it "el mar" while those like Santiago who "love her" call her "la mar" (Hemingway, *Old Man* 29-30). Without question, the sea is female for Santiago as he describes her "as feminine and as something that gave or withheld great favours, and if she did wild or wicked things it was because she could not help them. The moon affects her as it does a woman, he thought" (Hemingway, *Old Man* 29-30). There is an aura of mystery surrounding Santiago's description; he cannot fully understand her depths, or her possibilities, but he knows that he loves her nonetheless. The *Oxford English Dictionary* defines a "sea change" as "an alteration or metamorphosis, a radical change" ("sea change"). The term is originally from Shakespeare's *The Tempest* in which Ariel sings:

> Full fathom five thy father lies.
> Of his bones are coral made;
> Those are pearls that were his eyes;
> Nothing of him that doth fade
> But doth suffer a *sea-change*
> Into something rich and strange. (I.ii) [italics mine]

Critic Deirdre Pettipiece notes that the sea is the seat of life where "all biological creatures are born ... [and] It is potentially there, also, that deviations, mutations, or possibly new creations are born" (71). Therefore, the sea as a feminine being becomes an infinite source of possibility. However, in the Hemingway text "The Sea Change," the woman's struggle to acknowledge such possibilities becomes fundamental to her existence. In accepting and embracing her desires, she rids herself of patriarchal oppression, thus freeing herself to explore the depths of her psyche and sexuality. Her compulsion to have a lesbian affair becomes a way for her and her male partner to recognize that people contain enigmatic depths, which allow for a multitude and dichotomy of desires and emotions.

Much like "Hills Like White Elephants," "The Sea Change" begins in the middle and is anchored in dialogue. Within the first eight lines, Hemingway lays out the crux of the story. Immediately the reader is made aware that the couple are in the midst of a crisis as noted by the man's agitated tone, "All right … "What about it?" (Hemingway, "Sea Change" 397). The first lines spoken by the woman, "No, … I can't," relate that she has an innate desire which cannot be denied (Hemingway, "Sea Change" 397). The man, Phil, corrects her by stating, "You mean you won't," implying that her choice to have an affair is an act of free will and entirely within her control (Hemingway, "Sea Change" 397). This exchange occurs again with the woman finally retorting, "All right…You have it your own way," to which he replies, "I don't have it my own way. I wish to God I did," until she finally silences him with "You did for a long time" (Hemingway, "Sea Change" 397). This banter shows the presence of inequality in the relationship and that the time has come for the man to relinquish his power over her.

Although confronting the man, the woman is still confined within the narrative structure. The omniscient narrator refers to her as "girl" and she remains nameless throughout the work, while the man, who is first referred to as "the man," is later named, albeit once, by the woman who reduces him to "Poor Old Phil." Physically too, the woman seems to be challenging patriarchal oppression as Hemingway describes her wearing a plain "tweed suit" and having "hair [which was] cut short and [which] grew beautifully away from her forehead" ("Sea Change" 397). Her clothes reflect earth tones and are simple which is significant in Simone be Beauvoir's eyes as she equates decorative clothing as a "means of be[ing] offered" (471). Her choice in dress shows that she is no longer willing to portray herself as an object.

One of the few descriptive paragraphs in the story offers the reader much needed details about the couple while simultaneously adding to the silent tension between the two. Seated in a Paris café, Hemingway points out that the couple are "tanned" and "out of place" hinting that they have just returned from an ocean-side vacation ("Sea Change" 397). It is significant to note that only after having returned from the sea does the woman recognize her desire for another woman. The sea then becomes a symbolic medium, guiding the woman to acknowledge her emotions while making her aware of the depths of her sexuality. It is only fitting then that Phil's claim, "I'll kill her," referring to the other woman, breaks the silence of the paragraph (Hemingway, "Sea Change" 397).

In stating this, Phil has squarely placed the blame on the other woman, as if the woman across the table from him has no thoughts or wishes that he is not privy to. This one statement reveals that Phil cannot comprehend the fact that his female partner is capable of making such a choice. Her reply, "It won't make you happy," negates his misguided anger while reaffirming that her desires will not be denied (Hemingway, "Sea Change" 397). His further questioning of her, "Couldn't you have gotten into some other jam?" again insinuates that she has no control of her actions and is no more than an irrational, helpless creature who is at the mercy of circumstance (Hemingway, "Sea Change" 397). He cannot concede that she is an individual with the ability to make decisions. As a result, his misunderstanding of her leads to frequent contradictions. In one moment, he insinuates that she is consciously choosing to leave him, while in another he is inferring that she lacks the ability to make a clear choice. Furthermore, her response to him, "It seems not," draws attention to his shallow perception of her. Her use of the word, "seems," a synonym for "appears," denotes a surface understanding, a denial of substance. Therefore, Phil's concept of "woman" is only relevant in its relation to man; woman lacks the dynamic substance to be an independent creature. This echoes Virginia Woolf's statement in that "Women have served all these centuries as looking-glasses possessing the magic and delicious power of reflecting the figure of man at twice his natural size" (Woolf 35). As Woolf notes, this view of women in relation to men is centuries old and is most likely what prompts the woman to utter, "Poor old Phil" (Hemingway, "Sea Change" 398). The reader finally learns his name but only through the woman's epithet which describes his antiquated view of women.

Phil claims to understand "how it is" that she can carry on a sexual lesbian relationship, but again his understanding is shallow (Hemingway, "Sea Change" 398). He understands the sex act, but not the depth of the woman's psyche and emotions that surround her compulsion to have the affair. When Phil says that he understands, the woman assumes that he understands the full power of her emotions, which is that she is capable of having feelings for both him and the other woman. However, Phil, as aforementioned, cannot comprehend the notion that the woman even exists as a separate being with thoughts and feelings independent of his own. He sees the affair as no more than a betrayal, which is why he scoffs when she asks if he trusts her. When she says, "I'll come back if you want me" and is rebutted with his "I don't want you," there is a silence; she is shocked (Hemingway, "Sea Change" 398). Perplexed, she asks, "You don't believe I love you, do you?" (Hemingway, "Sea Change" 398). Again, his remarks are superficial and child-like as he mocks her further by repeating her own words back to her, "You have to [go], of course" (Hemingway, "Sea Change" 398). Her response, "I have to and you know it" foreshadows the final exchange (Hemingway, "Sea Change" 399).

But just as the tension rises to its apex, Hemingway diffuses it by focusing our attention on the bar and its patrons. Like the first descriptive paragraph, the second calms the anxiety and seems to call the reader back to the title and the sea imagery. The rising and falling of the character's angst mimics the movement of the sea's high and low tides. The man and woman's frustration are reminiscent of the turbulent waters of high tide. Their short but biting sentences force the reader to read with haste heightening the growing frustration between the characters.

In addition, the paragraphs serve to not only fill in much needed spatial details, but also slow readers down, allowing them to catch their breaths. Readers can then gain a greater perspective thereby becoming aware of the couple's anxiety. We are able to see the couple through the two men at the bar who decide that looking "Towards the barman was the [more] comfortable [direction]" and later, when Phil moves to the bar, the same men move twice in order to make ample room for the seemingly angered young man (Hemingway, "Sea Change" 399). Furthermore, their talk with the bartender of "inserting brandy" into a drink and gaining weight is frivolous and superficial (Hemingway, "Sea Change" 399). The fact that they are all men seems to highlight Phil's shared failure of not being able to see below the surface causing him to have only a superficial understanding of the world.

As the couple's conversation resumes, Phil's inability to understand the woman's desires causes him to harshly condemn her. He incorrectly quotes the neoclassical author Alexander Pope, stating, "Vice is a monster of such fearful mien ... that to be something or other needs but to be seen. Then we something, something, then embrace" (Hemingway, "Sea Change" 399). It is of important to note that Phil and Pope both value reason over emotion. By quoting this phrase, albeit incorrectly, Phil is trying to apply logic to the emotions. He is attempting to fit the profundity of desires within the confines of reason and logic. Furthermore, he condemns her act as "vice" imposing a strict morality that she immediately refuses to which he replaces "vice' with "perversion" (Hemingway, "Sea Change" 399). The woman also refuses the label of perversion because it denotes willfully acting in a way one believes to be wrong. Neither of these labels can be applied to her because her choice to acknowledge and be honest about her feelings and desires cannot be wrong. They initiate from the core of her being which is immune to an imposed morality. Phil's inability to correctly recite Pope affirms the idea that his reason is useless and ineffective when trying to understand the most profound aspects of being.

In their final confrontation, the woman discards Phil's effort to confine and define not only the depths of her psyche, but also her relationship with the other woman. She appropriates his own argument that "We're made up of all sorts of things" in order to awaken him to the deepness of one's psyche and emotions (Hemingway, "Sea Change" 400). There are elements of the self that cannot be explained, but exist nonetheless. It is significant that she uses his own words in order to free herself from his labels and oppression. If he does not understand her when she speaks her mind, it is necessary that she use her own voice to speak his words. He is paralyzed by his own words, his only response being "All right...All right" (Hemingway, "Sea Change" 400). He has relinquished his power and his sea change is almost complete. This power is transferred into her newly established will. Before the woman leaves, the conversation centers on her return to him after the affair. Hemingway uses variations of the word, "will" ("I will," "You'll see," "You...will") to affirm that the woman has asserted herself ("Sea Change" 400). She exercises her free will by obeying and acknowledging her deepest desires.

In relinquishing his power, Phil is equated with the woman as well as sharing the role of lover with the woman's lesbian lover. After the woman leaves, his sea change is absolute as the narrator informs us that "He was not the same-looking man as he had been before he told her to go" (Hemingway, "Sea Change" 400-1). The phrase "He was not the same-looking man" does not refer to any physical change, but rather a change in his perception. He tells the bartender, James, that "You see in me quite a different man" meaning that his sea change occurred deep within him (Hemingway, "Sea Change" 401). The syntax of the sentence calls to mind the profound depths Phil had to understand in order to begin to comprehend the woman's individual and profound range of desires. Hemingway does not write "You see me as..." because the word, "as" would show that Phil has not grown, but has stagnated and would only appear to be changed; Phil's change is deeper. However, this troublesome syntax assures the reader that Phil has begun to acknowledge that humans do not and cannot always be shaped and molded and confined to spaces labeled 'right' and 'wrong.' His sea change is realizing that humans have an enormous capacity for emotions and desires, which cannot be ignored without killing some part of the self. It is integral that the sea remain constantly in the background of the work as it emphasizes that humans, like the sea, are a profound source of possibility. There are depths waiting to be conceived of and explored which once found, cannot be denied. For Hemingway, the connection between humans and sea is a natural one because both contain the ability to harbor life, death, joys, fears, desires, creation, and destruction. Just below the surface of both humans and the sea lies a realm of possibilities, some of which can be explained and some that remain a mystery. Thus, Hemingway has created a story that entails all of these existential dichotomies but most importantly, the need for evolution, the need for a "sea change."

Works Cited

De Beauvoir, Simone. "The Lesbian." *The Second Sex*. NY: Vintage, 1974.

Hemingway, Ernest. *The Old Man and the Sea*. NY: Macmillan, 1980.

—. "The Sea Change." *The Short Stories of Ernest Hemingway*. NY: Macmillan, 1987.

Pettipiece, Deirdre Anne (McVicker). *Sex Theories and the Shaping of Two Moderns: Hemingway and H.D.* NY: Routledge, 2002.

"Sea Change." *Oxford English Dictionary*. <www.oed.com>. 2 Sept. 2006.

Shakespeare, William. *The Tempest*. NY: Arden, 2000.

Woolf, Virginia. *A Room of One's Own*. San Diego: Harcourt, 1981.

ERNEST HEMINGWAY'S CARIBBEAN GULF STREAM FRONTIER: AN EVOLVING ECOLOGICAL PERSPECTIVE

MARK P. OTT

According to James Brasch and Joseph Sigman's *Hemingway's Library: A Composite Record* Ernest Hemingway owned two books by James Fenimore Cooper: *The Last of the Mohicans*, and *The Two Admirals: A Tale of the Sea.* These two novels provide an intriguing entrance into Hemingway's understanding of the natural world. Nathaniel Philbrick calls Cooper "the originator of the sea novel," and his ability to write convincingly about both the land and the sea earned Hemingway's admiration. At a time when Hemingway was increasingly aware of his place in literary history, the Gulf Stream provided a background for him to write himself into the foreground of American culture.[1] Cooper, like Twain and Melville, was a writer that self-consciously shaped an American tradition that Hemingway yearned to be a part of, and the protagonist of his short stories, Nick Adams, is a recognizable descendant of Leather-stocking, Huckleberry Finn, and Ishmael.

Hemingway, like Cooper, created an artistic vision of the land, and an equally robust vision of the sea. Hemingway's frontier existed simultaneously as an intellectual construction, and, to him, as a physical fact. He sought open spaces, in Spain, Wyoming, Africa, or the Gulf Stream, far from the civilization of cities, because he firmly believed in the existence of "wild country," and his hunting and fishing renewed him. This essay explores how Hemingway wrote and thought about the natural world, especially the sea, through the publication of *A Farewell to Arms*

---

[1] Hemingway's library attests to this preoccupation with his place in American literary history, and his bookshelves contained some of the essential reading for a course in American Studies. In addition to Cooper, Melville, Stephen Crane, Henry Adams, Van Wyck Brooks, Waldo Frank, H.L. Mencken, F.O. Matthiessen, Jack Kerouac, and Norman Mailer were all represented on the shelves of the Finca Vigia, his home in Cuba. See Sigman and Brasch, *Hemingway's Library: A Composite Record.*

(1929) to the publication of *The Old Man and the Sea* (1952). Although his work has consistently been referred to as a form of literary naturalism, his novels after 1937, *For Whom the Bell Tolls* (1941), *Across the River and Into the Trees* (1950), and *The Old Man and the Sea* (1952), have enormous differences in terms of theme, style, and method. And though he once saw the Gulf Stream as a frontier, after studying it as a self-taught marine biologist, that view, too, evolved, and according to ichthyologist Henry V. Fowler, Hemingway "revised the classification for marlin for the whole North Atlantic" (Baker, *A Life Story* 264).

I. "An Unexploited Country"

The Frontier, the West, the Pastoral: these concepts in their overlapping imprecision apply equally well as tools for interpreting Hemingway's first impressions of the Gulf Stream. Since the West had been closed, in Frederick Jackson Turner's terms, since 1893, Hemingway had to find his frontier elsewhere. When Hemingway moved to Key West in 1928 and encountered the Gulf Stream, he saw it as a Pastoral space: Edenic, untouched, timeless, indifferent to civilization. Without sensing an inconsistency in his vocabulary, five years later, when he began writing for *Esquire*, Hemingway conceptualized the Gulf Stream as a frontier. As someone deeply influenced by Teddy Roosevelt, this vocabulary was reflexive. The word "frontier" pops up consistently in Hemingway's writing from 1929-1936, most frequently in his journalism and personal letters. As Patricia Nelson Limerick notes: "Frontier is an unsubtle concept in a subtle world" (25). Yet it is too easy to oversimplify Hemingway's understanding of the American West and the "frontiers" around him. There is enormous evidence that Hemingway's understanding of the Gulf Stream, and the people he encountered in Cuba, Key West, and Bimini, was much more nuanced than the overarching concept of the frontier would allow. Turner's frontier rested on a single point of view. In contrast, the evidence in Hemingway's writing and life serves to illuminate his multiple points of view on the Gulf Stream. Hemingway's frontier evolves, and the Gulf Stream of *The Old Man and the Sea* serves as a correction to the limitations of his initial perspective.

Hemingway's first articulation of his Gulf Stream frontier appears in 1936. In order to entice him to write for his new men's magazine, in 1933 Arnold Gingrich paid $3,000 towards the purchase of Hemingway's boat, *Pilar*. In return, Hemingway's first article for the magazine was about fishing: "Marlin Off the Morro: A Cuban Letter." In the twenty-five articles that Hemingway wrote from 1933-1936, the main subject of each piece was Hemingway's public persona, and his leisure activities. His frontier article, entitled "On the Blue Water: A Gulf Stream Letter," was one of his last pieces for the magazine:

> In the first place, the Gulf Stream and the other great ocean currents are the last wild country there is left. Once you are out of sight of land and of other boats you are more alone than you can ever be hunting and the sea is the same as it has been since before men ever went on it in boats. In a season fishing you will see it oily flat as the becalmed galleons saw it while they drifted to the westward; white-capped with a fresh breeze as they saw it running with the trades; and in high, rolling blue hills the tops blowing off them like snow as they were punished by it so that sometimes you will see three great hills of water with your fish jumping from the top of the farthest one and if you tried to make a turn with him without picking your chance, one of those breaking crests would roar down on you with a thousand tons of water and you would hunt no more elephants, Richard, my lad. (On the Blue Water 228-29)

The first sentence leaps out: "the last wild country there is left." Hemingway sees the stream as a place to explore, conquer, exploit, apparently blind to the fisherman that have been working here for hundreds of years, and the ecological damage his presence may incur.

Yet even within that same article, Hemingway recognizes his own complex feelings for the Gulf Stream: it is not just a space to be conquered. A relationship can be established with the stream, heightening one's own human experience through intimate contact with nature. Hemingway continues: "But there is great pleasure in being on the sea, in the unknown wild suddenness of a great fish; in his life and death which he lives for you in an hour while your strength is harnessed to his; and there is great satisfaction in conquering this sea it lives in" (234). The key phrase here, of course, is "in his life and death which he lives for you in an hour while your strength is harnessed to his." A timeless, universal struggle takes place here on the stream, and Hemingway's life is enriched through this recognition. The unification within the "great fish" can exist simultaneously with the act of conquering for Hemingway, as at this point in his life, he recognized no conflict within his own values.

For him, a wilderness was something that was spoiled and destroyed by the encroachment of civilization, as that contact eroded the regenerative power of nature. In "Big Two Hearted River Part I," Nick laments the "burned over country" but finds solace in watching trout in a stream: "They were very satisfactory" (In Our Time 134). Outside of his creative work, Hemingway referred to the world around him using a language of frank assessment that jars us today. In a later *Esquire* essay, or "letter" entitled "He Who Gets Slap Happy," Hemingway wrote:

> America has always been a country of hunters and fishermen. As many people, probably, came to North America because there was good free hunting and fishing as ever came to make their fortunes. But plenty came who cared nothing about hunting, nothing about fishing, nothing about the woods, nor the prairies...nor the big lakes and small lakes, nor the sea coast, nor the sea, nor the mountains in summer and winter...nor when the geese fly in the night nor when the ducks come down before the autumn storms... nor about the timer that is gone...nor about a frozen country road...nor about leaves burning in fall, nor about any of these things that we have loved. Nor do they care about anything but the values they bought with them from the towns they lived in to the towns they live in now; nor do they think anyone else cares. They are very sure no one cares to read about hunting and fishing because they don't. So I say to hell with them. (48)

By embracing the beauties of the Gulf Stream and elsewhere, Hemingway was rejecting the narrowness of an urban perspective, and declaring emphatically that the beauty of the American landscape was a solitary pleasure that must be experienced to be understood.

Hemingway had fished since he was a small boy; photos exist of a three-year-old Ernest, cane pole in hand, trying his luck off a dock in Petosky, Michigan. While his fishing for trout in his twenties could be seen as a natural extension of his boyhood hobby, Hemingway's interest in saltwater fishing was completely different. Soon after his first fishing trip to Cuba in 1932, Hemingway became passionately involved in deep-sea fishing for marlin and tuna. Like his deep lifelong engagement with bullfighting, Hemingway's interest and devotion were instantly established. The unknown depths of the Gulf Stream were especially intriguing to Hemingway, and he became increasingly proficient as a saltwater fisher-man. As the "great white hunter" Phillip Percival had guided him on safari in Tanganyika, so Hemingway would be a Leather-stocking-like pathfinder to others in search of enormous game fish. In the same essay, Hemingway wrote:

> Because the Gulf Stream is unexploited country, only the fringe of it ever being fished, and then only at a dozen places in thousands of miles of current, no one knows what fish live in it, or how great size they reach or what age, or even what kinds of fish and animals live in it at different depth. When you are drifting, out of sight of land, fishing four lines, sixty, eighty, 100 and 150 fathoms down, in water that is 700 fathoms deep, you never know what may take the small tuna that you use for bait and every

time the line starts to run off the reel, slowly first, then with a scream of the click as the rod bends and you feel it double and the huge weight of the friction of the line rushing through that depth of water while still you pump and reel, pump and reel, pump and reel, trying to get the belly out of the line before the fish jumps, there is always a thrill that needs no danger to make it real… Or it may be some fish that you will never see at all that will head straight out to the north-west like a submerged submarine and never show and at the end of five hours the angler has a straightened-out hook. There is always a feeling of excitement when a fish takes hold when you are drifting deep. (Blue Water 229-230)

The remote, "unexplored" nature of the stream would at first enthrall Hemingway, and later inspire him to immerse himself in the vocabulary and practices of marine biology. It is also intriguing to note how Hemingway's language establishes his dual perspective; he is unapologetically a hunter of big fish, but also appreciative of natural mysteries of the Gulf Stream.

Hemingway's unintentional advertising in *Esquire* was also an unsubtle admission of his longing for company. Far away from intellectual equals and practicing writers, Hemingway launched a steady stream of letters to friends such as Archibald MacLeish, John Dos Passos, Max Perkins, and others to join him on the Gulf Stream. In an April 8th, 1933 letter to Janet Flanner, Hemingway wrote:

Look, why don't you come to Havana? I'm going over there in three days in a thirty four foot boat fixed up for fishing. We fished along that coast 65 days last year, from this time on. It is wonderful. The gulf stream [sic] runs almost black and comes right in to the shore. The marlin swordfish go by, swimming up the stream like cars on a highway. You go in to shore in the boat and look down to see the wrinkles in the white sand through the clear water. It looks as though you would strike bottom. They have beaches miles and miles long, hard white sand and no houses for twenty miles. We go out in the morning and troll the stream go in to swim and get back somewhere at night. Sometimes sleep on the boat. Sometimes on the town. (386-387)

The Gulf Stream was a garden of pleasures and plenty to share with deserving and appreciative guests. Unlike other sedentary urban writers, Hemingway's individual path had to be charted in pastoral terrain. Leo Marx writes:

The dominant spirits of this body of writing (pastoralism)….tend like Ishmael to connect the recovery of self with the recovery of the natural, and to represent their deepest longings in numinous visions of landscape. In one way or another, they all lend expression to what may be called the pastoral impulse: a desire, in the face of growing power and complexity of organized society, to disengage from the dominant culture and to seek out the basis for a simpler, more satisfying mode of life in a realm "closer," as we say to nature. (Pastoralism 54)

Marx calls this model an American "fable," yet in the case of Hemingway, the fable seems to be "true." He fled from big city America to the remote reality of the Gulf Stream, and he found, as his writing testifies, a more satisfying life, deeply connected to the natural world. As a wealthy young writer, Hemingway was able to escape the pressures and anonymity of regular employment, and replace them with a "frontier" on which he would be center stage. Paradoxically, as he cherished his isolation on the stream, by publishing his accounts of fishing, Hemingway acted as a metaphorical pathfinder to the Gulf Stream to a larger American public, crafting an image that bolstered a nascent tourist industry.

II. The Gulf Stream as Muse

Thus, in the midst of his fragmented life of the 1930s, Hemingway's singular preoccupation was the Gulf Stream. The height of the marlin season runs from late April to August, and, from 1932 to 1937, Hemingway arranged his life to spend those months on the Gulf Stream. Fishing logs exist from 1932, 1933, 1934, 1936, and 1939.[2] To read the logs carefully is to recognize that Hemingway's creative life and his broader understanding of the natural world were in constant metamorphosis. One day with stunning aggression he would pursue a pod of whales with a harpoon, the next he would dwell on the beautiful colors of a marlin's stripes. Hemingway sought to kill the same animal life he revered. Yet to him there was no inconsistency in this behavior. Raised by a physician father who was a serious naturalist, hunter, and fisherman, by the 1930s Hemingway had reconciled the paradox of his pursuit of game with a very serious conservation ethic. These two perspectives that existed as Hemingway's duality would be transformed by his immersion in the Gulf Stream.

---

[2] There have only been three scholarly articles that examine these fishing logs: Janice F. Byrne's "New Acquisitions Shed Light on 'The Old Man and the Sea.'" *The Hemingway Review.* 10:2 (Spring 1991): 68-70; William Brasch Watson's. "Hemingway in Bimimi: An Introduction." *North Dakota Quarterly.* 63:3 (Summer 1996) 130-144; and Linda Patterson Miller's "The Matrix of Hemingway's *Pilar* Log, 1934-1935." *North Dakota Quarterly.* 64:3 (Fall 1997): 105-123.

Dense in observed detail, the fishing logs give convincing evidence of Hemingway's education as an aspiring marine scientist, while showing his progression from a novice saltwater fisherman to an acknowledged expert, who would later contribute to authoritative texts such as *American Big Game Fishing* (1935), *Atlantic Game Fishing* (1937), and *Game Fish of the World* (1949). The logs record mundane details, such as the menu for lunch on July 30, 1934: "macaroni with meat, avacado [sic] salad, ham, fruit salad." The logs also contain the more intriguing details of catching a barracuda the next day: "Fish had hit so hard on a tight line that he was hooked in the gills. We noticed sepia black oozing from the wound the gaff made. Carlos opened him and in the belly found a small octopus freshly swallowed and a very large squid that had been sliced in two places." The economy and clarity of the description signals a shift in Hemingway's writing style, foreshadowing later work. For example, on May 17, 1932, Hemingway recorded:

> Hooked Marlin opposite Cojimar 2 jumps threw hook—930 swam at beach 3pm—Saw first big striped marlin tail at least three feet behind teaser deep down—back a foot or more across came to surface when we curled boat but [illegible] down before we saw baits (sky was very overcast) and had strike from another marlin.

Hemingway is trying to create an objective document, representing unadorned what he observed in a narrative that uses precise descriptive phrases—"big striped marlin tail at least three feet"—in order to "see exactly" the world of the Gulf Stream. Hemingway connects the behavior of the marlin with the overcast sky to understand their interdependence in a way that will be essential to Santiago's narration. For literally hundreds of pages in the fishing logs, Hemingway crafts short, precise, representational descriptions of what he observed on the Gulf Stream. He would of course use that knowledge later in his fiction. In *The Old Man and the Sea*, Santiago is aware of what is beneath the surface of the ocean. He has studied the Gulf Stream, and he is aware of the organic unity that exists within nature. In the fishing logs, Hemingway is learning what exists beneath the iceberg.

The basic form begins with a notation about the fuel status, the weather (sky, clouds, wind, temperature) a description of the Gulf Stream, a list of passengers, and the time of departure. The fishing logs are written in English, but Hemingway uses Spanish names for the marine life. The Cuban fishermen refer to sharks as dentuso, and dolphins as dorado. Writing in 1935, Hemingway noted the struggle to identify the different species of marlin: "White marlin are called aguja blanca, striped marlin are called casteros or aguja de casta; black marlin are called pez grande, or aguja negra. Blue marlin are confounded with the black marlin are called, sometimes azules or aguja bobos" (Connett 81). This Cuban vocabulary was completely new to Hemingway when he first fished from the Anita from Joe Russell in 1931. In bullfighting and big game hunting, Hemingway had been an autodidact, creating his own reading lists, and asking questions of acknowledged experts. Just as he had learned about modernism at the knee of Gertrude Stein, Hemingway would learn about fishing at the knee of Carlos Gutierrez.

A Cuban commercial fisherman, Gutierrez had been fishing the Gulf Stream since 1884, when he was six years old (Baker, Life 228). Since 1912, the fifty-four year-old Gutierrez had been keeping a record of all his catches, with dates and weights. Hemingway, the good student, would follow his example. Taking place on July 14, 1932, the first conversation between Hemingway and Gutierrez was transcribed by Hemingway himself, and scribbled onto the cover of a "Standard School Series" marble notebook, his first makeshift log. Writing in fragmented sentences, Hemingway took down Gutierrez's responses to his questions. Through examples from the extremes of his own experience, Gutierrez educates Hemingway of the basic parameters of the marlin season, explaining breeding habits, how to hook them. What Hemingway writes down indicates what he did not know, providing the index for his subsequent education. He notes an aguja (black marlin) getting so large that it looked like a whale and may leap over a man alone in a small boat, an image that surely would have stimulated Hemingway's Melville-fed imagination. Hemingway's transcription of Gutierrez's lecture also set the pattern for his own log entries; if possible, everything about the Gulf Stream should be quantified: the swiftness of the wind, the depth of the water, the gasoline left in the tanks, the barometric pressure, etc. Janice Byrne correctly asserts that this interview demonstrates that "Hemingway began gathering material for The Old Man and the Sea possibly as early as 1932 and continued to record and refine his data thereafter" (Byrne 70).[3]

In this initial fishing log entry, and in just a few sentences, the seeds emerge that would germinate twenty years later during the composition of

---

[3] Michael Culver asserts that the story is founded upon a combination of commercial fisherman Carlos Gutierrez's experience and the actual events of the Hemingway-Strater Bimini trip of 1935 (31-37). Dos Passos suggests that a shark attack on a tuna Hemingway caught near Bimini in 1933 or 1934 provided the impetus for the story (60-67). Rose Marie Burwell claims that Hemingway found inspiration for the marlin off Bimini in 1936 (61).

The Old Man and the Sea (1952). Carlos tells Hemingway's about a marlin reduced to a skeleton by sharks, leaving only the head and shoulders. The skeleton weighed 12 arrobas (or 300 pounds). This skeleton marlin may be the first instance of shark ravaged fish to impress itself on Hemingway's consciousness; he would see many more "apple-cored" marlin over the years before he began composing *The Old Man and the Sea* in 1947. Yet Hemingway also notes that, if a female marlin is hooked, the males rush the boat and refuse to leave. Hemingway would revisit this aspect of marlin behavior in his essay "Marlin Off Cuba," expanding on his shorthand:

> Marlin when they are paired are very devoted. The fishermen claim the male fish always hangs back until the female fish has taken a bait, but since the male is often only a fraction of the size of the female this may not be true altruism. I know that we have frequently hooked the female fish of a pair and had the male fish swim around all during the fight, staying close to the female until she was gaffed. I will tell an incident that anyone is at perfect liberty to doubt but which will be couched for by Captain Joe Russell and Norberg Thompson of Key West who were on the "Anita" at the time when we hooked one fish out of a pair of white marlin. The other fish took a bait a few seconds later but was not hooked. The hooked fish was brought promptly to gaff and the unhooked marlin stayed close beside it, refusing a bait that was passed to it. When the hooked fish was gaffed the unhooked fish swam close beside the boat and when the hooked marlin was lifted in over the gunwale, the unhooked fish jumped high in the air close beside the boat as though to look and see where the hooked fish had gone. It then went down. I swear that this is true but you are quite at liberty to disbelieve it. The hooked fish was a female full of roe. (77)

Indeed, this small moment underscores the transformation that occurs in Hemingway's thinking about the Gulf Stream and its connection to mankind. *To Have and Have Not* was written from 1933-1937, and, in that novel, when Harry Morgan dies, his wife screams and cries to mourn his death. In the novella, Santiago's mourning is not public, but manifests itself in the observations he makes on the Gulf Stream. Santiago narrates:

> He remembered the time he had hooked one of a pair of marlin. The male fish always let the female fish feed first and the hooked fish, the female, made a wild, panic-stricken, despairing fight that soon exhausted her, and all the time the male had stayed with her, crossing the line and circling with her on the surface. He had stayed so close that the old man was afraid he would cut the line with his tail which was sharp as a scythe and almost of that size and shape. When the old man had gaffed her and clubbed her, holding the rapier bill with its sandpaper edge and clubbing her across the top of her head until her colour turned to a colour almost like the backing

of mirrors, and then, with the boy's aid, hoisted her aboard, the male fish had stayed by the side of the boat. Then, while the old man was clearing the lines and preparing the harpoon, the male fish jumped high into the air beside the boat to see where the female was and then went down deep, his lavender wings, that were his pectoral fins, spread wide and all his wide lavender stripes showing. He was beautiful, the old man remembered, and he had stayed. (49-50)

The fact that the marlin had "stayed," having stood by his mate's side, enduring her death was a model of heroic behavior for Santiago, as his own perseverance in the face of this trial is strengthened by his memory of his wife. Thus, where Marie Morgan is shown mourning in isolation on a dark dock in Key West, Santiago handles his grief by turning to the Gulf Stream for sustenance and models of endurance. In 1932, Hemingway is a novice to the world of the Gulf Stream and he is gathering raw material. By 1934, he has become a marine scientist, an authority on marlin behavior, stating further in his essay that he has no great respect for them since "the black marlin is a stupid fish," and that "the meat of the very big old black fish is almost uneatable" (64). Then, by 1947, when he is composing the novella, Hemingway is a wizened intimate of the Gulf Stream, able to appreciate the marlin as a spiritual equal to Santiago, a brother and a partner.

Other passages in the log celebrate the rejuvenating powers of the stream, affirming again, Hemingway's understanding of it as a pastoral space. On May 15th, Hemingway wrote:

> ....
> Pauline had (good) strike-fish
> took 50 yards line pulled out
> at 1220—as we were going
> (illegible) beach above pavilion—
> *most wonderful water and*
> *swimming ever in my life*—(italics mine)
> coming out at 230 Grant
> hooked marlin (32)

The phrase in italics is striking: "the most wonderful water and swimming ever in my life." Hemingway's impression is immediate, unfiltered, and unadorned. This experience was one of the most marvelous of all those in his thirty-two years of life. The waters of the Gulf Stream transformed Hemingway; they were unique, fertile, life-giving. At a time in his life when he felt besieged by urban critics, they were a whole new world.

By the time Hemingway resumed marlin fishing in 1933, much had happened in his life. He had hunted from July to October in Wyoming. *Death in the Afternoon* had been published to deeply unsatisfying reviews. And Hemingway had driven from Key West to Piggott, Arkansas, for the holiday season. When the dust had settled, and Hemingway finally found himself back on the deck of the *Anita* on January 25th, his passion for fishing had crystallized. It was a narcotic-like alternative to the complicated world on land. Again, he maintained a fishing log, and again, he would mine the month of April for images for both *To Have and Have Not*, and *The Old Man and the Sea*. Noting each species of marine life he encountered, on April 21st Hemingway notes that he sees two loggerhead turtles mating. This image reoccurs in Book Three (Winter) of *To Have and Have Not*. Hemingway creates a conversation between Harry Morgan and his wife, Marie, prior to their lovemaking. Morgan has already lost his arm in a gunfight. In a passage that is not pleasant to read, Hemingway creates a dialogue with Harry as the first speaker:

> "Listen, do you mind the arm? Don't it make you feel funny?
> "You're silly. I like it. Any that's you I like. Put it across there. Put it along there. Go on. I like it, true."
> "It's like a flipper on a loggerhead."
> "You ain't no loggerhead. Do they really do it three days? Coot for three days?"
> "Sure. Listen, be quiet. We'll wake the girls." (113)

The loggerhead turtle was listed as a "threatened species" in 1970, which makes it an apt metaphor for Morgan. Although there is no evidence that Hemingway knew of the decline in the loggerhead population, he certainly must have been aware that they frequently ate the marine debris found floating in harbors. At this point in the novel, Morgan, barely scavenging for a living off the Gulf Stream, has taken on the qualities of a loggerhead, fulfilling Hemingway's determinist design for the novel. In *The Old Man and the Sea*, Hemingway would again use the image of the loggerheads making love, writing: "(Santiago) had a friendly contempt for the huge, stupid loggerheads, yellow in their armour-plating, strange in their love-making, and happily eating the Portuguese men-of-war with their eyes shut" (37). Significantly, Hemingway feels liberated here to express his "contempt" for loggerheads in a way that his naturalist design for *To Have and Have Not* restricted him. In the universe of the Gulf Stream, Harry and Marie Morgan are the Darwinian equivalent of scavengers, eating the Portuguese men-of-war, "the falsest thing in the Ocean" (35).

The Gulf Stream was very much on Hemingway's mind when he was on his safari in Tanganyika from December 20, 1933, to February 28, 1934. Hunting on the African frontier and fishing the Gulf Stream were parallel activities for Hemingway: both settings placed him in an environment where he could define himself within the context of enduring natural forces. The harsh African landscape contrasted jarringly with the fertility of the Gulf Stream, churning Hemingway's imagination. When he returned to Key West, he immediately resumed his fishing schedule, and began composing *Green Hills of Africa*. Not a novel, or a traditional travel narrative, *Green Hills of Africa* gives further evidence that Hemingway was a writer in metamorphosis throughout the 1930s. In the foreword, Hemingway wrote: "The writer has attempted to write an absolutely true book to see whether the shape of a country and the pattern of a month's action can, if truly presented, compete with a work of imagination" (iii). The phrase "absolutely true" carries extra weight, and signals that Hemingway is focusing on observation. Like the minutiae of the fishing logs, the experience of Africa must be given over to the reader through details of meals, weather, conversations, and animals. It would be in *Green Hills of Africa* that Hemingway would make his longest and most lyrical evocation of the Gulf Stream as a unifying symbol for humanity, foreshadowing the themes of *The Old Man and the Sea*. The passage is central to understanding the Gulf Stream's importance to Hemingway in the years he was preparing the fishing log. Hemingway begins:

> If you serve time for society, democracy, and the other things quite young, and declining any further enlistment make yourself responsible only to yourself, you exchange the pleasant, comforting stench of comrades for something you can never feel in any other way than by yourself....(148)

In the first few lines, Hemingway is responding to the critics of *Death in the Afternoon*, and his articles in *Esquire*, affirming that this writing has "value absolutely." Affirming the connection between Africa and the Gulf Stream through the euphoria of his frontier individualism, Hemingway expresses his disdain for the fashionable Marxism sweeping across urban intellectual circles. He continues:

> ...(W)hen, on the sea, you are alone with it and know that this Gulf Stream you are living with, knowing, learning about, and loving, has moved, as it moves, since before man, and that it has gone by the shoreline of that long, beautiful, unhappy island since before Columbus sighted it and that the things you find out about it, and those that have always lived in it are permanent and of value because that stream will flow, as it has flowed, after Indians, after the Spanish, after the British, after the Cubans...(149)

Searching for language that captures both the enduring majesty of the Gulf Stream and his disdain for the man-made corruption within urban environments, Hemingway continues:

> ...(A)ll the systems of governments, the richness, the poverty, the martyrdom, the sacrifice and the venality and the cruelty are all gone as the high-piled scow of garbage, bright colored, white-flecked, ill-smelling, now tilted on its side, spills off its load into the blue water, turning it a pale green to a depth of four or five fathoms as the load spreads across the surface, the sinkable part going down and the flotsam of palm fronds, corks, bottles, and used electric light globes, seasoned with an occasional condom or a deep floating corset, the torn leaves of a student's exercise book, a well-inflated dog, the occasional rat, the no-longer-distinguished cat; all this well-shepherded by the boats of the garbage pickers who pluck their prizes with long poles, as interested, as intelligent, and as accurate as historians; they have the viewpoint; the stream; with no visible flow, takes five loads of this a day when things are going well in La Habana and in ten miles along the coast it is as clear and blue and unimpressed as it was ever before the tug hauled out the scow; and in the palm fronds of our victories, the worn light bulbs of our discoveries and the empty condoms of our great loves float with no significance against one single, lasting thing—the stream. (148-150)

The Gulf Stream exists outside of the structure of man-made time, fashion, empires, and the power of its current absorbs the real and metaphorical garbage generated by civilization. To Hemingway, art connected to a regenerative muse endures, as the Stream renders other transitory preoccupations of man irrelevant. Inscribing himself within its metaphorical waters, Hemingway thus draws strength for the indifference of his position from the stream, which "will flow, as it has flowed."

Here Hemingway is also outlining what he considered the symbolic potential of the Gulf Stream. In the preface to the first printing of *Virgin Land: The American West as Symbol and Myth*, Henry Nash Smith stated that "myth" and "symbol" were used to designate "the same kind of thing, namely an intellectual construction that fuses concept and emotion into an image" (xi). Hemingway's "feeling," that "comes when you write well and truly of something" is here wedded in his love to the symbolic reality of the Gulf Stream, something that is "blue" in its purity, and God-like in its indifference to the venality of man. In his creation of an Eden-like image of the Gulf Stream, Hemingway is outlining the symbolic terrain for *To Have and Have Not* and *The Old Man and the Sea*. They will take place in a seascape both imagined as a timeless, fertile space, and as an actual site of man-made violence, and predatory fishing. In the scope of his language, Hemingway is revealing that his symbolic Gulf Stream is, at this point, unreconciled with his activities, as there is no recognizable conflict between sport and nature.

Also in *Green Hills of Africa*, Hemingway made his first comments about Herman Melville. Hemingway's discovery of the Gulf Stream coincided with the "Melville Revival" of the late 1920s. Publication of Raymond Weaver's *Herman Melville, Mariner and Mystic* (1921), Melville's posthumous "Billy Budd, Foretopman" (1924), and Lewis Mumford's *Herman Melville: A Study of His Life and Vision* (1929) sparked a reevaluation of his work by students of literature and history (Robertson-Lorant xv). By 1932, when Hemingway was fully confronting the Gulf Stream for the first time, "the vogue of Herman Melville was at its peak" (Shumway 180). Hemingway wrote:

> We have had writers of rhetoric who had the good fortune to find a little in a chronicle of another man and from voyaging, of how things, actual things, can be, whales for instance, and this knowledge is wrapped in rhetoric like plums in a pudding. Occasionally it is there, alone, unwrapped in pudding, and it is good. This is Melville. But the people who praise it, praise it for the rhetoric which is not important. They put a mystery in that is not there. (20)

Although Hemingway does not admire the language Melville used to transform his own experiences into fiction, he recognizes a shared appreciation for the "plums" or actual observations of the whales. In 1934, Hemingway professes not to believe in the "mystery" of the whales that was so important to Melville. Instead, he approached the natural world from the viewpoint of a scientist, and a hunter.

When Hemingway had returned from Africa, he found waiting for him a letter from Charles B. Cadwalader, Director of the Academy of Natural History in Philadelphia. Cadwalader inquired if he would be interested in cooperating with Academy scientists in conducting research in Cuban waters. There was a need to remedy the "lack of knowledge concerning the classification, life histories, food (and) migrations of the … sailfish, marlin, tuna and other large game fishes (and) to secure specimens and information in order that our knowledge of these fish may be advanced" (Martin 5). Criticism of the number of days that Hemingway spent on the Gulf Stream may have spurred him to invite promptly Cadwalader to join him on the Gulf Stream. With *Esquire* providing an audience, Cadwalader's presence would encourage Hemingway to take his observations more seriously in a way that expanded on his boyhood instincts as a naturalist. In his reply to Cadwalader, Hemingway wrote: "it would be very interesting to have a complete collection of these fish and determine scientifically which are truly different species and which are merely sexual and age variations of the same fish" (Reynolds 1930s 171). On July 18th, when Hemingway and crew arrived in Havana for the marlin season, Cadwalader and ichthyologist Henry Fowler were there to meet him.

Most of the entries in the Anita logs followed a specific shorthand form, beginning with the time of departure, the temperature, wind direction, and a list of passengers. The increase in the amount of detail in the 1934 log is striking. Quoting the complete entry in the Pilar log for July 31st illustrates the change:

> The density of detail establishes that Hemingway was no longer just creating notes for himself; the document has a full narrative structure, complete characters, and a plot full of digressions. The details are more explanatory than evidentiary. Hemingway notes the bait—"green teaser"—which engine they are using, and the specific mistakes that Carlos made in boat handling. Hemingway is creating a document that is meant to teach the reader why things happened, rather than merely record their occurrence. Now that Fowler and Cadwalader are on board, the fishing trip has become a scientific expedition, and he must create a record of appropriate depth, specificity, and gravity. The log is also meant to supplement the scientific data that they are gathering. Hemingway notes their actions—sketching, taking photos and specimens—and uses his own descriptive language to fill in the scene: "We noticed sepia black oozing from the wound the gaff made. Carlos opened him and in the belly found a small octopus freshly swallowed and a very large squid that had been sliced in two pieces." Hemingway is asking the question, "Why is this barracuda bleeding black?" As a scientist, he must cut it open to find the octopus and the answer to his question. At the same time he is crafting evocative phrases—"sepia black oozing from the wound," and the "small octopus freshly swallowed"—he is learning about life below the surface of the Gulf Stream.

Perhaps still stung by criticism of *Death in the Afternoon* and early responses to *Green Hills of Africa*, Hemingway also presented his most elaborate definition of sport in "Marlin Off Cuba." He writes:

> As I see big-game fishing with rod and reel it is a sport in which a man or woman seeks to kill or capture a fish by the means which will afford the fisherman the greatest pleasure and best demonstrate the speed, strength and leaping ability of the fish in question; at the same time killing or capturing the fish in the shortest time possible and never for the sake of flattering the fisherman's vanity, using tackle unsuitable to the prompt

capture of the fish. I believe that it is as bad to lose fish by breaking unsuitable tackle in an attempt to make a light tackle record as it is to allow animals to escape wounded in an attempt to get a record bag or a record head. Talk of giving the fish a sporting chance on excessively fragile tackle seems nonsense when one realizes that the sporting chance offered the fish is that of breaking the line and going off to die. The sporting thing is to kill your fish as promptly as possible on suitable tackle which does not prevent him running or pulling or jumping to the best of his ability, while you fight him as rapidly as possible to kill him as quickly and mercifully as possible (70).

As Hemingway spent more and more time on the Gulf Stream, he came in more intimate contact with members of the sporting class, such as Michael Lerner, S. Kip Farrington, Zane Gray, Dick Cooper, Tommy Shevlin, and Winston Guest. Competing against each other and sharing a common interest in record keeping and conservation, they recognized the need to create a formal organization.

A small circle of big game fisherman finally put together a governing body called the Bahamas Marlin and Tuna Club on November 23rd, 1936. In an article in the New York City World Telegram, Ray Trullinger wrote:

> Another new big fish angler's club has just bloomed in our midst, and judging from the eligibility requirements, it doesn't appear the Membership Committee ever will be snowed under with applications....Officers of the new club include Ernest Hemingway, president; Michael Lerner, Thomas Shevlin and A.O.H. Baldridge, vice presidents; Julio Sanchez, treasurer; and Erl Roman, historian. (Trullinger).

According to Trullinger, the noteworthy rules were: "1. All fish must be hooked, fought, and brought to gaff by the angler unaided. 6. A mako shark is considered a game fish and should be gaffed and tail-roped. A mako may not be killed by any means other than a club." As an officer of the club, which would evolve into the International Game Fish Association, Hemingway was now ineligible to hold fishing records. Hemingway would serve as vice president of the IGFA from 1940 until his death in 1961 (IGFA). The organization had close ties to the American Museum of Natural History from its earliest days that were forged by Hemingway. Francesca LaMonte, an associate curator of fishes for the museum, served as secretary and as trustee until her retirement in 1978.

III. Transformations of Philosophy and Technique

The evolutionary nature of Hemingway's thinking about the Gulf Stream is one of the most intriguing dimensions to the aesthetic and philosophic differences between *To Have and Have Not*, and *The Old Man and the Sea*. Indeed, to read the fishing logs as an agent of Hemingway's transformation is also to understand the extraordinary stylistic between these two works. In the former, Harry Morgan, the sea-captain protagonist, calls another captain "brother," stating: "Most everybody goes in boats calls each other brother" (83). Santiago, in the latter, calls the great marlin brother: "Never have I seen a greater, or more beautiful, or a calmer or more noble thing than you, brother. Come on and kill me. I do not care who kills who" (92). The difference in the use of that one word summarizes the transformation that took place in Hemingway's thinking of the Gulf Stream, as in the former he sees only his fellow man in the brotherhood, and in the latter it has been extended infinitely. If, in the 1930's his characters are descendants of Leatherstocking, finding solidarity with other cowboys of the sea in times of crisis, by the late 1940's when he is creating Santiago's character, the brotherhood has been extended into the natural life of the Gulf Stream: the fish, the birds, the stars, and the sea itself. Hemingway grew from a novice saltwater fisherman into a serious student of marine biology, and an authority on big game fishing. He grew to see the Gulf Stream not as a frontier, but as an extension of the universal harmony of the natural world. Moreover, as he integrated himself into the seascape, he recognized the river of time that washes over his life, and his mortality, when put "against one single, lasting thing—the stream" (*Green Hills* 150). His protagonist of *To Have and Have Not*, Harry Morgan, very much the cowboy conqueror of the Gulf Stream, will give birth to Santiago of *The Old Man and the Sea*, a character who would state: "You did not kill the fish only to keep alive and to sell food, he thought. You killed him for pride and because you are a fisherman. You loved him when he was alive and you loved him after" (105).

Works Cited and Consulted

Baker, Carlos, ed. *Ernest Hemingway: Selected Letters 1917-1961*. New York: Scribner's, 1981.

—. *Hemingway: A Life Story*. New York: Scribner's, 1969.

Bercovich, Sacvan, and Myra Jehlen, eds. *Ideology and Classic American Literature*. Cambridge: Cambridge University Press, 1986.

Brasch, James D. and Joseph Sigman. *Hemingway's Library: A Composite Record*. New York: Garland Publishing, 1981.

Burwell, Rose Marie. *Hemingway: The Postwar Years and the Posthumous Novels*. New York: Cambridge University Press, 1996.

Byrne, Janice F. "New Acquisitions Shed Light on 'The Old Man and the Sea.'" *The Hemingway Review* 10.2 (1991): 68-70.

Cadwalader, Charles M. B. *Letters to Ernest Hemingway, 1934-1935*. Incoming Correspondence. The Hemingway Collection. John F. Kennedy Library, Boston.

Connett, Eugene V., ed. *American Big Game Fishing*. Lyon, MS: Derrydale, 1993. Facsimile reprint of the 1935 edition.

Culver, Michael. "Sparring in the Dark: Hemingway, Strater, and 'The Old Man and the Sea.'" *The Hemingway Review* 11:2 (1992): 31-37.

Day, Jane. "Hemingway in Bimini." *South Florida History Magazine* 4 (1989): 5-9. 24.

Dos Passos, John. "Old Hem Was a Sport." *Sports Illustrated* 29 June 1964: 60-67.

Farrington, S. Kip. *Atlantic Big Game Fishing*. New York: Kennedy Bros. Inc., 1937.

Fowler, Henry W. Letter to Ernest Hemingway, 8 August 1935. *Incoming Correspondence*. The Hemingway Collection. John F. Kennedy Library, Boston.

Hemingway, Ernest. *By Line: Ernest Hemingway, Selected Articles and Dispatches of Four Decades*. Ed. William White. New York: Scribner's, 1967.

—. "Cuban Fishing." In Vesey-Fitzgerald and LaMonte. 156-160.

—. *Death in the Afternoon*. New York: Scribner's. 1932.

—. *Ernest Hemingway: Selected Letters, 1917-1961*. Ed. Carlos Baker. New York: Scribner's, 1981.

—. Fishing Log. 7-20 June 1932. Box 88. The Hemingway Collection. John F. Kennedy Library, Boston.

—. Fishing Log. 25 January to May 15 1933. Box 88. The Hemingway Collection. John F. Kennedy Library. Boston.

—. Fishing Log. 28 July, 1934 to 2 February 1935. Box 88. The Hemingway Collection. John F. Kennedy Library. Boston.

—. *Green Hills of Africa*. New York: Scribner's, 1935.

—. *In Our Time*. New York: Scribners, 1925.

—. "Introduction." *Atlantic Game Fishing*. By Kip Farrington, Jr. Lyon, MS: Derrydale Press. 1937,

—. *Islands in the Stream*. New York: Scribner's, 1970.

—. "Marlin Off Cuba." In Connett. 55-81. Includes photographs and charts.

—. "Marlin Off the Morro: A Cuban Letter." *By Line: Ernest Hemingway*. Ed. William White. New York: Scribner's, 1967. 138-144.

—. *The Old Man and the Sea*. New York: Scribner's, 1952.

—. "On the Blue Water: A Gulf Stream Letter." *By Line: Ernest Hemingway*. Ed. William White. New York: Scribner's, 1967. 236-244.

—. "Out in the Stream: A Cuban Letter." *By Line: Ernest Hemingway*. Ed. William White. New York: Scribner's, 1967. 169-175.

—. *To Have and Have Not*. New York: Scribner's, 1937.

A History of the IGFA. Ft. Lauderdale, FL: International Game Fishing Association, 1991.

Limerick, Patricia Nelson. *The Legacy of Conquest: The Unbroken Past of the American West*. New York: W.W. Norton, 1987.

Marx, Leo. *The Machine in the Garden: Technology and the Pastoral Ideal in America*. New York. New York: Oxford U P, 1967.

—. "Pastoralism in America." *Ideology and Classic American Literature*. Sacvan Bercovitch and Myra Jehelen, eds. New York: Cambridge University P, 1986. 36-70.

Martin, Lawrence H. "Ernest Hemingway, Gulf Stream Marine Scientist: The 1934-35 Academy of Natural Sciences Correspondence." *The Hemingway Review* 20. 2 (2001): 5-15.

Miller, Linda Patterson. "The Matrix of Hemingway's Pilar Log, 1934-1935." *North Dakota Quarterly* 64.3 (1997): 105-123.

Mumford, Lewis. *Herman Melville*. New York: Harcourt, Brace & Co., 1929.

Reiger, George. *Profiles in Saltwater Angling: A History of the Sport—Its People and Places, Tackle and Techniques*. Englewood Cliffs, NJ: Prentice Hall, 1973.

Reynolds, Michael. *Hemingway's Reading, 1910-1940*. Princeton: Princeton U P, 1981.

—. Hemingway: The 1930s. New York: W.W. Norton, 1997.

LIVERPOOL JOHN MOORES UNIVERSITY
LEARNING SERVICES

Robertson-Lorant, Laurie. *Melville: A Biography*. New York: Clarkson Potter, 1996.

Shumway, David R. *Creating American Civilization: A Genealogy of American Literature as an American Discipline*. Minneapolis: U Minnesota P, 1994.

Smith, Henry Nash. "Symbol and Idea in Virgin Land." Bercovitch and Jehlen, eds. *Ideology and Classic American Literature*. Cambridge: Cambridge University Press, 1986. 21-35.

Virgin Land: *The American West as Symbol and* Myth. Cambridge: Harvard U P, 1950.

Tompkins, Jane. *West of Everything: The Inner Life of Westerns*. New York: Oxford U P, 1992.

Trullinger, Ray. "New Big Fish Club Is Organized, But It's Awfully Hard to Crash." *New York City World Telegram* 23 November 1936. Page unavailable.

Vesey-Fitzgerald, Brian, and Francesca LaMonte, eds. *Game Fish of the World*. London: Nicholson & Watson, 1949.

Watson, William Brasch. "Hemingway in Bimimi: An Introduction." *North Dakota Quarterly* 63.3 (1996): 130-144.

Weaver, Raymond. *Herman Melville, Mariner and Mystic*. New York: George H. Doran, 1921.

TENNYSON'S MARITIME INFLUENCE ON MELVILLE'S *JOHN MARR*: AN IDYLL SPECULATION

KAREN LENTZ MADISON

In the literary world inhabited by Herman Melville and Alfred, Lord Tennyson, the two appear to be independent barques adrift on a nineteenth-century linguistic ocean. That both authors lived in different cultures is a given, but their literary connections and their common experience of despair and isolation necessitated their negotiations of the chasm created by an era marked by doubt and duty. As these authors develop projects involving the lives of seafaring souls, Melville's *John Marr and Other Sailors* and Tennyson's *Enoch Arden,* the two utilize the language of isolation, with its recognition of both a sailor's need for interaction and dependency and the loneliness incurred by its absence. Both works are recognized for their richness of verse and portrayal of agony resulting from isolation.

Even though there is no evidence of Melville's sailors ever having visited Tennyson's library, the British subject was well aware of literary movements and tastes in the United States, from his being published and received with acclaim here in the 1830's to his eventual collaboration with Arthur Sullivan and American producer Augustin Daly in a celebrated 1892 American production of *The Foresters* (*Letters*, III, 429, 431). Added to this publication and presentation acumen was his interest in the sea and seafarers apparent in such works as the 1842 "Ulysses" or his later 1889 "Crossing the Bar."

Schooled by his disinherited father, the Reverend George C. Tennyson, who predicted that his son "should be the greatest Poet of the Time" (Tennyson, *Collection* 2) and under whose tutelage young Tennyson tapped an extensive library of classics, the five year old was inspired to write a line he considered to be greater than " ... Byron's or   Scott's ... 'With slaughterous sons of thunder rolled the flood'" (2). Years later at Trinity College, he excelled, even while complaining that "the studies of the University were so uninteresting, so much matter of fact. None but dry-headed, calculating, angular little gentlemen can take much delight in them" (4).

On the other side of the Atlantic, Melville's situation was similarly privileged. He devoured the extensive library that his father, an importer of French dry goods (Parker 1), would eventually be forced to sell due to business losses. Unlike Tennyson's father, Melville's finds his son "very backward in speech & somewhat slow in comprehension," although he does recognize where the writer's future talent would lie: "as far as he understands men & things [, he is] both solid & profound, & of a docile & amiable disposition" (Sealts 17).

Young Melville attended a series of elementary schools culminating in Albany Academy up until the time of his father's death in 1832. His curiosity, genius, and inculturated upper-middle class sensibility directed his self-education at the fireside school, just as he had Redburn remember foggy Saturdays "when school-boys stay at home reading *Robinson Crusoe*" (Sealts 16). Although the young man, to his regret, never attained the same level of mastery in the classics that Tennyson did, the American continued studies in the natural sciences (Sealts 20), which, supplemented with his sea experience, served him well in his literary endeavors.

All the while, and well into his career as a novelist, he read many of the same works Tennyson had read or was reading, as well as various editions of Tennyson's works. Melville did welcome into his library the influence of the poet laureate. In fact, Melville's library held copies of three different 1870 editions of *The Holy Grail, and other Poems* (Sealts 219), as well as a variety of Tennyson's other works.

One can see the attraction for him. The two shared a poetic and sensual awareness of the sea and an intense sense of melancholia stemming from disappointment and predisposition, both traits creating a trans-Atlantic, *ubi sunt* connection. In Tennyson, it was apparent in works like "Marianna in the South," *In Memoriam*—and in much of his *oeuvre*. An obvious example can be found in Melville's copy of the 1855 edition (Sealts 219) of *Maud, and Other Poems*. The speaker says in "Maud":

> Do we move ourselves, or are moved by an unseen
> hand at a game
> That pushes us off from the board, and others
> ever succeed?
> …

However we brave it out, we men are a little
    breed. (23)

These lines remind us of Chapter 132, "The Symphony" in *Moby Dick*, published in 1851:

What is it, what nameless, inscrutable, unearthly thing is it; what cozening, hidden lord and master, and cruel, remorseless emperor commands me ... Is Ahab, Ahab? Is it I, God, or who, that lifts this arm? (406)

The language and philosophy of both works are similar to Diogenes Teufelsdroch's anguished questioning of his existence in Thomas Carlyle's *Sartor Resartus*: "Who am I; what is Me? A Voice, a Motion, An appearance—Some embodied, visualized idea in the Eternal Mind?" (88) Not only had Tennyson been friends with Carlyle, Melville had borrowed the work in 1850 (Sealts). More than likely, he also had the 1849 volume of Carlyle in the *Modern British Essayists* series from this time (Sealts 198-9).

Another *ubi sunt* poem, "Break, Break, Break," was in the 1861 edition of *The Poetical Works of Alfred Tennyson*, also found in Melville's library:

Break, break, break,
    At the foot of thy crags, oh Sea!
But tender grace of a day that is dead
    Will never come back to me (I: 255)

This melancholia had long been a part of Tennyson's character:

In my youth I knew much greater unhappiness than I have known in later life. When I was about twenty, I used to feel moods of misery unutterable! ... The smallness and emptiness of life sometimes over-whelmed me. (Tennyson, *Collection* 4)

And in Melville, similarly, we can find such despair in his later works. During the years just prior to the Civil War, he realized that he would never be financially secure and suffered from a severe and disabling case of rheumatism during which he seriously examined the poetry of Hunt, Shelley, Thomson, Spenser, and of course, Tennyson (Sealts 112). At this point, it appears that his enforced convalescence and concentration yoked with his declining literary influence resulted in the bulk of his poetic *oeuvre*, beginning with his 1857 *Poems*.

Along with his recurring bouts of rheumatism, he continued his study of poetics and poets, including Matthew Arnold, a poet whose naturalist sensibilities in the 1867 "Dover Beach" (found in the 1871 *New Poems* in Melville's library) can be associated with Tennyson's "honest doubt" and questioning verse: "... [W]e are here as on a darkling plain/Swept with confused alarms of struggle and/flight,/Where ignorant armies clash by night" (96).

Although we can find Arnold's influence in Melville's work, we must temper it with the knowledge that Arnold was influenced by Tennyson, despite the younger poet's later criticism of his elder. Anyone doubting the Laureate's influence on Arnold can find evidence in Tennyson's letters. There we find that Aubrey de Vere wrote to Isabella Fenwick in 1850 concerning the Laureate's predisposition to be "surrounded ... by young men ... who believe no more in Christianity than in the feudal system." Her remark had been prompted by the departure of the two poets as they traveled together from Cheltenham to Crewe (*Letters* III, 340).

Unlike Arnold, well known were Tennyson's personal vacillations between upholding the status quo—belief and duty—and deploring it. One of the most famous examples of this struggle could be found in 1854, when Tennyson's Victorian devotion to duty mingled with his aversion to the existing state of affairs. His outrage about a discrepancy in numbers and reporting in *The Times* concerning an incident in Balaclava where soldiers had fallen because of "some hideous blunder" (Shannon and Ricks 1-2) found its way—in two different versions—into Melville's library, one printed in the 1855 *Maud and Other Poems* and the other in the 1861 *The Poetical Works of Alfred Tennyson.* The second version held nothing back, revealing his support for those whose fate, like his, was determined by forces beyond their own control:

> "Forward the Light Brigade!"
> Was there a man dismayed?
> Not though the soldier knew
> Someone had blundered:
> Their's not to make reply,
> Their's not to reason why,
> Their's but to do and die ... *(Poetical*, II: 177)

And in a similar galloping meter, Melville's "Sheridan at Cedar Creek" from his 1866 *Battle Pieces,* also recognized predetermined fate while raggedly triple-rhyming men into the valley of death:

> They cheered him in the looming,
> Horseman and horse they knew.
> The turn of the tide began,

The rally of bugles ran,
He swung his hat in the van;
The electric hoof-spark flew. (116-7)

He continued his discussion of fate in "The Armies of the Wilderness":

> Obscure as wood, the entangled rhyme
>> But hints at the maze of war—
> Vivid glimpses or livid through peopled gloom,
>> And fires which creep and char—
> A riddle of death, of which the slain
>> Sole survivors are. (103)

And like these slain, sole survivors, Melville found the riddle of gaining acceptance for these poems, during his lifetime, to be one he never solved. Nevertheless, he continued his poetic endeavors, weaving a doomed volume of poetry and a tale of doomed love and disbelief in his 1876 religious epic *Clarel*. Even after his trip to the Holy Land, Clarel says, "They wire the world—far under sea./They talk; but never comes to me/A message from beneath the stone" (498). Even as he attempts to believe, in the closing lines of the work, Clarel can only speculatively do so: "Even death may prove unreal at the last,/And stoics be astounded into heaven" (499). Of his work and his life, Nathaniel Hawthorne recalled that Melville

> had "pretty much made up his mind to be annihilated" ... He can neither believe, nor be comfortable in his unbelief; and he is too honest and courageous not to try to do one or the other. (Parker 300)

Hawthorne's observation might have been a profound observation about a Romantic novelist, but it was merely an accurate observation of a Victorian poet, for even in his mature years; the two voices in his *In Memoriam* were never at peace. On one hand, Tennyson assured the Queen that he was her Poet Laureate, representing her will and position. But on the other hand, he was Melville's spiritual and emotional doppelganger. In June of 1879, the Prime Minister's daughter, Mary Gladstone, said of the poet's "unbelief":

> I am disappointed in his religion. It is purely founded on the chaos and failure of a godless world, and there is a want of reverence which is a shock from one who speaks of the 'worlds' great altar stairs, that lead through darkness up to God.' (Tennyson, *Collection* 62-3)

The poets' similarities might have been the basis of Hawthorne's appreciation for the Laureate:

> I was indescribably sensible of a morbid painfulness in him, a something
> not to be meddled with. (Tennyson, *Collection* 35)

Relating to the despair and sense of isolation found in both poets, that Melville would be interested in the inspiration for *In Memoriam*, Arthur Hallam, should not be surprising. Sometime between 1863 and 1870, Melville acquired a copy of *Remains in Prose and Verse of Arthur Henry Hallam* in an edition published by Ticknor and Fields in 1863. Had he not been primed by Tennyson's *In Memoriam*, which Melville had read in 1850 and returned to specifically in 1871 (Sealts 219),[1] Melville, of course, would have had no obvious reason to be interested in Hallam.

In *Remains*, edited by Hallam's father, the historian Henry Hallam, Melville would have met a bereaved father who by the time of the book's second edition in 1853 (the one reprinted by Ticknor) had lost not one but two sons. In Arthur, Melville met a student of poetry who had every advantage that Melville lacked to become a poet.[2] In Hallam's love of Dante and Shakespeare, of Wordsworth and Shelley, even in his fits of depression, Melville would have recognized a kindred spirit of the kind he often sought in real life—Jack Chase, Richard Henry Dana, Nathaniel Hawthorne. And he would have recognized, when he read of Arthur's death in Vienna at age 22 how easily he himself might have died at age 22 in the Typee Valley. When he set seriously to work on *John Marr*, Melville had lost one son to suicide and another to obscurity on the west coast. By 1886, the kindred spirit was the father who, Empedocles-like, had outlived his progeny and his age.

Besides the personal and emotional influences found in *In Memoriam*, another work would profoundly affect Melville's *John Marr and Other Sailors with Some Sea Pieces* (1888). Although William Shurr has observed a connection between Tennyson's "The Lotos Eaters" and *John Marr*, *Enoch Arden, ETC.*, written in 1861-2, ought to be considered even more indicative of Tennysonian influence. Both works feature narrative poems recounting sailors who, for reasons beyond their own control, lose everything they hold dear.

---

[1] He also might have read the 1853 description in *Notes and Queries* of Hallam's grave, which is near the sea at the parish Church of St. Andrew in Clevedon: "rounding a green shoulder, you come suddenly upon it, like a ghost" (*Notes* 221).

[2] Hallam's connections also brought Tennyson advantage with Edward Moxon and literary magazines of the day: "If Hallam was a powerful persuader, so too was his money" (Ricks 71).

Relatedly, Tennyson's wife remembered him reading to the family George Crabbe's "The Parting Hour" (Scott 11), from his 1812 *Tales* (Tennyson, *SE* 592), and Melville had read the same poem in his copy of Crabbe's 1819 *Tales of the Hall* (Bryant 3), which was more than likely an influential text about a missing sailor for both their story lines. Moreover, Herman Melville couldn't have been unaware of *Enoch Arden*. During the War, his good friend Henry T. Tuckerman would have reminisced about his visits in New York with Garibaldi in the early 1850's (Parker II: 488, 655) and also most likely would have been aware of, and talked to Melville about, the Italian's 1864 visit in April to Farringford, the Laureate's home. Tennyson's work was published soon afterward, in August, and Tuckerman would have let neither event pass unnoticed.

With Melville's version of the sailor tale, the author initiated his tale with a poetic prose headpiece, which is comparable to Tennyson's verse throughout his poem. Marr's isn't an unusual tale. He is an orphan who has sailed under numerous flags and who becomes disabled from a "crippling wound received at close range with the pirates of the Keys" (263).[3] Unable to support himself at sea, he moves from seaport to seaport, mending sails, eventually moving inland, with a sailor's instinctive wanderlust, settling in a sparsely populated prairie where he marries and begins a family. When his wife and baby die of fever, he refuses to leave the only family he has ever known. As a result, he suffers from an intense isolation only possible when others are nearby. Melville signals, in verse, how Marr counters the isolation by recreating his interactions with the men he had sailed with, attempting to connect:

> ... A beat, a heart-beat musters all,
> One heart-beat at heart-core '.
> It musters. But to clasp, retain;
>
> To see you at the halyards main—
> To hear your chorus once again! (268)

His obvious allusion to Matthew Arnold's "darkling plain" in the beginning of this verse section, "Once, for all the darkling sea,/You your voices raised how clearly,/Striking in when tempest sung ... " (*JM* 267),

---

[3] His background and physical description are identical to James Fenimore Cooper's biographical subject in his 1843 *Ned Myers; or, A Life Before the Mast*. Moreover, Melville's brother later ran the same Sailors' Snug Harbor that Myers retired to. Melville's portraits of sailors ashore did not need to be speculative. (Parker II: *651 ff*)

belies the only slightly less assignable affinity with Tennyson. Not only is the construct of the sailor's story an important element of the book, but like Melville's "Bridegroom Dick" or "Tom Deadlight," Tennyson's earlier companion poems to the 1864 "Enoch Arden," "Sea Dream" and "The Grandmother" and "Aylmer's Fields," similarly capture in verse others who experience what little life has to offer, whose isolated discourse tells of madness, despair, or suicide. Here, Sir Aylmer reveals the dilemma of death in life, a common Tennysonian theme:

> Staring for ever from the guilded walls
> On him their last descendant, his own head
> Began to droop, to fall; the man became
> Imbecile; his one word was "desolate":
> Dead for two years before his death was he. . . . (*EA* 94)

Unlike *John Marr*'s, *Enoch Arden*'s blank verse tale is told in extensive detail from childhood to manhood, building with an emotional intensity found in a lovers' triangle, which remains until the story's close. After being lost at sea for years, the sailor returns to find his family now the family of his friend and rival. On leaving the window where he's seen their happiness,

> Back toward his solitary home again,
> All down the long and narrow street he went
> Beating it in upon his weary brain,
> As though it were the burthen of a song,
> 'Not to tell her, never to let her know.' (43-4)

He, like Marr, almost loses his sanity, but his work and decision to tell his sad tale only to Miriam Lane, the local tavern owner, help him survive. Only moments before death does he give permission for her to inform family members that he has been on shore for a good while, employed at a variety of vocations, as had Marr been:

> Scorning at alms, to work whereby to live.
> Almost to all things could he turn his hand.
> Cooper he was and carpenter, and wrought
> To make the boatmen fishing-nets, or helped
> At lading and unlading the tall barks. . . . (44-5)

The two characters' choices in dealing with their fates are similarly motivated. Although both construct survival within a language of loss and isolation, these sailors find no safe harbor from a sea of troubles. Relating to Marr's being stranded on an island of prairie and Arden's being stranded on a tropical one, Shurr has equated the work with Tennyson's blissful life of the lotus eaters who are "'unconscious' of the loveliness of the setting" (143). But as with many Tennysonian characters, Marr and Arden "[wait] in an unmerciful landscape" (Ricks 280). The overall portrayal of Arden's reality is painfully candid and conscious, more in keeping with the destroyed psyche found in Melville's work. For Arden, his family's chances for survival would be completely destroyed by the revelation of his return, torn and weakened by allegiances to both fathers. For Marr, because his family lives only in memory, when he dies, they die too. In order to keep them "alive," his own sanity must be maintained. The conversations he has are a life raft in the midst of a culture remarkably sterile for all its lush agricultural fertility.

Significant to the development of *Marr* is the genre choice that Melville and his sister Augusta, as well as the rest of the reading public, were noticing in Tennyson's 1842 *Poems*—his English Idylls, the beginnings of the *Idylls of the King,* eventually released in 1859. A few years afterward, in 1861, Tennyson announced his latest publication, *Idyll's of the Hearth* (Scott 20), but he realized that he needed to avoid layering the poem with more Victorian, religious undertones than it already held.[4]

Thus, the Laureate changed the title to *Enoch Arden*, but the original had found its way into Melville's creative consciousness. *John Marr* is nothing if not a collection of idylls, pastoral poems, all within the mind of a man for whom the prairie was "a reminder of ocean" (265). Marr is adrift, isolated:

> [i]n some more enriched depressions between the long, green, graduated swells, smooth as those of ocean becalmed receiving and subduing to its own tranquillity [sic]. (266)

His creating connections with his compatriots serves the poem in much the same way that Tennyson's Arthur does: The "King [is] the complete man, the Knights are the passions" (*SE* 671). Tom Dean, Jack Roy, The Haglets,[5] all short (by Victorian standards), descriptive poems, attempt to

---

[4] Anyone who kept abreast of literary affairs was aware of the criticism that was leveled over Arden's failing in his moral duty to inform his wife that she was a bigamist. Tennyson's work viewed the tragedy with compassion toward all involved. (Scott 11-7)

[5] *Billy Budd* began as a "prose sketch and ballad thus placing the character in a situation" (Hayford 2) similar to the characters in *Marr*.

form an emotional fortress for a mind bereft of channels for even minimal engagement:

> Man keeps from man the stifled moan,
> They shouldering stand, yet each in heart how lone.
>> Some heaven invoke; but rings of reefs
> Prayer and despair alike deride
> In dance of breakers forked or peaked. (289)

Melville had read and related to the poetry that was Tennyson's "stifled moan," and nowhere is it more obvious than in John Marr's curse. His is similar to the plight of the subject of Tennyson's most famous idyll, the Lady of Shallott who resides on an island between "[l]ong fields of barley and of rye,/that clothe the wold and meet the sky" (*PW* I:38). She weaves the very fabric of her isolation from the voices of "reapers reaping early":

> She has heard a whisper say,
> A curse is on her if she stay
>> To look down to Camelot.
> She knows not what the curse may be,
> And so she weaveth steadily. . . . (39)

Like the lady, Marr will lose his sanity should he look directly at reality. He weaves his "shadows," his "prayer and despair," not only to dispel loneliness but also to retain the memories of those he loves, in order to give them life.

The sentiment echoes both Tennyson's personal and intense loneliness and the mind's engagement in his "In Memory," found in Melville's 1861 set of *Poetical Works*:

> *We may hold converse with all forms*
> *Of the many sided mind,*
> *And those whom passion had not blinded,*
> *Subtle-thoughted, myriad-minded,*
> *My friend, with you to live alone. . . , (*20)

Beyond the common texts that Melville and Tennyson had read, beyond the Laureate's works owned by Melville, beyond the correspondences of theme, beyond the shared language of isolation, and beyond the profound draw that the sea and its sailors held for each author is the circumstance that *Enoch Arden*'s blue and gold bound "publications [in America] were too numerous and their sale too rapid for accurate recording," most likely totaling over 400,000 the first year (*Letters* II, 428). On the first day alone, "[s]ome seventeen thousand copies were sold" (Scott 1). So recognized, perhaps *John Marr* would have finally visited Tennyson's library, but neither was to be. Over one hundred years have passed since its publication, and today many consider *Marr* an innovative and worthy mixed prose-verse (Renker 487). Regardless of its merits, it would be difficult to prove that *John Marr* in its completed form would exist had there been no maritime Tennyson.

Works Cited

Arnold, Matthew. *New Poems*. Boston: Ticknor and Fields, 1867.

Bryant, John. "From the Masthead." *Leviathan*. 6:1 (2004): 3.

Carlyle, Thomas. "The World Out of Clothes." *Sartor Resartus. English Prose of the Victorian Period. Ed. William D. Templeman and Charles Frederick Harrold.* New York: Oxford UP, 1938. 83-149.

Cooper, James Fenimore. *Ned Myers; or, A Life Before the Mast*. New York: Lee and Blanchard, 1843.

Hallam, Arthur Henry. *Remains in Verse and Prose of Arthur Henry Hallam*. Henry Hallam, ed. Boston: Ticknor and Fields, 1863.

"Hallam's Grave." *Notes and Queries*. Sept. 22, 1853.

Hayford, Harrison and Merton M. Sealts, Jr., eds. Introduction. *Billy Budd, Sailor: An Inside Narrative* by Herman Melville. Chicago: U of Chicago P, 1962.

Melville, Herman. *Clarel: A Poem and Pilgrimage in the Holy Land*. Eds. Harrison Hayford, Alma A. MacDougall, Hershel Parker, and G. Thomas Tanselle. Chicago: Northwestern UP, 1991.

—. *The Poems of Herman Melville*. Ed. Douglas Robillard. Kent, Ohio: Kent State UP, 2000.

Parker, Hershel. *Herman Melville: A Biography, Volume 1, 1819-1851*. Baltimore, MD: Johns Hopkins UP: 1996.

—. *Herman Melville: A Biography, Volume 2, 1851-1891*. Baltimore, MD: Johns Hopkins UP: 2002.

—. *Moby-Dick*. New York: Norton Critical Edition, 2002. Eds. Hershel Parker and Harrison Hayford. 2nd ed.

Renker, Elizabeth. "Melville the Realist Poet." *A Companion to Herman Melville*. Ed. Wyn Kelley. Malden, MA: Blackwell, 2006. 483-96.

Ricks, Christopher. *Tennyson*. New York: Macmillan, 1972.

Scott, P. G. *Tennyson's "Enoch Arden": A Victorian Best Seller*. Lincoln, England: Keyworth and Fry Ltd., 1970.

Sealts, Merton. M., Jr. *Melville's Reading*. Columbia: U of South Carolina P, 1988.

Shannon, Edgar, and Christopher Ricks. "'The Charge of the Light Brigade': The Creation of a Poem." *Studies in Bibliography*, 38 (1985): 1-38.

Shurr, William H. *The Mystery of Iniquity*. Lexington: UP of Kentucky, 1972.

Tennyson, Alfred, Lord. *A Collection of Poems by Tennyson*. Ed. Christopher Ricks. Garden City, NY: Doubleday, 1972.

—. *Enoch Arden, ETC*. London: Moxon, 1864.

—. *Letters of Alfred, Lord Tennyson*. Vols. I-III. Eds. Cecil Y. Lang and Edgar F. Shannon, Jr. Oxford: Clarendon P, 1990.

—. *The Poetical Works of Alfred Tennyson*, Poet Laureate, ETC. Boston: Ticknor and Fields, 1861. Vol. I.

—. *The Poetical Works of Alfred Tennyson*, Poet Laureate, ETC. Boston: Ticknor and Fields, 1861. Vol. II.

—. *Tennyson: A Selected Edition*. Ed. Christopher Ricks. Berkely, U of California P, 1989.

—. *Maud, and Other Poems*. Boston: Ticknor and Fields, 1855.

CHAPTER THREE:

THE FEARSOME SEAS: FACT AND FICTION

SUBMERGED REALITIES: SHARK DOCUMENTARIES AT DEPTH[1]

KATHRYN FERGUSON

> There isn't any symbolism. The sea is the
> sea. The old man is an old man. The boy
> is a boy and the fish is a fish. The sharks
> are all sharks no better and no worse. All
> the symbolism that people say is shit.
> What goes beyond is what you see beyond
> when you know.
> —Ernest Hemingway (780)

Richard Fitzpatrick caught his first Epaulette shark from the Coral Sea when he was eleven years old. He took it home, put it in his aquarium, and then transported the whole thing to school for show and tell. Some twenty years later, he is still playing show and tell with sharks, but to a much larger audience. His work has been seen on, amongst others, the Discovery Channel, the National Geographic Channel, the ABC, the BBC, the CBC, and Japan's NHK and TBS. As both a marine scientist and a director of Digital Dimensions in Townsville Australia, Fitzpatrick has been a subject of several documentaries, has filming credits on a wide range of documentary, corporate, and mainstream film projects, and has, with his business partner Brett Shorthouse, created a number of award-winning nature documentaries. Fitzpatrick has been senior biologist at Manly Oceanworld and Maui Ocean Center, a biologist at the Great Barrier Reef Aquarium, and has spent well over eight thousand hours underwater, a goodly percentage of that time with sharks. His aquarium has grown into a fully-tended aquatic film studio which includes a sixty cubic-metre tank and four thousand-litre tanks. In both studying and filming sharks, he has navigated through the maze of corporate television

---

[1] An earlier version of this essay appeared in *Revista Atenea* XXVI-1 (June 2006) Special issue on Humans and the Environment. We thank the journal for permitting us to re-print this essay.

expectations, and put them to the use of shark research and conservation.[2] Fitzpatrick's argument is straightforward and pragmatic: "very little is known about the basic biology and ecology of tropical sharks" (Fitzpatrick). We need to know more about sharks' biology, habits, and haunts before we can implement a successful and responsible preservation strategy for these animals and their environments. His assessment of commercial shark fishing is even more succinct: "shark fishing is just— it's unsustainable" (Fitzpatrick in Brook). Putting premises into practice, Fitzpatrick and Digital Dimensions have forged a unique relationship with Undersea Explorer, an environmentally responsible charter diving operation, that combines scientific research, documentary production, and eco-tourism: a sustainable shark industry in Australia's Coral Sea.

What I propose here is an historically contextualised examination of specific segments of the documentary work of Richard Fitzpatrick; Australia's "Shark Tracker." Fitzpatrick's work is a particularly apt point of departure, as he has been both the cameraman and the subject of underwater documentary films. Admittedly, my article looks at only a tiny portion of Fitzpatrick's documentary work, which is itself only a minute fraction of a vastly under-analysed genre, and thus must be considered as a discrete example rather than as representative of an entire sphere. My discussion stems from Bill Nichols' notion of an 'historical reality' wherein documentary representations of any given reality are understood as ontologically, rather than simply analogically, linked to the 'real world' ("The Voice of Documentary"; *Representing Reality*). Understanding any documentary reality as an historically constituted reality—one which is defined by its own contemporaneous positioning, which has, in turn, been shaped by historical forces—is particularly significant to any understanding of underwater documentaries because of the 'Otherness' of the environment which is depicted.

In thinking of 'the environment,' we too often neglect the vast submerged eco-systems that make up a huge portion of our world. This may be due in part to the fact that we tend to translate 'the environment' to '*our* environment' which is, for the most part, limited to land; we are terrestrial creatures. As Hemingway's disgruntled comment, which serves as an epigraph to this article, suggests, there is a well-established tradition of reading an oceanic text, not as a descriptive narrative of a unique environment, but as a simplified simulacrum symbolic of our own *a priori*

---

[2] The commercial success of Digital Dimensions has also allowed the company to offer stock footage to specific environmental protection groups.

world. Historically, this way of thinking has been mirrored in documentary commentary and theory. For example, in his 1974 otherwise inclusive history of non-fiction films, Erik Barnouw dismissed underwater documentary with a quick nod to the fact that Jacques Cousteau chronicled "a strange world" (210). I contend that it is precisely *because* of the ostensible 'Otherness' and 'strangeness' of the underwater environments—our alienation from them and our lack of understanding of them—that we need to recognise the historical bases and biases of our own prejudices and perceptions of that immense underwater bionetwork. As Fitzpatrick notes in *Richard Fitzpatrick and his Sharks*:

> Everything is related together ... Biodiversity is very important. There are things out there and inter-relationships we just don't know anything about at all, and we may not know about for generations. And if we destroy them now, we could be having a *huge* detrimental effect to the ecosystem—the whole world.

Keeping in mind John Corner's warning that theoretical work on documentaries "has often increasingly divorced itself from attention to specific practices and artefacts, setting up as a relatively autonomous discursive activity 'above' the level of both practice and practical criticism" (9), my article does not propose to institute a coherent or cohesive theory of underwater or shark documentary. Instead, I will put forward a brief examination of some of the specific elements of the historical reality that lies beyond and beneath a very small sampling of Fitzpatrick's underwater documentary endeavours. My article is, somewhat ironically, grounded in the water.

Anchor, Bruce, and Chum, Pixar's cartoon trio of twelve-stepping vegetarian sharks (2003), the internet's favourite digitally merged photograph of a South African Great White leaping at an American military helicopter in San Francisco Bay (Danielson), and Damien Hirst's pickled Australian Tiger shark (1991) all point towards the increasing lack of distinction between what is 'real' and what is 'illusion,' and do so specifically in the world of sharks. Indeed, in a world where eighty percent of shark species may be endangered, and humans still kill up to a hundred million sharks annually; where flavourless shark fin is an illicit gourmet status symbol while the cheapest choice on the menu at the local fish and chip shop is most likely to be flake; and the redolent 1975 soundtrack from *Jaws* still has cultural currency, it is arguable that such a line has been practically erased.[3]   The uneasy oscillations of fear and fascination, fact and fiction, art and science that thrum through our contemporary impressions of sharks seem to portend a particularly thorny state of affairs confronting shark documentarists aiming to portray sharks and their underwater environments realistically. With a market increasingly demanding their nature and wildlife documentaries 'red in tooth and claw' with "higher tempo—much more action" (Landin 16), there seems little space for anything but spectacular scenes showing as much blood, gore, and carnage as possible. Peter Steinhart has labelled the exaggerated emphasis on death and violence in nature films as "eco-porn" ("Ecoporn") or "outdoor porn" ("Wildlife Films" 41), suggesting that 'the kill shot' in nature documentaries has become equivalent to 'the money shot' in pornography. The histrionic combination of blood and bubbles in rigidly segmented timeframes is increasingly being demanded and expected of underwater documentaries. Fitzpatrick sums up the filmic conundrum facing shark documentarists neatly: "we are probably responsible for people's [exaggerated] perceptions of sharks ... Yeah, documentary makers have been responsible for changing people's perceptions of these animals" but adds that if he were "to make a shark documentary about what sharks are doing normally, people would fall asleep" (Fitzpatrick in R. Williams).

The creation of a shark documentary is thus no simple process of relentlessly recording 'what sharks are doing normally': on the contrary, it would seem that the documentary, albeit perhaps reluctantly, reinscribes at least some portion of the exaggerated mythologies and fictions about what sharks are *not* doing normally. With this knowledge, one might glibly conclude that there is no real possibility of any inherent biological or ecological reality to be found in shark documentaries, and consequently the only pertinent questions remaining entail quantifying the value of such documentaries as highly stylised nautical fiction.[4] This line of reasoning,

---

[3] *Jaws*'s lingering ability to contaminate our perceptions of sharks may go even further than imagined. In *Jaws* (1975) a Louisiana licence plate is removed from the belly of a Tiger shark. In *Deep Blue Sea (1999)* the exact same plate is removed from the teeth of a Tiger shark.

[4] For a history of the truth/fiction debate specifically in terms of wildlife documentary, Bousé offers an excellent recounting in his third chapter, "Science and Storytelling" (86-123). A valuable point to emerge in the truth/fiction debate regarding wildlife documentary is the issue of animal cruelty. George James brought this point to horrifying precedence in 1983 in his own animal documentary *Cruel Camera* on the CBC's *Fifth Estate*. The program showed that many 'natural' events in wildlife films had been ruthlessly staged. The most notorious

however, would not go far in explaining the long-standing dearth of critical or theoretical discussions, not only about shark documentaries specifically, but about underwater wildlife documentaries as a whole. Theorists have been debating the 'truth' content of documentaries for long enough that critics, such as Brian McIlroy, were confident in claiming over ten years ago that "it is now common to read that, theoretically speaking, documentary and narrative fiction film 'proper' are indistinguishable as constructed realities" (288). Linda Williams, alternatively suggested in 1993, that "an overly simplified dichotomy between truth and fiction is at the root of our difficulty in thinking about the truth in documentary" (20). That same year, Brian Winston argued that, in order to survive, the documentary form needed to once and for all privilege art over science that that, in the end, it would be "necessary for the documentary, to negotiate and escape from the embrace of science" (56-57). Science and storytelling, it would seem, make each other uneasy. Or, as Julian Petley neatly summed it up in 1996: "Fact plus fiction equals friction" (11).

Bill Nichols has noted that although in recent years the linkage of documentary and fictional space within single texts has led to a questioning of the reality of documentary footage, he believes that in documentary films "some quality of the moment persists outside the grip of textual organization" (*Representing Reality* 231). If, as Susan Sontag contends, photographs not only "give people an imaginary possession of a past that is unreal, they also help people to take possession of space in which they are insecure" (9), it follows that underwater films about sharks might well be construed, especially by those preferring to remain top-side, as the ultimate in psychologically satisfying photography, as they facilitate the comfortable imaginative appropriation of 'some quality of the moment' from a largely unknown and particularly precarious space. However, even within the specialised realm of animal documentary, underwater criticism is conspicuous by its scarcity. In 1966, John Warham's *The Technique of Wildlife Cinematography* justified the fact that it did not include marine animals in its topics by asserting that "those whose subjects are laboratory animals like fish...have available to them techniques and specialized gear generally quite inapplicable in the free world outside of the laboratory" (9). Perhaps that is understandable for an

---

was Disney's *White Wilderness* (1958) that passed off the intentional herding of pet lemmings off a cliff, several hundred kilometres south of their natural habitat, as natural behaviour. It is important to note here that *not all* animal documentarists practice, condone, or allow these practices.

author writing during an era when Jacques Cousteau, Peter Parks, and Hans and Lotte Hass were still trailblazers in the field of openwater underwater film production, and the BBC2's June 1968 programme on plankton had not yet "astounded viewers, most of whom had no idea that such life forms existed" (Parsons 253). However, some thirty-four years later it is less understandable when Derek Bousé admits in 2000 that, in his historical study of *Wildlife Films*, he had

> not dealt with films about underwater creatures—cetaceans, crustaceans, fish, and so on. I see underwater films ... operating by somewhat different codes and conventions because of the conditions under which they are made, the behaviour of underwater creatures themselves, and several other factors. (xiii)

Bousé does not explain what the 'several other factors' are, but does go on to suggest that a book, such as his own, "can and should be written about films dealing with underwater life" (xiii). The elision of underwater documentary from critical discourse has meant that we have not thought, to any significant degree, about what exactly it means to film an underwater environment, about the documentary representation of that underwater environment itself, or how we have come to think what we do about that 'Othered' space and its inhabitants.

In 1997, Fitzpatrick financed a portion of his ongoing research on the White Tip Reef sharks at Osprey Reef by agreeing to be the subject of *Australie: Les Requins de la Grande Barrière* (1997) as a part of Canal Plus' Dans la Nature series.[5] In 2002, he similarly agreed to be the subject of *Shark Tracker* (2002) and *Richard Fitzpatrick and his Sharks* (2002) at Raine Island to partially finance the first successful satellite tagging of a Tiger shark in Australian waters.[6] In 2003 he returned to tag three more

---

[5] Osprey Reef is an isolated seamount approximately 330 Kilometres northeast of Cairns in the Coral Sea. It is about 70 nautical miles outside of the Great Barrier Reef Marine Park Authority's jurisdiction, and thus extremely vulnerable to raiding by floating fish processing plants. Fitzpatrick has been studying the White Tips at North Horn since 1995, and, to date, has captured and tagged twenty-eight of the thirty identified White Tips. With Andy Dunstan of Undersea Explorer, a database is maintained that monitors the growth and reproductive rate of the population. The data collected thus far clearly indicates that if the resident population of sharks were to be significantly depleted, the slow growth and reproductive rates of sharks would guarantee that the health of the entire reef would be detrimentally affected by the loss of its apex predators.

[6] Raine Island is a thirty-two hectare coral cay six hundred and twenty kilometres northwest of Cairns near the northern tip of Cape York. As the largest green turtle

Tiger sharks and be a part of *Raine Island: Nature's Warzone* (2003). All of these documentaries highlight the fact that humans and documentary cameras are visitors to the reef rather than inhabitants. The mechanical sound of breathing through a regulator during underwater scenes, an emphasis on means and length of travel, the gear required to get into the water and stay there for a longer than a breath-length, and footage of humans on land all serve as reminders of the very basic differences between living *on* land and living *in* the sea. Fitzpatrick makes the point clear: "we must always remember that in here [the ocean] that's the sharks' home—that's their home—its not ours, and we're visitors to that ... It's their world; we have to be respectful when we visit." In 2004 it seems rather obvious that to represent the lives of sharks accurately and effectively one must get in the water; we must visit their world. There are between 465 and 480 species of sharks in the world, and although some live in fresh water and some live in salt water, they all live in water. For our contemporary sophisticated tastes, any documentary that presented sharks exclusively by looking down on them from the dry perspectives of land or deck would be laughable, and even a documentary shot exclusively in a large aquarium would be disappointing.

What is easy to forget is that, until the last half of the nineteenth century, almost all depictions of sea creatures were conventionally described from the perspective of the shore. Marine animals were usually portrayed either alive at the water's surface or dead and desiccating on land. In 1731, for example, J.J. Scheuchzer published his very successful 750-plate tome depicting a natural science perspective of the Biblical scenes wherein all aquatic animals are depicted on top of or out of the water. When John Singleton Copely painted *Watson and the Shark* in 1778 and showed only the parts of the shark that are above the water line, not only was he creating a dramatic representation of man's struggle against nature, he was also adhering to the 'natural' and naturalists' way of illustrating sharks. Even by 1852, Sir William Jardine's *Fishes of British Guiana* in The Naturalist's Library series has most of its fish posed unconvincingly on dry rocks at the water's edge. There was no underwater perspective to expect or demand from those who took it upon themselves to represent the submerged world. Most people did not know how to swim, and although Aristotle discusses the use of diving bells, it

---

rookery in the world and the most significant tropical seabird nesting site, Raine Island is Australia's most protected natural space and closed to all except a limited number of researchers. Each year, as thousands of turtles migrate to the island, Tiger sharks (usually solitary and elusive creatures) gather to prey on the turtles.

was not until 1535 that the first true diving bell was invented. Even though the first diving suit was tested in the Thames in February of 1715, it was not until 1825 that a workable, yet still dangerous, model for a breathing apparatus was designed.

It would not be until after the English aquarium craze of the 1850s that the 'natural' and 'correct' way of depicting marine life would shift from looking downwards on the subject to an edge-on perspective.[7] Arguably, the 'proper' way of depicting marine life was dependent more upon the lifting of the exorbitant British tax on glass in 1845 and the English middle-classes' obsession with domestic fashion, than it was on a scientifically driven campaign for biological accuracy. Before the English aquarium fad it was close to unthinkable to view marine life face to face, as the only natural perspective hitherto had been from the shore. Although some marine naturalists may well have known exactly what a shark would look like head on or from the side in, say 1806, it simply was not done to illustrate a shark from any perspective but from above; the perspective from which most people would have seen marine life. With the intro-duction of the domestic aquarium in the last half of the century, everyone came to know that the 'correct' way of viewing sea creatures was up close and eye-to-eye. However, even by the summer of 1922, when E.J. Pratt wrote "The Shark," underwater perspectives of pelagic creatures, those which did not fit in the household tank, were still largely reserved for educated specialists and enthusiastic naturalists.[8] Pratt's 'common man' narrator watches a shark from a Newfoundland wharf on the east coast of Canada, describing only that which is above the surface; the way that sharks would be seen 'naturally':

> He seemed to know the harbour,
> So leisurely he swam;
> His fin,
> Like a piece of sheet-iron,
> Three-cornered,
> And with knife-edge,
> Stirred not a bubble
> As it moved

---

[7] Stephen Jay Gould discusses this transition in "Seeing Eye to Eye, Through a Glass Clearly" (57-73).

[8] There was a brief period from 1870-1890 where public aquariums were popular. However, as Lynn Barber points out, when experts began to garner better and more sophisticated research facilities, "the public aquaria…sank into mere vulgar amusement" and most public aquariums were re-fitted for other uses (124).

With its base-line on the water (1-9).

In 1958, all of that would change, at least in Britain, when Hans and Lotte Hass began their *Diving to Adventure* television series for the BBC. Ten years later, Jacques Cousteau was asked to make a television series on underwater life. For the next eight years, *The Undersea World of Jacques Cousteau* brought the underwater world to countless homes around the world—in colour. Although Cousteau's *The Silent World* (1956) and *World Without Sun* (1966) had both won Academy Awards for best documentary, it was with the paradigm shift, again domestic rather than scientific, of television programming that radically changed the 'correct' and 'common' way to depict sharks.[9] It was not until television brought the ocean into the homes of the western world in the last half of the twentieth century that audiences generally came to expect to be able to see a shark portrayed in his or her own natural habitat—from a 360-degree perspective in colour.

Obviously, that radically truncated account elides a myriad of detail and a great deal of both naturalist and technological history. However, the argument I would like to draw from that brief recounting is that sharks have, for quite some time now, looked the same. What has changed is the human perspective of what is to be expected when we see sharks represented. Admittedly, something of an obvious pair of statements, but what is implicit in that pairing is a recognition, not only that strategies of sight and thinking arise within social contexts, but that our contemporary notions of what it means to document a shark accurately, truthfully, and even scientifically have a very brief pedigree in the world of natural history. Most of us have taken pleasure in watching the work of underwater documentarists, and it is, for many of us, the only glimpses we have had of submerged worlds beyond the city aquarium. Although we may not have watched a full documentary on the undersea world since grade school, when presented with an underwater documentary, we still fully expect our sharks and other aquatic animals to be presented to us in a certain way, and within their own marine environment.

---

[9] In 1998 it would be admitted that a diver had faked the bends for *The Silent World*. Much more troubling, however, was the revelation that on the *Undersea World* documentaries, Cousteau crew had poured chlorine bleach into a tank containing an octopus to get the famous footage of an octopus climbing out of a tank onboard the *Calypso* and throwing itself back into the ocean. Even more problematic is the death of two sea lions who died because of the amount of time they had been kept out of the water in order to get sufficient footage for *Undersea World*.

Fitzpatrick, who has been fascinated with sharks for most of his thirty-four years, and is an articulate and able speaker, could very quickly, easily, and efficiently stand beside a whiteboard and explain to most members of a television audience pretty much all they could understand about shark biology and the importance of apex predators in maintaining a healthy reef ecosystem. He could probably even do it without a white-board. But that is not how we want or expect our environmental science to be served; we want real images of the real world showing us things we are not likely to see, ironically, outside of our own lounge rooms. We want our fish and marine scientists in the water, and we want our water bottled. As Susan Sontag points out, "reality has always been interpreted through the reports given by images, but it was not until the middle of the nineteenth century, with the invention of photography, that "the new age of non-belief strengthened the allegiance to images" to the extent that they became a supplement rather than a complement to the real (153). Sontag goes on to argue that, to some extent, we have begun to rely entirely upon images for our perceptions of reality, and that "the primitive notion of the efficacy of images presumes that images possess the qualities of real things, but our inclination is to attribute to real things the qualities of an image" (158). We have begun to interpret reality through the images presented to us by popular media, as much as we interpret those same images from our own experiential reality. This is particularly true of the underwater environment, which is, for many of us, 'known' and 'experienced' exclusively through filmic mediums. Unfortunately, the highly fiction-alised realms of movies such as *Jaws* and *Deep Blue Sea* have tended to eclipse, by simple popular sensationalism, any realistic appreciation of sharks as a natural, indeed necessary, part of a healthy reef ecosystem.

Today, images are premised on a certain epistemology and have an always already authority to dictate our expectations of reality. Our estimations of what is the 'correct' way of seeing marine life have been modified dramatically over the years, as has the experiential weight that we attribute to those images. Watching documentary footage in which Fitzpatrick tail ropes a 3.4 metre Tiger shark, measures her, attaches a tracking device to her dorsal fin, releases her, swims with her to make sure she is fine, and then sends her on her way with a hug and fond pat is quite a different experience than reading this relatively bland sentence. Indeed, what Fitzpatrick actually does with sharks is almost impossible to believe *until* we see the entire process laid out in front of us as a fully explicated and evidenced process of valuable environmental research. The process is not quite believable, intellectually intelligible, or environmentally relevant until we see the practical processes and scientific reasons for tagging a huge fish represented sequentially as part of a coherent whole. The documentary thus emerges as a highly effective way to communicate information that would otherwise be incredible—or, as Fitzpatrick would have it, put us to sleep. Indeed, our alienation from the underwater environment makes, not only the practical physical realities of Fitzpatrick's research almost beyond belief, but leaves much of the everyday moment to moment and mundane realities of the underwater world as inconceivable and unknown. Fish that change sexes, snails with harpoons, curious cod, amiable poisonous snakes, technicolour octopi, and sharks that like a bit of a scratch once they get to know you are just a sampling of those things which have to be seen to be believed; and we want to see them under-water, not from shore and *definitely* not dead and dehydrated on a biologist's bench.

When the *Endeavour*'s naturalist, Joseph Banks, sailed the east coast of Australia with Captain Cook in 1770 he paid scant scientific attention to the one-hundred and twenty-three species of sharks that reside on the Great Barrier Reef. A journal entry from earlier in the journey suggests that may have been, at least in part, due to the fact that, at least for that expedition, sharks were more interesting as crew rations than biological subjects:

> Up at 5 this morn to examine the shark who proves to be A blew Shark *Squalus glaucus*, while we were doing it 3 more came under the Stern of which we soon caught 2 which were common grey Sharks *Squalus Carcharias*, on one of whom were some sucking fish *Echinus remora*. The seamen tell us that the blew shark is worst of all sharks to eat, indeed his smell is abominably strong so as we had two of the better sort he was hove overboard (Banks, *Endeavour Journal*).

Banks' interest in sharks as a comestible commodity,[10] rather than an

---

[10] Here, it should also be recalled here that Banks was, in part, the instigator of Australia's disastrous whaling and sealing industries that blunderingly exhausted their resources within fifty years. In 1806, his advice was:

After the seals have been once effectually disturbs their diminished quantities will not then afford sufficient encouragement to induce Americans or Frenchmen to interfere with our colonists; but there can be no doubt that at all times hereafter seals will be attainable in great quantities … by stationary fishers, who know the course they take in their migrations, and can intercept them in their progress by nets and other contrivances. Thus, if we encourage our new settlers to disturb as speedily as possible every seal station they can discover, we shall receive from them an immense supply of skins and oil, in the first instance; shall prevent the interference of foreign nations in future in the sealing fishery; and secure ourselves intrinsic part of a fascinating ecosystem has been, thankfully, challenged by contemporary naturalists and scientists who are beginning, albeit slowly, to convince the western world that sharks are worth more alive than dead. This would seem particularly true of the Great Barrier Reef where tourism to the reef in 1998 was estimated to be worth over a billion dollars (*State of the GBR: Tourism*) whilst controlled commercial fishing on the reef in 1996 accounted for the, relatively small amount of $143,000,000 (*State of the GBR: Fisheries*). Dean Miller's ongoing research at James Cook University in Townsville has unequivocally convinced him that, in regard to the responsible and sustainable use of sharks at the Great Barrier Reef, "there is no better avenue than tourism" especially "when compared to extractive industries" (Miller). Live sharks can be revisited and respected: dead sharks are, per pound, worth half as much as halibut—once.[11]

Many of Fitzpatrick's documentaries are filmed onboard the *Undersea Explorer*, which is a recognized leader in responsible Australian marine eco-tourism. The shark attract dives offered by Undersea Explorer are featured in several shark documentaries, and are, in Miller's estimation, "a great conservation tool for sharks" as they allow tourists to see firsthand, and television audiences to witness vicariously, that, despite the bad media spin, sharks are not "senseless eating machines with a taste for human flesh, but are amazing animals born from millions of years of evolution" (Miller). Sharks indubitably play a role in attracting tourist, especially diving tourist, dollars to the Great Barrier Reef, and thus are key players as well as primary stakeholders in the success of their own preservation. Digital Dimensions and Undersea Explorer are currently engaged in lobbying to have the perimeters of the Great Barrier Reef Marine Park expanded to protect a larger area of the vulnerable world heritage site, and thus protect more of the isolated communities of sharks inhabiting the outer, and so far unprotected, reefs.

In his book *Age of Extremes,* Eric Hobsbawm highlights the difficulty of writing contemporary histories: "If the historian can make sense of this century," he contends, "it is in large part because of watching and listening" (x). As air-breathing land animals, our own reality-based experience of the underwater world, and particularly the realm of sharks,

---

a permanent fishery hereafter, because it will be carried out by means which none but stationary fisherman can provide. (Banks, "Remarks").

[11] In *Richard Fitzpatrick and his Sharks*, Brett Shorthouse notes that the same might be said of Fitzpatrick: "He's worth a lot more to me alive and in one piece than he is dead."

may well be largely limited to watching and listening to the work of documentarists. Fitzpatrick's work plays a pivotal role in what is an ongoing process of scientific evaluation and increasing public awareness of an oceanic environment that might otherwise remain a largely misunderstood and concomitantly neglected realm. The 'otherness' of the underwater world, renders it an environment more vulnerable than most to misrepresentation and exploitation. As Bill Nichols points out, documentary films have the ability to change the way we see our world, and sometimes to 'correct' the erroneous impressions given by popular sensationalism:

> Documentary film has a kinship with those other nonfictional systems that together make up what we may call the discourses of sobriety. Science, economics, politics, foreign policy, education, religion, welfare—these systems assume they have instrumental power; they can and should alter the world itself, they can effect action and entail consequences (*Representing Reality* 3).

Documentary's often unique way of directly connecting a reality to an expositional purpose has been brought to good use by Fitzpatrick and others like him.

Rather than expounding upon the ever-popular and unrealistic themes of 'eco-porn,' Fitzpatrick leans towards showing us how little we actually know about sharks, and how that ignorance is far more dangerous to us and to the welfare of reef eco-systems than any shark is likely ever to be. It would be very easy to sensationalise what Fitzpatrick does with sharks; there are lots of teeth, thrashing tails, and anxious moments. However, rather than demonstrating how vulnerable humans are to sharks, we begin to see how vulnerable sharks, and concomitantly the ecologies of the underwater world, are to us. The three species with which Fitzpatrick's research is primarily concerned are unprotected and dangerously exposed not only to commercial over-fishing, sports fishing, and illegal finning, but also to death as discarded bycatch. In *Les Requins De La Grande Barrière*, Fitzpatrick loses Jesabel, a White Tip at Osprey reef. In *Richard Fitzpatrick and His Sharks* Jesabel is still missing, and Nicole, the Tiger shark that is tagged in the documentary, is post-scripted as being found suffocated in Barramundi fishing nets less than four months after she was tagged. A sad reminder of what animal is in peril underwater—it is not human, and it is not a metaphor.

Works Cited

Banks, Joseph. *Endeavour Journal*, 11 April 1769 (Series 03:227) "South Seas." 1769. State Library of New south Wales. Available: <http://www.sl.nsw.gov.au/banks/series_03/03_227.htm.7Feb. 2004>.

—. "Some Remarks on the Present State of the Colony of Sidney, in New South Wales, and on the Means Most Likely to Render It a Productive Instead of an Expensive Settlement: June 4, 1806." *Historical Records of New South Wales*. Ed. F.M. Bladen. Vol. VI. Sydney: Government Printer, 1898. 89.

Barnouw, Eric. *Documentary: A History of the Non-Fiction Film.* Revised Edition. 1974. Melbourne: Oxford UP, 1983.

Benchley, Peter, Carl Gottlieb, *Jaws.* Prod. Zanuck/Brown Productions. Universal Pictures, 1975.

Bousé, Derek. *Wildlife Films.* Philadelphia: U of Pennsylvania P, 2000.

Brook, Simon and Roland Théron, *Richard Fitzpatrick and His Sharks.* Prod. Georgia Watson-Crabbe Sylvie Barb. Télémages International, 2002.

Copeman, Clive, *Raine Island: Nature's Warzone.* Prod. Jeremy Hogarth/Digital Dimensions. National Geographic, 2003.

Corner, John. *The Art of Record: A Critical Introduction to Documentary.* Manchester: Manchester UP, 1996.

Danielson, Stentor. *Shark "Photo of the Year" Is E-Mail Hoax.* 2002. National Geographic News. Available: <http://news.nationalgeographic.com/news/2002/08/0815_020815_photoofthe year.html. 17 Feb. 2004>.

Fitzpatrick, Richard. *Tiger Shark Tagging: Raine Island--Field Report.* 2002. Great Barrier Reef Research Foundation. Available: <http://www.barrierreef.org/research/current/tigershark.cfm. 20 Feb, 2004>.

Gould, Stephen Jay. *Leonardo's Mountain of Clams and the Diet of Worms.* Sydney: Vintage, 1999.

Hemingway, Ernest. "Letter, 13 September, 1952 to Bernard Berenson Regarding *the Old Man and the Sea*." *Ernest Hemingway, Selected Letters, 1917-1961*. Ed. Carlos Baker. New York: Scribner, 1981. 780-81.

Hirst, Damien. *The Physical Impossibility of Death in the Mind of Someone Living.* 1991. Saatchi Gallery, London.

Hobsbawm, Eric. *The Age of Extremes: A History of the World, 1914-1991*. New York: Pantheon, 1994.

Landin, Bo. "Scandinature Films: Truth & Consequences." *RealScreen* 1.12 (1998): 16-20.

McIlroy, Brian. "Observing and Walking the Thinnest of Lines: Phenomenology, Documentary Film and Errol Morris." *Recherches Semiotique/Semiotic Inquiry* 13.1-2 (1993).

Miller, Dean. E-mail letter to the author. 25 March 2004.

Nichols, Bill. *Representing Reality: Issues and Concepts in Documentary.* Bloomington: Indiana UP, 1991.

—. "The Voice of Documentary." *New Challenges for Documentary.* Ed. Alan Rosenthal. Berkeley: U of California P, 1988. 48-63.

Parsons, Christopher. *True to Nature: Christopher Parsons Looks Back on 25 Years of Wildlife Filming with the BBC Natural History Filming Unit.* Cambridge: Patrick Stephens, 1982.

Payron, Stephane, *Les Requins De La Grande Barrière.* Prod. Canal Plus, 1997.

Petley, Julian. "Fact Plus Fiction Equals Friction." *Media, Culture and Society* 18.1 (1996): 11-25.

Powers, Donna, Wayne Powers, *Deep Blue Sea.* Prod. Tony Ludwig Akiva Goldsman, Alan Riche. Warner Brothers, 1999.

Pratt, E.J. "The Shark." *The Collected Poems of E.J. Pratt.* Ed. Northrope Frye. Toronto: Macmillan, 1962. 5.

Sontag, Susan. *On Photography.* Ringwood: Penguin, 1984.

Stanton, Andrew, Bob Peterson and David Reynolds, *Finding Nemo.* Prod. Graham Walters. Walt Disney Pictures/Pixar Animation Studios, 2003.

State of the Great Barrier Reef World Heritage Area 1998: Fisheries. 1998. Great Barrier Reef Marine Park Authority. Available: <http://www.gbrmpa.gov.au/corp_site/info_services/publications/sotr/ 1998/fisheries_frame.html. 9 February 2004>.

State of the Great Barrier Reef World Heritage Area 1998: Tourism. 1998. Great Barrier Reef Marine Park Authority. Available: <http://www.gbrmpa.gov.au/corp_site/info_services/publications/sotr/ 1998/tourism_frame.html. 9 February 2004>.

Steinhart, Peter. "Ecoporn." *Audobon* 85.3 (1983): 22-25.

—. "Wildlife Films: End of an Era?" *National Wildlife* 18.1 (1980): 36-45.

Warham, John. *The Technique of Wildlife Cinematography.* London: Focal P, 1966.

Williams, Linda. "Mirrors without Memories: Truth, History and the New Documentary." *Film Quarterly* 46.3 (1993): 9-21.

Williams, Robyn, *Tracking Sharks: Interview with Richard Fitzpatrick.* Prod. ABC Radio National, 2 November 2002.

Winston, Brian. "The Documentary Film as Scientific Inscription." *Theorizing Documentary*. Ed. Michael Renov. London: Routledge, 1993. 37-57.

Shark Films: Cinematic Realism and the Production of Terror

Graham Benton

The paradigmatic "monster" of the sea in the contemporary popular imagination is the man-eating shark, and the paradigmatic shark film remains 1975's *Jaws*. The celebrated 30th anniversary of the blockbuster roughly corresponds with the release of *Open Water*, a small, independent film involving sharks and scuba divers abandoned at sea. This moment of confluence invites an exploration of the evolution of the shark movie genre: while such a project risks criticism on the grounds of significance and value, I argue that this approach provides a unique lens through which to interrogate broader issues of representation and the aesthetics of contemporary filmmaking. That is, these two films, produced thirty years apart, signal divergent relationships to the cinematic and literary conventions of the "real," and by pairing the two, I want to interrogate the category of "realism" and chart some observations that are made under the banner of this notoriously thorny and theoretically-unfixed term.

My analysis is triggered by the claim recently advanced by Rebecca Onion and which is evident in the title of her essay: "Sharksploitation! *Jaws* and the Sad Decline of the Shark Movie." Why, she asks, has no shark movie since *Jaws* managed to have such an effect on its audience? It is not for lack of trying. The immense popularity of *Jaws* not only enabled three vastly inferior sequels to be made, but also paved the way for numerous lower-grade films wherein grossly exaggerated and caricatured carcharodon generally get bigger ("Megalodon," "Meg") or smarter ("Blue Demon," "Dark Waters," "Deep Blue Sea," "Shark Hunter") and always more blood-thirsty ("Red Water," "Blood Surf"). We get "Shark Attack," "Night of the Shark, "Shark Hunter," "Shark Zone," and, in a rare demonstration of restraint in the genre, simply "Shark!" There are mutant sharks, genetically-modified sharks, fresh-water sharks, and even, in something called "Raging Sharks," radioactive sharks driven into a frenzy by consuming crystals dropped into the Bermuda Triangle as a result of an "alien intergalactic car crash" (elasmodiver.com).   As the *Jaws* sequels and outlandish imitations proliferate—all of which are predicated on fantasy and excess (bigger, smarter, more murderous)—it's not a surprise, writes Onion, that an authentic low budget movie (speaking about *Open Water*) would be hailed as a revelation.

To look first at the movie which spawned this phenomenon, however, it must be recognized that much ink has been spilled concerning *Jaws* and its role in ushering in the blockbuster era of Hollywood. It was the first movie to open simultaneously on hundreds of screens, it was backed by the most expensive advertising campaign to date, it was the first film ever to make 100 million dollars, and it still ranks seventh all-time in adjusted box office profit ("Jaws"). The commercial success of *Jaws*, moreover, fortuitously coincided with the rise of popular culture studies, and thus the film became an object of inquiry for academic investigations from a variety of methodological perspectives: psychoanalysts, feminists, Marxists, and myth critics all found *Jaws* a rich and compelling text.

A few sample citations may demonstrate the wildly energetic interpretive schemes mapped onto the movie. According to Dan Rubey,

> In *Jaws* the shark reflects a disguised hated of women and the preoccupation of our society with sadistic sexuality, a view of business as predatory and irresponsible in human terms, and a fear of retribution for the atomic bombing of Hiroshima. The film resolves these issues and fears by externalizing them from the protagonists and solving them in a macho-fantasy, which denies any possibility of concerted social action, excludes women as weak and ineffectual, and erases the past and its guilts. (1)

For Jane Caputi, "*Jaws* emerges as a full-blown male nightmare, not only of castration, but also of abortion […] this great white shark […] represents the untamed female, the Mother, the vagina dentata, the Lesbian, the White Goddess, […] the wild, the unconscious" (35-36). For Peter Biskind, *Jaws* is a tale of liberalism at sea at odds with its land-based representations of conservative domesticity; and in the impressionistic, short book by Antonia Quirke, we get this description of the shark: "all the things this creature has been! A dirty old man racked with longing. An insatiable psychopath forced to repeat a sin. A scarlet pimpernel leaving a toothy plume. An insolent catwalk model. A Bond adversary salivating at the possibility of an equal opponent" (67). Thus, shark as rapist, shark as female avenger in patriarchal world, shark as communist threat, shark as corporate capitalism, shark as avenging angel of death.

Into this maelstrom appears an early but still very astute critical assessment by Fredric Jameson in "Reification and Mass Utopia in Mass Culture." To quote at length:

> critics [...] have tended to emphasize the problem of the shark itself, and what it 'represents:' such speculation ranges from the psychoanalytic to historic anxieties about the Other that menaces American society—whether it be the Communist conspiracy or the Third World—and even to internal fears about the unreality of daily life in American today, [...] Now none of these reading can be said to wrong or aberrant, but their very multiplicity suggests that the vocation of the symbol—the killer shark—lies less in any single message or meaning than in its very capacity to absorb and organize all of these quite distinct anxieties together. As a symbolic vehicle, then, the shark must be understood in terms of its essentially polysemous function rather than any particular content attributable to it by this or that spectator. Yet it is precisely this polysemousness which is profoundly ideological, insofar as it allows essentially social and historical anxieties to be folded back into *apparently* 'natural' ones, to be both expressed and recontained in *what looks like* a conflict with other forms of biological existence. (142, my emphasis).

Now this attention to the "apparently 'natural'" is the hinge upon which my analysis turns: I argue that *Jaws* succeeded (commercially, artistically, and as an object of academic interest) in part because of the filmmakers' attention to a certain kind of authenticity. Much care was given to make the action "believable," and Spielberg's work is often referred to in terms of its "pseudo-realism." However many "ideological" subject positions one may grant to the shark, these are always subsumed under the recognition of the (ir)rational fear of the primordial, threatening, Other.

Despite many charges that the film—in its drive to shock and scare—grossly distorts its representation of shark behavior, some care has been given to verisimilitude. In the lengthy documentary that accompanied the 30th-anniversary re-issue of *Jaws*, the director, producers, actors, and screenwriters repeatedly come back to the issue of realism and the importance of believability. Robert Benchley, the original screenwriter and author of the novel upon which the film is based, said he first lit on the idea of the killer shark after reading a newspaper account about an incident wherein four bathers had been killed by a single marauding shark in one afternoon. In the film, the shark is alleged to be 26 feet long; in reality, great white sharks have been found to reach 21 feet. This is not, therefore, an unfathomable stretch outside the purview of the possible. Spielberg employed marine biologists as consultants, and the mechanical shark models were meticulously designed to mimic typical shark movements.

Even as the filmmakers strove for a certain kind of realism, critics, too, were attuned to what Jameson, as cited earlier, termed "natural anxieties." Notes Peter Biskind about a shift halfway through the film:

> In an abrupt change of focus, the political categories with which *Jaws* had flirted are suddenly naturalized. Brody's moral cowardice in the face of social pressure is subsumed by 'real' physical cowardice: fear of the shark. Even the psychosocial elements in his phobic fear of the water become secondary to the actual physical menace of the shark—which we see and experience with him. There are monsters beneath the sea which, as Quint later finds out, threaten real castration and death. Thus the psychological associations that have accrued to the shark during the first part of the movie (when, in fact, the shark was rarely seen—therefore serving as an ideal vehicle for such anxieties) fall away in the face of concrete, not metaphorical danger. (6)

Similarly, Quirke suggests that "[Spielberg] wants to make us see, even if in doing so we leave the world of make-believe and join the world of believe. And when you do get to look into this thing, into this mouth, your literal-mindedness catches up with you as the image slowly drifts back the harder you stare, from three dimensions back to two [...] We have believed enough in *Jaws* that no phoney gill could ruin it for us now" (83-84).

To leave the world of "make-believe" and join the world of "believe," as she puts it, is eased by the fact that there is one scene in the movie which makes use of footage of an actual Great White Shark: Spielberg hired the Australian filmmakers of *Blue Water, White Death* to film sharks in the sea, and this material was then spliced into the scene of the marine biologist Hooper being attacked in his underwater cage. The dramatic footage at once troubles the line of fact and fiction and simultaneously opens up a host of questions regarding "reality" and the documentary tradition. While such an investigative pursuit remains beyond the scope of this present paper, it cannot go unnoticed that documentaries *on* sharks are perennially popular, and have been so partly as a result of the success of *Jaws*.

Film and film series such as *Anatomy of a Shark Bite*, *Great White Death*, *Jaws of the Pacific*, *Island of the Shark*, *Operation Shark Attack* (volumes 1-5), *The Science of Shark Attacks*, and, most bluntly, *"Shark!"* all demonstrate that there are "uneasy oscillations of fear and fascination, fact and fiction, art and science that thrum through our impression of sharks" (Ferguson 117). Postmodern film theorists recognize that narrative feature films and documentaries alike are indistinguishable as constructed realities, and in her work on shark documentaries, using Bill Nichols' framework of fictionality in documentary, Kathryn Ferguson notes that "in recent years the linkage of documentary and fiction space within single texts has led to a questioning of the reality of documentary footage" (119). More interestingly for my present concerns, Ferguson then sets this observation alongside Brian Winston's assertion that "in order to survive, the documentary form need[s] once and for all to privilege art over science [so] that in the end, it would be necessary, for the documentary, to negotiate and escape from the embrace of science" (Ferguson 119). I want to reverse the poles of this binary—to look not at the fictionalization of the shark documentary but at the documentarianization of shark fiction. If, as Ferguson claims, *Jaws* is "highly fictionalized" and tends "to eclipse, by simple popular sensationalism, any realistic appreciation of sharks as a natural and necessary part of a healthy reef ecosystem" (124), then does the incorporation of documentary footage into the film allow, in the words of Bill Nichols, "some quality of the moment to persist outside the grip of textual organization" (qtd. in Ferguson 119)? For Antonia Quirke, all the various symbolic investiture in *Jaws* falls away when the shark first breaks the surface of the water next to the boat: "from this moment he's also simply a species enemy. He exists, and like all monsters, he is far, far older than us" (67). Ironically, Quirke goes on to declare that the footage of a real shark in this film

> makes the fiction lose focus. It's the shark's least characteristic moment. The attack cannot seem personal because we know it's no longer a story. Animals can't act.
>
> In only one sense is it frightening. We vault out of a yarn about a shark's animosity toward human beings into proof of the fact. Here's an actual shark looking vicious and un-restrained and filled with ugly things. Out to get us. Still, the shaken and blurred verite camera giving that authentic feel is just too much pushy camera work trying to inject excitement into an unexciting scene. It's only because he has no alternative that Spielberg must cut quickly. Everything must be blurred, not through choice, but necessity. And the violence must go on and on, flatly, because it has no meaning. (80-81)

A curious turn indeed, because if the makers of shark documentaries are commonly accused of manipulating shark behavior toward the "unnaturally violent"—Ferguson quotes one such producer who claims if sharks were filmed as they naturally were the audience would fall asleep—

then the violence filmed as it actually exists *empties* meaning when contextualized within the fictionalized filmic space.   This idea of a "necessary violence that has no meaning"—that which cannot be decoded with the interpretive tools of literary criticism—is very much responsible for the manufacture of terror that drives the film *Open Water*.

As noted earlier, this film is extremely simple in its narrative structure: a workaholic yuppie couple takes time off from their hectic schedules for a weekend of scuba diving off an unnamed tropical island. (The movie was shot in Bermuda.) The dive-boat captain miscounts the number of divers aboard, and the submerged couple is left behind; three-quarters of the film simply records their conversation and actions as they tread water and fight off sharks as they await rescue.

It is a horror film, yet certain filmic techniques work to increase its credulity. We are boldly informed by the film poster that this is "based on a true story." (Indeed, this is the only bit of information we are given, with no mention of actors or director which might draw attention to the artifice of the production.)   Also, the director repeatedly stresses in interviews that "we were just trying to tell that story in the best and most accurate and realistic way we could" (Kentis). This involved the use of hand-held waterproof digital cameras whose aesthetic, according to Dan Kaye, "impacts a sense of realism" because "the digital-video immediacy builds a sense of realism and dread" (Kentis). Most sensationally for the promotional campaign of the movie, *real* sharks were used; this is not the animatronic creation of Spielberg, or the CGI wizardry of later shark films. After the actors were lowered into the ocean, fish offal was dumped around the pair to pull up sharks into the camera frame. Not surprisingly, the actors have claimed in interviews that the terror we witness on their faces during the movie is not really "acting." (Interestingly, as the terrified characters try to determine what behavior may deter attacks, they draw on information derived from watching the Discovery Channel's *Shark Week*, a notorious and oft-repeated omnibus of shark attack documentaries. To have characters in a fictional film adopt survival strategies culled from artificially-constructed documentaries deepens and ironizes the very troubled lines of realism and cinematic license that this essay addresses.)

Many reviewers, uneasily confronted with this kind of filmmaking, curiously resort to a critical discourse that stresses the uninterpretability of the sharks: according to reviewer Stephanie Zacharek in Salon.com, "the sharks are majestic and menacing" but they are also "unreadable. It's impossible to know their intentions." [The directors] "didn't intend to make an enjoyably shivery B-movie: *Open Water* is ultimately a serious film about the unknowability and uncontrollability of nature." For *Stylus Magazine*, the movie enacts a "fear of being stranded in an environment that is not so much malicious as it is entirely indifferent to the survival of humans." And finally, to return *Salon*, Zacharek ultimately condemns the film because she feels the decidedly unHollywood ending is sadistic and cheap: "Nature is cruel and unforgiving, and sometimes movies are too."

All these observations on the fundamental forces of nature and man's ability (or inability) to survive in these elements suggest that the narrative participates in the category of naturalism. If realism is commonly held to be a mode of writing or filming that gives the impression of faithfully recording an actual way of life (and I recognize this to be a broadly conceived definition), naturalism is a narrower, more deliberate aesthetic and philosophical approach that presents human beings as passive victims of natural forces and their environment. Not to drift too far in the current of my analysis, but associations may be drawn between *Open Water* and Stephen Crane's 1897 short story "Open Boat," about four men adrift off the coast of Florida. Both are based on "real" events, both invoke the terror of the sea, both make use of naturalist techniques, and both raise questions of the limits of authenticity and the destruction of genre borders. The way the film *Open Water* borrows (consciously or unconsciously) on the emotive power of Crane's "Open Boat" suggests that something new is going on here; that perhaps there is an undertow to the dominant postmodern paradigm which celebrates self-reflexivity, irony, and self-conscious artifice.

As technology becomes more advanced, commercial moviemaking has increasingly capitulated to lifelike filmic effects that paradoxically have severed most connections with profilmic reality. By extension, technology's inexorable march toward ever finer attention to accuracy and verisimilitude has revived the perennial problem of thinking about realism in film. In his later, wildly successful film *Jurassic Park*, Spielberg brings dinosaurs "back to life" with technological virtuosity. However, this film ultimately fails (in the eyes of Antonia Quirke) because this particular "pursuit of reality has nothing to do with art. We finally go to see the dinosaurs a quarter of a way into the movie, and all we could say was 'well done!' One of the enemies of fiction is our growing capability to see through it" (84).

In contrast, Antonia Quirke continues, the rubber shark in *Jaws*

has a reality far in excess of, say, the computer-generated sharks of *Deep Blue Sea*. In *Jaws* the event is actually enacted and an action surely must be undergone for it to have any reality. Here there really is a simulacrum of a shark heaving onto a transom, half sinking a ship beneath him, straining and straining to reach Quint. And Shaw is not lying on some blue screen imagining how teeth might feel if they closed around his ribs. The actor and machine were there, one day in 1975, acting out 'Death by Shark' in 1975 no matter if those closing teeth are false. (84)

"Death by Shark"—as a set piece—resonates with the recently translated work of Serge Daney who defends André Bazin, a maligned proponent of realist cinema, from what he perceives to be facile, overdetermined postmodern assaults on realism. Daney advocates for the power of the unedited moment by looking specifically at those films in which humans and animals share the screen. Writing of the crocodile attack in the 1948 movie *Louisiana Story* (which could just as well be a shark attack in *Open Water*), Daney writes: "What justifies the prohibition of editing, of fragmentation, is not only [...] the exploitation of the depth of field, the birth of cinemascope, or the ever-greater mobility of the camera in an increasingly homogenous space but also, and above all, the *nature* of what is being filmed, the status of the protagonists (in this case men and animals) who are forced to share the screen, sometimes at the risk of their lives" (32-33). Via a theoretical move indebted to the work of Jacques Derrida, Daney suggests filmmakers should not split or cut the screen through artificial editing techniques, but "should show the split occurring *on* it; not break continuity but make a rupture stand out." Shark films, perhaps, literalize this desire for "difference, rupture, discontinuity" because sharks are creatures of the sea who invoke fear in humans whose natural habitat is land. The most terrifying moments in *Jaws* are the moments when the shark breaks through the interface of land and water, penetrating and threatening our illusion of security. According to Dan Rubey,

Spielberg's film captures these moments of primal terror because his sense of realism demanded that the film be shot with all the principals (including the shark) in the frame. The usual technique of cutaway shots and close ups would have saved Universal the price of the three mechanical sharks used in the film. But then the film could only have suggested, rather than actually shown, the shark breaking into the human space of the characters. (12)

Of course the shark increasingly violates the boundaries of human space up to and through the climactic death scene of Quint. The real articulation of terror, here, culminates in one long, difficult, shot. The shark's increasing incursion into our territory gets cast finally in psychological terms. The primary interfaces—land and sea, above and below, inside and out—are finally those, indexically speaking, of our own bodies. The shark, therefore, is "a perfect image for the violation of this barrier, because it tears its victims apart. It is an instrument of dismemberment, of violation of the integrity of the body" (Rubey 12).

I want to conclude, then, with two suggestive quotations. The first, again from Dan Rubey, describes the production of "real" terror elicited from watching *Jaws*: "*Jaws* is not escapism. It is a skillfully crafted articulation of the concerns and fears of our society in images ideally suited to them and in part derived from them, organized in terms of the ways in which we see reality and understand our own experience" (13). The second is Ernest Hemingway's infamous and disingenuous response to critics of his classic late novella: "There isn't any symbolism. The sea is the sea. The old man is an old man. The boy is a boy and the fish is a fish. The sharks are all sharks, no better and no worse. All the symbolism that people see is shit. What goes beyond is what you see beyond when you know" (780). I believe that *Jaws* and *Open Water* oscillate between these two positions: they articulate our fears and instill terror precisely because they cannot so easily be interpreted, categorized, and finally defused. As divergent yet important variations on the shark tale, they are focal points on a screen that charts our anxiety about comprehending that which resides under the sea and our inability to fully capture that which lies beneath the surface of the text.

Works Cited

Biskind. Peter. "Jaws: Between the teeth" *Jump Cut: A Review of Contemporary Media.* No. 9 (1975). <http://www.jumpcut.org/archive/onlineessays/JC09folder/Jaws/html>.

Caputi, Jane. *Goddesses and Monsters: Women, Myth, Power, and Popular Culture.* Madison, WI: Ray and Pat Browne Books, 2004.

Daney, Serge. "The Screen of Fantasy (Bazin and Animals)" Mark A. Cohen, trans. *Rites of Realism.* Ivone Margulies, ed. Durham: Duke University Press, 2003. 32-41.

Elasmodiver.com. "Shark Movies and Documentaries" <http://www.elasmodiver.com/Sharks%20on%20film.htm>.

Ferguson, Kathryn. "Submerged Realities: Shark Documentaries at Depth." *Revista Atenea* XXVI.1 (2006): 115-129.

Hemingway, Ernest. "Letter, 13 September, 1952 to Bernard Berenson" *Ernest Heminway, Selected Letters, 1917-1961.* Ed. Carlos Baker. New York: Scribner, 1981. 780-81.

Jameson, Fredric. "Reification and Utopia in Mass Culture." *Social Text* 1 (1979): 130-148.

Jaws. Dir. Steven Speilberg. Universal Pictures, 1975.

"Jaws." *Internet Movie Database*. <http:// imdb.com>.

Kentis, Chris. Interview with Dan Kaye. *Horrorchannel.com*. 3 Oct. 2004. <http://www.horrorchannel.com/index.php?name=news&file= article&sid=3602>.

"The Making of Jaws." Dir. Laurent Bouzereau. Universal Pictures. 2004.

Onion, Rebecca. "Sharksploitation! Jaws and the Sad Decline of the Shark Movie." *Slate.com*. 16 June 2005. <http://www.slate.com/id/ 2120876/>.

Open Water. Dir. Chris Kentis. Plunge Pictures, LLC., 2003.

Quirke, Antonia. *Jaws*. London: British Film Institute, 2002.

Reimink, Troy. Rev. *"Open Water"* Stylus Magazine. 20 August 2004 <http://www.stylusmagazine.com/articles/movie_review/open-water.htm>.

Rubey, Dan. "The *Jaws* in the Mirror." *Jump Cut: A Review of Contemporary Media*. No. 10-11 (1976): <http://www.jumpcut. org/archive/onlineessays/JC10-11folder/JawsRubey.html>.

Zacharek, Stephanie. Rev. of "Open Water," dir. Chris Kentiss. *Salon.com*. 12 June 2006 *LexisNexis*. <http://www.lexisnexis.com>.

CHAPTER FOUR:

MARITIME HISTORIOGRAPHIES

"WHERE ELSE TO ROW BUT BACKWARD?" WALCOTT'S VOYAGE THROUGH HISTORY

MAEVE TYNAN

Postcolonial literature proliferates with both real and symbolic voyages aimed at mitigating the sense of historical displacement ushered in by colonialism. Connecting all class of colonial traveller—colonialist, labourer and slave (as well as migrant and exile), the trope of the voyage encapsulates the uprooting effect of Imperialism. The sea as medium for the passage operates as an interstitial site that both conjoins and separates colonizer and colonized. The voyage metaphor has a particular resonance in a Caribbean that clearly bears the scars of historical rupture. This essay seeks to chart Caribbean poet Derek Walcott's engagement with the voyage motif as a means of coming to terms with a degraded colonial past. Sharing with Stephen Dedalus the attitude famously expressed in Joyce's *Ulysses*, "History is a nightmare from which I am trying to awake," Walcott's Odyssean travellers opt to voyage *through* history, a dynamic quest into the future that repudiates the past and grounds his poetics in the here and now (42). The figure of the rower who simultaneously travels backwards to move forwards epitomises the difficulties facing the postcolonial writer who wishes to transcend traditional historical dis-courses, as well as stressing the faith required to journey into the unknown.

Walcott's well-documented rejection of history reaches its apogee in a 1974 essay titled "The Muse of History" in which he categorically "refuses to recognize it as a creative or culpable force" (37). His poetics "neither explains nor forgives history" claiming instead that "amnesia is the true history of the New World" (37-39). Concomitant with this denunciation of history is a refusal to engage with the degradations of a colonial past on a creative level. In another statement essay published in the same year he declares: "[t]he degradations have already been endured; they have been endured to the point of irrelevancy" (*Caribbean* 53). In the Caribbean, traumatic regional stereotypes born of the area's downtrodden past, such as Trinidadian writer V.S. Naipaul's assertion that "History is built around achievement and creation; and nothing was created in the West Indies" (20), or Victorian traveller James Anthony Froude's damning verdict that, "There are no people there in the true sense of the word, with a character and purpose of their own" (quoted in Walcott, *Air* 36), are combated not by the production of a counter-catalogue of local achievement but the unceremonious dumping of the yardstick.

The strategic benefits of deposing the historical muse are manifold in postcolonial nations which are frequently read to be historyless, cultureless, underdeveloped or derivative and are accustomed to having their past record relegated to the footnotes of historical discourse, assuming they are accounted for at all. Walcott's poem "The Sea is History" which first appeared in *The Star-Apple Kingdom*, reiterates this refusal to become embroiled in traditional historical discourse. The poem is structured around a simple question and answer scheme, which Rei Terada reads as a "mock catechism of Afro-Caribbean history" (Terada 168). The questioner is representative of the colonizing culture interrogating the colonial subject as to the viability of his history—"Where are your monuments, your battles, martyrs?"(Walcott, *Sea* 364). The catalogue of monuments, battles, martyrs reveal an assumption as to what constitutes a legitimate history—in this case the elements of a military history. This is followed by a request for evidence of a distinct cultural history in the Caribbean—"but where is your Renaissance?" (364). Over the course of the poem, the questioner pumps the colonial subject for evidence of military conquests, a mythology, cultural production, an account of life after political independence. Though the colonial subject is seemingly subservient, addressing his answers respectfully to "Sirs" (364), the content of these answers abrogate the categories of the colonial culture, rendering them defunct. In this manner the poem serves as a "classic model of the dialectical counter-discourse with the traditional idea of history" (Ismond 9). In a reading of "The Sea is History" at York University in 1989, Walcott expanded on what the discourse of history as examined in the poem signified for him:

> When somebody asks you where is your history or where is your culture, or what you have done, the question comes from a presumption of people who believe that history represents achievement ... So if someone asks me, as a Caribbean person: "Where is your history?" I would say: "It is out there, in that cloud, that sky, the water moving." And if the questioner says: "There's nothing there," I would say: "Well, that's what I think history is. There's nothing there." The sea is history. (Walcott, *Sea*b 24)

Walcott counters the conception of Western Imperial history by propounding an alternative definition. This is achieved through listing the various stages of Western civilization and matching each with a corresponding, parallel experience of the Caribbean past. In doing this Walcott stresses the equivalence of New and Old World thus refuting the charge of "historylessness" that has been leveled at the Caribbean in the judgment of Froude, and of Naipaul after him. This approach enacts a process of Creolization whereby foreign models are reengineered to provide local configurations. In response to the initial question "where" Caribbean history can be located, the answer provided is in "[t]he sea. The sea has locked them up. The sea is History" (*Sea* 364). The sea for Walcott, here and in his others writings "gives you an idea of time that makes history absurd" (*Omeros* 158). In contrast to a European conception of history validated by the "visible presence of ruins" (*Muse* 44), Walcott offers a conception imagined by the fresh newness and beauty of the organic world, history as natural history. As mentioned previously, these vying histories might be understood as a dispute between a sanctioned, empirical history "chronicled successively by epochs as a record of achievement" (*Sea*b 24) and an "imaginative" historical record that seeks a fusion with place and imagination. The sea is indifferent to the cataloging of military conquest, the erecting of monuments, the vanity of rulers. As historical record it is "an epic where every line was erased// yet freshly written in sheets of exploding surf" (*Omeros* 296), suggesting the impermanence of human achievements, "Nothing can be put down in the sea. You can't plant on it, you can't live on it, you can't walk on it…The sea does not have anything on it that is a memento of man" (White 158-9).

Walcott's Caribbean history sets out by outlining the progress of Western civilization. Dipping into the spiritual history of the West, Walcott pairs scenes from the Bible with corresponding moments of the African diaspora. Despite the horror and trauma of the Middle Passage, the history of the black diaspora is shown to capitulate "a parallel, equal in depth, of self-achievement" (Ismond, 54). Thus Genesis for the Afro-Caribbean population was "the lantern of a caravel" (Walcott, *Sea*a 364), which signified their "journey into bondage" (Ismond 54); "Exodus" is signaled by the "packed cries, the shit, the moaning" (Walcott, *Sea*a 364); the sacred relics that compete in equivalence to the "Ark of the Covenant" are provided by the souls lost in transit—" [b]one soldered by coral to bone,/ mosaics/ mantled by the benediction of the shark's shadow" (364). Here, as in other works, the natural world is imbued with the ability to provide spiritual blessing. The parallels continue—"the plucked wires/ of sunlight on the sea floor" equates the "harp of the Babylonian bondage";

the "white cowries clustered like manacles/ on the drowned women" are the "ivory bracelets of the Song of Solomon" (364/5).

From religious analogues Walcott moves to mythological allusions. In his account of the "brigands who barbecued cattle" (365) we find a subtle reference to Odysseus's ill-fated crew who signed their death warrants by eating the cattle of the sun-god, Hyperion. In a similar fashion the myth of Jonah is paired with the "tidal wave swallowing Port Royal"; still the interrogator insists "but where is your Renaissance?" (365). The cultural history of the Caribbean is also recorded in the sea, in the "gothic windows of sea fans"; "these groined caves with barnacles/ pitted like stone/ are our cathedrals" (365/6). Emancipation follows, the birth of independence heralded when "each rock broke into its own nation" (367). In Walcott's ironic configurations, the official duties of state are carried out by the animal kingdom, a state of nature. Thus he announces a "synod of flies," "bats like jetting ambassadors," "the mantis, like khaki police" (367) and so forth. Walcott is clearly enjoying himself here substituting the respected, government officials with a staff composed almost entirely of insects and reptiles.

However there is a sense that the history of Walcott's providing is somehow insufficient or deficient. For each response there is a doubt as to whether the replies can be entered into an official historical record. Having provided Caribbean equivalents to the Judaeo-Christian narrative at the core of Western civilization, the poet writes, "but the ocean kept turning blank pages// looking for History" (364). Later the testimony of "Bones ground by windmills/into marl and cornmeal" are said to be "not History," "just Lamentations" (366). Likewise the conversion of the African diaspora to Christianity was "not History/ that was only faith" (367). The insistent qualifications and classifications denote the capacity of the official European historical narrative to silence or obscure the history of the colonized country. As Terada suggests the idea of history being "locked up" suggests the past is "sunk in suppression" (169), which may support Walcott's contention that the legacy of colonialism was the inflicted "amnesia" that shaped Caribbean culture. The native tribes of the Caribbean region have been wiped out; its new inhabitants have all arrived from somewhere else. The history of the region has thus been marked by a rupture, a break, a violent erasure. The witnessing tribes are all dead. Therefore it is only the natural world that has remained present to survey all that has gone before. The rumours of a new beginning thus sound in the "salt chuckle of rocks" resonating in the "dark ears of ferns" (Walcott, *Sea*a 367):

in the dark ears of ferns

and in the salt chuckle of rocks
with their sea pools, there was the sound
like a rumour without any echo

of History, really beginning. (367)

What is heard is a "rumour without any echo," that is an independent sound which requires no exterior point of reference, no distortion in repetition. It is the sound of "History, really beginning" (367). If this is history "really beginning" what came before must have been a false start a "degradation... endured to the point of irrelevancy" (Walcott, *Caribbean* 53). It is implied by the genesis of this history in the natural world that it is here that the true story of the archipelago lies, in this second postlapsarian Eden. The tendency to analyze historical data in terms of military achievement and political prominence highlights the capacity of the official European historical narrative to silence or obscure the history of the colonized country which exists only in relation to "the history of Europe," a variant of its master narrative. Dipesh Chakrabarty sums up the problem thus:

> [I]nsofar as the academic discourse of history...is concerned, 'Europe' remains the sovereign theoretical subject of all histories, including the ones we call 'Indian,' 'Chinese,' 'Kenyan,' and so on. (383)

The "repressive strategies and practices" of the narrative of European history actively suppress colonial accounts of the world, thus acting as an instrument of control over subject peoples (388). In the poem "Origins" Walcott writes:

> I learnt your annals of ocean,
> Of Hector, bridler of horses,
> Achilles, Aeneas, Ulysses,
> But "Of that fine race of people which came off the mainland
> To greet Christobal as he rounded Icacos,"
> Blank pages turn in the wind. (11)

Colonialism virtually eradicated the indigenous people of the Caribbean, therefore all language and culture was brought over, either from Europe, Africa or Asia. As Stuart Hall reminds us, Caribbean people are "not just a diaspora and living in a place where the center is always somewhere else, but we are the break with those originating cultural sources as passed through the traumas of violent rupture" (284). Colonialism forcibly broke up linguistic, tribal and familial groupings leading to a fragmentation of tradition. Old World roots withered and died as empires imposed their own languages, religions and customs on those they governed. Walcott reads the diasporized population of the region as a community of "castaways," forced to make a new home in the Caribbean after the "shipwreck" of colonialism. The resultant sense of displacement accounts for the insistence of representations of a population in perpetual motion, of identities in flux, of cultures constantly being revised and redrafted on what Walcott dubs "islands [that] have drifted from anchorage" (*Origins* 12). He urges "all the decimated tribes of the New World who did not suffer extinction" to view their "degraded arrival ... as the beginning, not the end, of our history" (*Muse* 41). Faced with a New World the "castaway" must take up whatever tools are available to construct a satisfying cultural home. This introduces Walcott's trope of "craftsmanship" to account for the means by which the "castaway" accustoms himself to his new environment, where the tools employed to build this home are chosen pragmatically from what is readily available. For Walcott these include the imposed language and religion of the colonizer, strategically adopted as a means of survival and continuation. These complementary linguistic tropes therefore serve to account for the conversion of the displaced inhabitants of the Caribbean to the language and religion of the colonizer, while freeing up these conversions from a sense of guilt or shame. In "Crusoe's Island" Walcott identifies each individual in the New World as a "craftsman and castaway" (69) a "creator as well as a casualty of his or her history" (Pollard 43). In the poem "Names" which explores the difficulty of accepting imposed names for local realities, Walcott writes, "The African acquiesced,/ Repeated, and changed them" (42). This process of acquiescence, repetition and change denotes Walcott's prescription for creating an indigenous culture and identity out of a fractured past. As a poet of mixed racial heritage Walcott acknowledges that he is trawling through strange waters in his use of the English language, but feels, like African writer Chinua Achebe, that the language is flexible enough to carry the weight of their diverse experiences. Conscious of himself as both inheritor and interloper in a tradition not wholly his own, Walcott's response, sometimes uneasy, other times triumphal, is one of ultimate acceptance. If the Caribbean poet cannot claim to be fully "at home" in the English language, he can adapt that language to suit his own purposes. In poems like "The Schooner *Flight*" and *Omeros* we see this process of creolization in action, playing out the tensions between basilect and acrolect as well as all the other varieties of language available in the Creole continuum. While adopting remnants of the disparate cultures washed up on the shore, the castaway/craftsman indigenizes these fragments introducing a line of tension between cultural assimilation and a will to localism. Elsewhere Walcott would claim, "you build according to the topography of where you live" (*Caribbean* 56), denoting that culture and identity are created from and imbued with the vision and realities of the local landscape, the "way the wind bends/ our natural inflections" (*Names* 307).

The Walcottian voyager is therefore aware of the Siren song of history but chooses not to listen. As Shabine, the storyteller protagonist of Walcott's narrative poem "The Schooner *Flight*" remarks "I met History once, but he ain't recognize me" (350). Shabine who glosses his name as the "patois for/ any red nigger" is irrefutably a Caribbean creation, a hybrid by-product of colonialism, and in his own admission a historical nobody (346):

I'm just a red nigger who love the sea, /
I had a sound colonial education, /
I have Dutch, nigger, and English in me, /
And either I'm nobody, or I'm a nation. (4)

However as the line "nobody or a nation" testifies, what begins in division can result in multiplication as the traumatic fragmentation of self, caused by colonialism allows for broader representative capabilities (4). It is a corollary of Shabine being a "nobody" or "any red nigger" that qualifies him to be a "nation" (346). In refusing to choose between these seeming alternatives, Shabine emphatically lays claim to both. As Rei Terada maintains, "Shabine's either/or claim is really a reflexive proposition" and thus is not a "cause and effect that unfolds continuously but a constant tension, each part of which produces the other" (114). After a botched smuggling enterprise sees the establishment of a Commission of Inquiry, designed to make a scapegoat out of Shabine, the sailor/poet, sickened with the corruption of "this Trinidad, the Limers' Republic" decides to steal away aboard the schooner *Flight*, the vessel's name inferring both a journey into the future and an escape from the past (348). Betrayed by history, and unable due to his mixed heritage to side with white or black, Shabine occupies an interstitial site that contravenes binary divisions:

After the white man, the niggers didn't want me
When the power swing to their side.
The first chain my hands and apologize, "History";
the next said I wasn't black enough for their pride (350)

A mulatto that contains both sides of the black/white dichotomy within himself, with bloodlines linking him to both colonizer and colonized, Shabine refuses the imposition of a single, unitary identity, proclaiming, "I had no nation now but the imagination" (350). However as the figure of the rower in the poem *Another Life* reminds us, to progress forwards requires a backward trajectory, a traversal *through* the past, "[w]here else to row, but backward?/ beyond origins" (75). In coming to terms with the past, the contemporary voyage undertaken by Shabine shades into historical crossings; in Part 5 of the poem the schooner encounter the slave trading ships of the Middle Passage. Shabine is, through his contact with the slave ship, offered an opportunity to reconnect with the past, either through a union with his African ancestry or through an identification with the colonizer that would assert the primacy of his European heritage. Clearly capable of identifying with the ship's ghostly crew, referred to as "those Shabines" on deck; while Shabine can make out the "great admirals" shouting "hoarse orders" his black ancestors are invisible, being confined to the notorious slave holds, "our fathers below deck too deep, I suppose, / to hear us shouting" (352/3). The initial reaction to invoke the suffering ancestor dissolves as Shabine refuses to allow history to define his identity, "we stop shouting. Who knows/ who his grandfather is, much less his name?" (353). If History won't recognize Shabine, he likewise gives short shrift to the discourse, being cognizant that the archipelago is "not marinated in the past" (*Muse*, 54).

The figure of the "castaway," the "eternal wanderer" or the "fortunate traveller" recurs throughout Walcott's literary career. He repeatedly invokes the allegory of the journey to signify an evolution or an ability to cross boundaries, transcend binaries and achieve a more holistic vision. Rajeev Patke observes of the postcolonial trope of travelling that the "end of voyaging is to find oneself where one has dispelled the tension produced by displacement, in a stasis of fulfilment" (Patke 208). In the poem *Epitaph for the Young*, Walcott's lyrical self-quest is a symbolic voyage, traveling in a circular motion, to return the poet to his initial point of departure, or in his own words "[t]o travel away from places is to know/ your doorstep better and the pride of possession/ Or the pride of dispossession" (47). In a similar fashion, Shabine's circular voyage both begins and ends in the Caribbean, eschewing the divisiveness of political allegiances for a nomadic life threading the various islands of the archipelago with the line of his passage. When Shabine announces "I taking a sea bath, I gone down the road" (346) we can understand this immersion as a baptismal rite of sanctification or rebirth. The trans-formative potentiality of the voyage motif therefore relies not only on the shift of geographical location but on the internal catharsis that such a journey affects.

A later poem *Omeros* also explores the realm of the symbolic voyage as the character Achille under the influence of a sunstroke delirium travels back to Africa, three hundred years previous to his present existence. This psychological return to Africa that Achille embarks on is overshadowed by a problem that every postcolony must face. In truth the return to a pre-colonial past is utopian. One of the main problems is that the Africa that is imagined is one that no longer exists. The roots to which the colonized direct their gaze are withered and dead. This imagined, pure, pre-colonial Africa cannot be addressed as a presence; rather it is a narrated and created absence. If both Achille and Shabine are offered an opportunity to reestablish the umbilical link to an African culture of origin, it is worth noting that the veracity of both accounts is called into question, Achille suffering at the time from severe sunstroke, Shabine's vision occurring during a period of convalescence after a near drowning.

This spiritual quest of Achille is a quest for self-knowledge. We are informed by the character Seven Seas, "His name / is what he out looking for, his name and his soul" (154). However having healed a wound brought on by a colonial past, the "homesick shame / and pain of his Africa," Achille must now return to his hybrid present (134). If Africa is a necessary port of call on a journey to self-knowledge it by no means constitutes the destination. The roots to which Achille "returns" are im-agined and based on a need of the fisherman to renegotiate his identity as opposed to a firm point of origin from which this culture derived. Achille's journey therefore is into an "Africa of the heart." The artificiality of this imagined homeland is emphasized in that the scene which Achille's delirium conjures up "was like the African movies/ he had yelped at in childhood" (133). The culture he must create belongs in the future not in the past. Stuart Hall contends:

> Silencing as well as remembering, identity is always a question of producing in the future an account of the past, that is to say it is always about narrative, the stories which cultures tell themselves about who they are and where they come from. (283)

Achille's journey highlights Walcott's position on the formation of cultural identity: while celebrating the complex sources of cultural inheritance, there is no going back, to Africa or anywhere else. Rather than "wailing by strange waters for a lost home" the castaway must look into the future, inventing a culture from the various crates and broken vessels washed up on the shore (Walcott, *Muse* 44).

In the Caribbean this inability to reconnect to the culture of origin affects the culture of the colonizer also. In *Omeros* the character Major Dennis Plunkett returns to London for a visit only to be overwhelmed by how much it and he have changed, "[t]he bombsites had become/ cubes of blue glass and indifferent steel" (251). The unfamiliarity of voices and traffic reduce him to tears and he is attuned to the knowledge that he is in fact playing the role of the British Major, "[r]inging the porter,// his pitch kept wavering on the proper language/ and the correct key- not a plea, but an order./ This tightened his jawline and increased his hatred" (252). Walcott speculates that the Major's life "might have ended/ that way" had he allowed himself to be overpowered by this fiction of himself that clung to a glorious past and could not appreciate how the island archipelago was now in fact his spiritual home. Instead he writes "The Major waited till his rage/ ebbed and…was ready to go back home" (252/3).

The voyage motif in Walcott's poetics therefore, most frequently depicts the journey as a rite of passage undertaken to further ground the individuals in their native land. The outward journey thus constitutes simultaneously the route home. Two opposing forces operate in tandem on the postcolonial poet; the centrifugal pull of diaspora, exile and self-exile and the centripetal draw of a return or a homecoming. However, it is worth noting that the majority of Walcott's work resists the straight-forward resolution of the *nostos* which is constantly deferred. Homecoming can be a difficult concept for the postcolonial writer when home itself frequently denotes an imagined state. In the poem "North and South" he would write, "I accept my function/ as a colonial upstart at the end of an empire, / a single, circling, homeless satellite" (11). The tension between the adopted home and the culture of origin, the pull of foreign publishers and readerships, and the yearning for homecoming preserve the equilibrium of centrifugal and centripetal forces. As Seven Seas explains to the poet-persona in *Omeros*:

> there are two journeys
> in every odyssey, one on worried water,
>
> the other crouched and motionless, without noise.
> For both, the "I" is a mast; a desk is a raft
> for one, foaming with paper, and dipping the beak
>
> of a pen in its foam, while an actual craft

carries the other to cities where people speak
a different language, or look at him differently,

while the sun rises from the other direction
with its unsettling shadows, but the right journey
is motionless; as the sea moves round an island

that appears to be moving, love moves around the heart
with encircling salt, and the slowly travelling hand
knows it must return to the port from which it must start. (291)

Works Cited

Chakrabarty, Dipesh. "Postcoloniality and the Artifice of History," *The Postcolonial Studies Reader.* Eds. Bill Ashcroft, Gareth Griffiths, Helen Tiffin. London: Routledge, 1995. 383-388.

Joyce, James. *A Portrait of the Artist as a Young Man.* London: Penguin Books, 1916.

—. *Ulysses.* London: Penguin Books, 1922.

Hall, Stuart. "Negotiating Caribbean Identities," *Postcolonial Discourses: An Anthology.* Ed.Gregory Castle. Oxford: Blackwell Publishers, 2001. 280-293.

Ismond, Patricia. *Abandoning Dead Metaphors: The Caribbean Phase of Derek Walcott's Poetry.* West Indies: University of West Indies Press, 2001.

Naipaul, V.S. *The Middle Passage.* London: Picador, 1962.

Patke, Rajeev S. *Postcolonial Poetry in English.* Oxford: Oxford University Press, 2006.

Terada, Rei. *Derek Walcott's Poetry: American Mimicry.* Boston: Northeastern University Press, 1992.

Walcott, Derek. "Air." *The Gulf.* London: Jonathon Cape, 1969 36-7.

—. "Another Life," *Another Life: Fully Annotated.* Boulder: Lynne Rienner Publishers. 1973. 1-153.

—. "Crusoe's Island," *Derek Walcott: Collected Poems 1948-1984.* London: Faber and Faber. 1965. 68-72.

—. *Omeros.* London: Faber and Faber, 1990.

—. "Names," *Derek Walcott: Collected Poems 1948-1984.* London: Faber and Faber. 1976. 305-308.

—. "North and South," *The Fortunate Traveller.* London: Faber and Faber, 1982. 11-16

—. "The Caribbean: Culture or Mimicry," *Critical Perspectives on Derek Walcott*. Ed. Robert D. Hamner. Washington, DC: Three Continents Press. 1976. 51-57.

—. "The Muse of History," *What the Twilight Says*. Kent: Faber and Faber. 1974. 36-64.

—. "The Sea is History," *Frontiers of Caribbean Literature in English*. Ed. Frank Birbalsingh. London: Macmillan Caribbean.1989. 22-29.

—. "The Sea is History," *Derek Walcott: Collected Poems 1948-1984*. London: Faber and Faber. 1979. 25-28.

—. "The Schooner *Flight*" *The Star-Apple Kingdom*. London: Jonathon Cape Ltd., 1979. 3-20.

White, J.P. "An Interview with Derek Walcott," *Conversations with Derek Walcott*. Jackson: University Press of Missippi, 1990. 151-174.

THE DISCOVERY OF THE HAWAIIAN ISLANDS: A CASE OF HUMAN-BIRD MUTUALISM

TOM LESKIW

Humans have been, and continue to be, a restless lot. Despite this, our self-image is one of being semi-sedentary, especially when we consider the exploits of truly migratory species such as caribou and wildebeest, shorebird and salmon. However, the scope and arduous nature of non-human migration should not obscure the fact that we, too, are a migratory species: in our daily commute to work, our weekend and vacation journeys in search of recreation, the flight from winter's cold by legions of "snowbirds," and initially, the human race's peregrinations outward from our evolutionary cradle in Africa. Since long before recorded history, humans have observed the comings and goings of other animals. The scientific study of migration began with Aristotle's speculation in book eight of *Historia Animalium* about what happened to swallows in winter. Today, wild creatures continue to pique our interest as we study their migratory patterns and technology has played a pivotal role in providing the answers to the long-standing questions of their points of origin and their destinations.

Seas have served as barriers to travel since time immemorial and crossing them has often entailed the crossing of a frontier. The Hawaiian Islands—geologically speaking, mere specks of rock—are renowned as the most isolated archipelago in the world, as they are situated 2,400 miles from California, 2,500 miles from Alaska, and 2,240 miles from Tahiti. This remoteness, arguably representing the ultimate frontier, prompts several questions with regard to the ways in which they were discovered and what could have possessed mariners to set out across the Pacific considering the exceptionally long odds of encountering land.

Voyagers from the Marquesas discovered the Hawaiian Islands 1,600 years ago. It was the Polynesian mariners' intimacy with the sea that enabled them to use a number of subtle clues for navigation: clouds, water color and taste, wave patterns, currents, presence of seabirds, fish, and plants, and the position of stars and planets. Harold Gatty, the aviation pioneer whom Charles Lindbergh called the "Prince of Navigators," suggested that it was birds that led ancient mariners to Hawaii. As Rachel Carson writes in *The Sea Around Us*:

> Students of primitive navigation believe that the migration of birds had meaning for the Polynesians, and that they learned much from watching the flocks that gathered each year in the spring and fall, launched out over the ocean, and returned later out of the emptiness into which they had vanished. Harold Gatty believes the Hawaiians may have found their islands by following the spring migration of the golden-plover from Tahiti to the Hawaiian chain, as the birds returned to the North American mainland. (192)

The plover's migration route strongly suggested the presence of land to the north, prompting the Polynesian explorers to sail in that direction and eventually discover the Hawaiian Islands. As critical as celestial navigation was to their success, it is important to note that the correct compass heading required to reach the Hawaiian Islands from Tahiti could only have been confirmed *following* successful landfall by the first mariners.

Apparently, long-distance flights of the Pacific Golden-Plover (*Pluvialis fulva*) also served as inspiration to early British explorers. In 1773, Captain James Cook sailed the waters of Tahiti during his second expedition. He was on a mission to find *Terra Australis Incognita*, the "Great Southern Continent" purported to lie somewhere between New Zealand and Australia. Naturalists aboard the H.M.S. *Resolution* noted the presence of the Pacific Golden-Plover. The first recorded specimen was collected on 26 August 1773 at Matavai Bay, Tahiti. Subsequently, the species was first scientifically described by naturalist J.R. Forster. The Tahitians informed Cook and his naturalists that the species did not nest in the islands, flying north each spring. Cook wondered if perhaps the small shorebird might breed on the elusive continent that he and his men were seeking. In 1778, Captain Cook was on his third expedition, seeking the elusive Northwest Passage. During late summer, in the North Pacific /Bering Sea, his crew spotted a Pacific Golden-Plover, which seemed to be migrating south. Cook wondered if the birds knew something about geography that he didn't: "Does this not indicate," he wrote, "that there must be land to the north where these birds retired in the proper season to breed?" (Johnson, "The Pacific Golden-Plover" 140) Cook's insight is regarded as the first written statement by a European concerning migration in the northern Pacific region.

By the time Cook reached the Hawaiian Islands in 1776, voyages between Hawaii and Tahiti had ceased. Cook and his crew were astounded to find a thriving civilization in such a remote location. The subject of how a Stone-Age people, lacking compass, sextant or chronometer could have found the islands was widely debated. Cook, for one, believed the natives had finely honed wayfinding skills. In 1769, while in Tahiti, he took a native sailor named Tupaia aboard the *Endeavour* and let him navigate the ship 300 miles south to the island of Rururu. The expedition sailed westward on various courses to New Zealand, then to Australia, then northward through the Great Barrier Reef, touching at New Guinea. Throughout this entire convoluted voyage, Cook was astonished to discover that whenever Tupaia was asked to point out the direction in which Tahiti lay, he could do so without access to the ship's charts or compass.

The daily lives of Polynesian mariners were dependent upon an intimate knowledge of the Earth's sky and waters. The Pacific Golden-Plover, is known as *kolea* in Hawaii, an onomatopoetic word that mimics the species' three-syllable flight call. That the explorers' nautical knowledge should be informed by the study of this shorebird's annual migration comes as no surprise. What *is* surprising, however, is the degree to which man's relationship with the *kolea* is mutualistic, where the association actually benefits both species. Mutualisms have been divided into two categories: obligate and facultative. While facultative mutualisms are beneficial but not essential to survival and reproduction of either party, obligate mutualisms are those that are essential to the life of one or both associates. Information is sometimes the currency in mutualisms, and in the case of *kolea*-Polynesian explorer mutualism, the *kolea* traded information (the presence of the Hawaiian Islands) for food (expanded foraging opportunities following colonization by man). The discovery of the Hawaiian Islands aided by the *kolea*'s migration flight was a boon to seafaring Polynesians. We will never know how many of their expeditions navigated a course destined never to encounter land, perishing in the process. Following the explorers' successful landfall, the Pacific Golden-Plover benefited from the islands' subsequent habitat alteration. However, because man and the *kolea* are not essential to the survival of each other, their association represents facultative mutualism.[1]

---

[1] There are other examples of human-bird mutualism, such as that of the Boran people of Africa with a bird known as the honeyguide, where human hunting parties are often joined by the Greater Honeyguide, *Indicator indicator,* which leads them to bee colonies. When searching in unfamiliar areas, the average search time by the Borans was reduced from 8.9 hours when they were unguided to 3.2 when they were guided and the efficiency in locating beehives increased by 64%

Native Polynesians intuited the location of the Hawaiian islands by watching the *kolea*'s spring migration. In the absence of the plover, who can say if they had been inclined to set out to discover other lands? Many aspects of the *kolea*'s life history lend credence to Gatty's theory. The species winters over a vast area, about half the circumference of the Earth—ranging west to Africa and south to New Zealand and Australia. Fossilized bones 120,000 years old found in Pleistocene lake deposits on Oahu evidence the species' long presence in Polynesia (James 221). The bird is easy to locate on its wintering grounds and close studies by professional and amateur alike are aided by the species' attachment to a particular place, the degree to which it exhibits site fidelity. Wintering territories are vigorously defended, as the same individual returns each year to the same patch of grass. For instance, a banded bird returned for 27 consecutive years to Bellows Air Force Station in windward Oahu, a record for shorebirds. Interestingly enough, various Hawaiian place names touch on the species attachment to a particular site, such as *Papakolea* (Plover Flats) on the Big Island and *Puukolea* (Plover Hill) on Molokai.

Residents of Polynesia continue their close observations of the *kolea* to this day. The "Krazy for Kolea Kontest"—founded in 1997 by the nonprofit organization Nene O Molokai—is held annually on that island to spot the first returning "fall" bird each August. An interactive website, "Kolea Watch," encourages observers to report the spring exodus of the *kolea* (Kolea Watch). The long tenure of humans observing the pattern in the *kolea*'s spring northward migration predates their written language. The birds' exodus is uncannily consistent; on Oahu, the migration starts within 2 days of April 24, making it one of the most precise internal calendars discovered in animals. Prior to their departure for their breeding grounds, the birds abandon their territories, gathering over a several-day period. The flock—known as a congregation of plover and consisting of up to 200 individuals—usually departs just prior to dusk. The birds fly in

---

Borans use fire and smoke to drive off the bees, break open the nest and remove the honey, but leave larvae and wax behind which are left for the birds. The use of fire and smoke reduces the bird's risk of being stung and in turn, the humans gain accessibility to nests. According to the Borans, the honeyguide informs them of the location of honeybees, from the compass bearing of bird flight, the duration of the bird's disappearance and height of perch and by the "indicator call." There are indications that this association originated quite some time ago: pictographs indicate that humans have collected honey in Africa for 20,000 years. Birds and Borans can survive without the other, but because each benefits from their association, this is also an example of facultative mutualism (Dean 99-100).

circles or make angled ascents to a great height before starting their northward journey (Henshaw 249).

In contrast to many long-distance migrant shorebirds, the *kolea*'s numbers are thought to be stable, not requiring special management efforts to stabilize their population. In fact, the *kolea* have benefited from the discovery of the Hawaiian Islands in several ways. The arrival of Polynesian explorers from the Marquesas around 400 AD unleashed a process of deforestation and as a result, less than 50 percent of the original forest cover remains. The conversion of forests to grasslands has actually benefited the plover because the *kolea* prefer microhabitats where plant cover is short or absent, allowing ease of movement and relatively unobstructed vision while on the lookout for predators (Johnson, *Birds of*).

New or expanded habitat niches include grazing lands, grassy borders of airport runways, cemeteries, athletic fields, parks, golf courses, and military bases, as well as paved surfaces adjacent to grass and other low vegetation from which the plovers glean insects. As the lowland forests gave way to sugarcane cultivation, the *kolea* moved into cane fields, foraging on caterpillars of two widespread and destructive cutworm species.[2] Annual sugarcane harvest followed by tilling created large, barren tracts of land, facilitating *kolea* foraging opportunities. Where suitable habitat such as pastures occur, Pacific Golden-Plover ranges to at least 2,500 meters in elevation, which furnishes foraging opportunities over a substantial portion of each island that has experienced forest to grass conversion. Widespread planting of ironwood (*Casuarina*) trees also helped the plover, which often can be found foraging on the dense, insect-rich mats of shed foliage. Actual scientific data on how the deforestation of the Hawaiian Islands benefited the *kolea* are lacking and can only be inferred based on the *kolea*'s preference for open habitats with low-growing vegetation. However, a contemporary comparison of the ways in which deforestation may have benefited the *kolea* can be seen in the relationship between the recent deforestation of the Amazon and the American Golden-Plover, a close relative of the *kolea*. Research has revealed that the widespread conversion of rainforest to pasture in South America has created new habitats for migrating and wintering American Golden-Plovers (Stotz 608). Furthermore, favorable habitats resulting

---

[2] On a different register, a more recent manifestation of the benefits derived from the mutualistic relationship with the *kolea* is through the biocontrol of agricultural pests such as cutworms, grasshoppers, beetles, grubs, roaches, and semi-poisonous millipedes. Some of these pests are considered to have a substantial adverse economic impact upon a variety of agricultural products that include sugar cane.

from settlement in the Eastern U.S. may have prompted some birds to eschew their autumnal migratory flight to the Amazon and winter instead in the United States (Paulson 121).

In contrast, evidence of the *kolea*'s habituation to humans is abundant. Flocks utilizing traditional nighttime roosting areas (beaches, rocky points, tops of mangrove trees) are found in parking lots and on levees and flat roof tops—the latter site also offering protection from cats (Johnson, *The Use of* 45). Sites illuminated by streetlights may offer protection from introduced Barn Owls and feral cats. In addition, plovers have been observed foraging on human foods such as bread, rice, French fries, and apples, and an injured bird ate earthworms, insects, and snails from the hand of its benefactor while in captivity. The availability of these supplemental foods may be a factor in the species changing its migration habit, as it is now a year-round resident on Oahu. However, the *kolea*'s close association with humans does have its price, such as the exposure to agrichemicals like those used at golf courses and on lawns and potential human-introduced predators that include mongoose, Barn Owl, and feral house cat. A scat analysis failed to detect *kolea* remains in Barn Owl or feral house cats, but *kolea* remains were discovered at a Barn Owl roost on Kaula Island, Hawaii. From a historical perspective, the *kolea* were utilized by the early Hawaiians, plucking its golden feathers for capes and feathered staffs, often without killing them. Yet while Early Hawaiians snared the *kolea* for food, plover hunting was banned in Hawaii in 1941.

Technology has unlocked a treasure trove of the *kolea*'s secrets. We can now state that this species can fly nonstop for at least 70 hours, flapping its wings twice a second to sustain speeds up to 65 miles per hour (Johnston). The *kolea*—those that winter as far south as Australia—are capable of flying up to 6,260 miles nonstop, even though unable to glide or soar to conserve energy. The plover's trans-Pacific flight is made possible by the accumulation of fuel in the form of fat, increasing its body weight by as much as 64% in the weeks prior to its migration (Johnson, *Birds of*). About one month after the vernal equinox, *kolea* begin to grow restless, each bird departing the territory it has vigorously defended since fall. For several days, they mill about, swelling in number. Flocks form along shoreline and grassy headland. Then, as dusk falls, the congregation—in the ultimate act of faith—lifts off, circles, and begins its 2,500-mile flight over the Pacific Ocean. Human eyes follow the flock until tiny specks dissolve into darkness. To the north, a bright pinpoint of light, *Hoku-pa'a*, the "immovable star," shines. It is this beacon, Polaris—the North Star—that will guide the birds' movements through the sky for the next two nights until they reach what the Hawaiians call *Kahiki,* the *kolea*'s Arctic breeding grounds.

Native cultures demonstrate that technology is but one part of the puzzle to understanding a creature. Hawaiians have long acknowledged their debt to the *kolea*. The long association with and careful observation of the *kolea* has inspired its inclusion into Hawaiian dance, song, and legend. The hula *kolea* is performed in a kneeling position, with the dancers forming a single row facing in the same direction. Arms, heads, and bodies imitate the movements of the plover. Still performed today, there is no instrumental accompaniment to the *kolea* hula.

The 3,000-mile, nonstop flight back to their Arctic breeding grounds requires substantial energy reserves. In preparation, the *kolea* gorge on their favorite foods; a bird weighing 110 grams in March may grow to 180 grams by late April. Their weight gain and annual exodus were well-known to native Hawaiians and resulted in the following chant (Pukui):

When the feathers darken on the breasts,
The kolea returns to Kahiki to breed
The kolea eats until he is fat, then returns to the land
from which he came!

When there is a desire for plovers,
The child to be born will travel to Kahiki
The plover can only cry its own name
The egg of the kolea is laid in a foreign land.

In addition, native Polynesians regard birds as potential gods or spirit beings. Oral histories recount how migratory birds or those that nest in high cliffs serve as messengers for the *alii* (kings). Acknowledging the part the *kolea* played in the discovery of the islands, legend holds that the birds are sent, generally in pairs, to act as scouts or to carry messages from island to island. The trans-Pacific *kolea*-man association is depicted on a 1984 U.S postage stamp commemorating the 25th anniversary of Hawaiian statehood. A *kolea* is shown in flight, ahead of a traditional Polynesian sailing vessel, inspiring the navigators onward.

H.W. Henshaw, in his landmark 1910 paper in the *Auk*, "Migration of the Pacific Plover to and from the Hawaiian Islands," touched on our sense of wonder for the species' twice-annual migration:

When we consider the number of miles traveled, the widely different characters of the regions chosen for summer and winter abodes, and the perils necessarily attending the passage between them, the migration of no other of our birds appears so wonderful as that of the Golden-Plover. (245)

Ecologists estimate that the Hawaiian Islands were colonized by plants and animals at the rate of one species every 100,000 years. The slow, millwheel grinding of time and isolation produces new species, the raw materials being storm-blown birds or floating seed pods. Exploration, for shorebird and human alike, is evolutionarily adaptive; that is, the trait confers an advantage to its bearer in terms of contributing to successful survival and reproduction. As Joy Harjo—poet, performer, writer, musician and part-time resident of Hawaii—observed, "There has to be power or sustenance in migration or the world would be without humans, most plants and animals." Chickens, pigs, taro root and coconut trees are among the animals and plants that have accompanied ocean voyagers in search of new lands to colonize. We readily acknowledge them as our "partners in migration." The *kolea* has played a pivotal—albeit under-appreciated—role in the human exploration of the Pacific frontier.

Works Cited

Carson, R.L.. *The Sea Around Us*. New York, New York: Oxford University Press. 1950.

Dean, W.R.J., W.R. Siegfried, I.A.W. MacDonald. "The Fallacy, Fact, and Rate of Guiding Behavior in the Greater Honeyguide." *Conservation Biology* 4.1 (1990): 99-100.

Henshaw, H.W. "Migration of the Pacific Plover to and from the Hawaiian Islands." *Auk* 27.3 (1910): 245-262.

James, H.F. "A Late Pleistocene avifauna from the island of Oahu, Hawaiian Islands." *Documents des Laboratoires de Géologie de la Faculté des Sciences de Lyon* 99 (1987): 221-230.

Johnson, O.W. "The Pacific Golden-Plover (*Pluvialis fulva*): Discovery of the Species and Other Historical Notes." *Auk* 110.1 (1993): 140.

Johnson, O.W., P.G. Connors. American Golden-Plover (*Pluvialis dominica*), Pacific Golden-Plover (*Pluvialis fulva*). In *The Birds of North America*, No.201-202 (A. Poole and F. Gill, eds.). The Academy of Natural Sciences, Philadelphia, and The American Ornithologists' Union, Washington D.C. 1996. <http://bna.birds.cornell.edu/BNA/account/American_Golden-Plover/FOOD_HABITS.html>

Johnson, O. W., R.M. Nakamura. "The Use of Roofs by American Golden-Plovers, *Pluvialis dominica fulva* wintering on Oahu, Hawaiian Islands." *Wader Study Group Bulletin* 31 (1981): 45-46.

Johnston, D.W., R. McFarlane. "Migration and Bioenergetics of Flight in the Pacific Golden Plover." *Condor* 69 (1967): 164.

Kolea Watch: Student Science With Native Shorebirds. Hawaii Nature Center. 10 November 2006. <http://www.hawaiinaturecenter.org/kolea/index.html>.

Paulson, D.R., D.S. Lee. "Wintering of Lesser Golden-Plovers in Eastern North America." *Journal of Field Ornithology* 63 (1992): 121-128.

Pukui, M. K. *Olelo Noeau: Hawaiian Proverbs and Poetical Sayings.* Honolulu: Bishop Museum Press, 1983.

Stotz, D.F., R.O. Bierregaard, M. Cohn-Haft, P. Petermann, J. Smith, A. Whittaker, S.V. Wilson. "The status of North American migrants in central Amazonian Brazil." *Condor* 94 (1992): 608-621.

THE AVIARY OF OCEAN: MELVILLE'S TROPIC-BIRDS AND ROCK RODONDO – TWO NOTES AND AN EMENDATION

R. D. MADISON

I

Of the various elements of the maritime world that have found their way into the nautical fiction and poetry of Herman Melville, perhaps the most elusive are seabirds, and perhaps the most ephemeral is sea language itself. In her forthcoming work *Cannibal Old Me*, Mary K. Bercaw Edwards explores the influence of varieties of spoken word on Melville's writings, especially the early fiction. Her work necessarily uses tools developed by folklorists to identify influences that might be regarded as fuzzily "cultural" by stricter genetic critics—that is, critics who explore literary, biographical, and psychological influences on the conception and birth of a text. How do you show the influence of a conversation when all we have is a report of the kind of conversation that took place or, at best, a literary transcription of such a conversation?

Just as there are verbal fingerprints that can be used to track the relation between two written texts, there are strands of DNA that can be extracted from literary and non-literary traces of sailor speech and which, used responsibly, can provide convincing, elucidatory analogues to Melville's writings.

An analogue to her own work might be the attempts of Melville scholars to determine what Melville knew about natural history. In the late forties and early fifties, Elizabeth S. Foster and Tyrus Hillway explored Melville's geological and zoological knowledge in relation to published sources ("Geology" 1945, "Another" 1951; "Geological" 1949, "Amateur" 1951). During their exchange, early Melville enthusiast Robert Cushman Murphy, the world's living authority on pelagic birds, published his *Logbook for Grace* (New York: Macmillan, 1947), the description of the young biologist's own whaling voyage of nearly forty years earlier.

And it is Murphy's *Oceanic Birds of South America*, two heavy green volumes published by the American Museum of Natural History in New York in 1936, which is the single most valuable work in sorting out Melville's birds.

It was Murphy's book (and a chance encounter with a conservation-stamp illustration of a Fairy Tern) which led me to the recognition of Melville's "white noddy," in "The Strange Fowl of 'Benito Cereno'" (Fowl 15-16). In the same issue of *Extracts*, Mary K. Bercaw Edwards published her note expanding Willard Thorp's and Kendra Gaines's identification of *The Penny Cyclopaedia* as Melville's intellectual warehouse during his novelist years (Infusion 9-13). In that article, Bercaw identified *The Penny Cyclopaedia* as the source for Melville's technical nomenclature of sharks in *Mardi*: "Only the Latin names were given for most of the sharks," Bercaw wrote, "and none of the common names Melville used were mentioned. They must have come from some other source—if he did not simply remember (or make up) names he used." (12) Now we would identify that "source" as sailor lore or, to use Bercaw's current phrase, "sailor talk"—to which, of course, Melville himself must be assumed to have been a contributor, leavening an already rich loaf.

Murphy's reports of sailor talk, along with his own observations, in the "Strange Fowl" note and in a later note on "The Haglets" (Haglets 79-84), matching Melville's own details with descriptions of the appearance and behavior (ethology) of candidate species led me to determine, as far as possible, a) what Melville had seen, and b) what his thoughts were when he incorporated his bird imagery into a given work. Sometimes Melville is too general for us to come to a conclusion, as in the hierarchical descriptions in the third sketch of "The Encantadas," addressed below. More often Melville, who turns out to have been an accurate observer, gives either ample enough or critical enough detail for a useful identification, one which in the context of further "sailor talk" (or "birder talk") can provide a fairly reliable gloss on Melville's use of the image. Recently I used this process to gloss a passage in *Clarel*, yielding, I must say, a rather unglamorous result when Agath's "sea-hawk" turned out to be a Galapagos Gull (*Companion* 295-296).

More recently still, in a chapter of her manuscript Bercaw quotes this passage from *Typee*: "The splendid long drooping tail-feathers of the tropical bird, thickly interspersed with the gaudy plumage of the cock, were disposed in an immense upright semicircle upon his head, their lower extremities being fixed in a crescent of guinea-beads which spanned the forehead" (*Typee* 77). For the Melville scholar accustomed to source hunting, this passage practically screams "stolen," but a check of the usual victims (in this case, as Bercaw points out, C. S. Stewart's *A Voyage to the South Seas* [1831] as a verbal source, but likely also David Porter's *Journal of a Cruise* [1815, 1822] for a visual "reminder"—whether of a real experience or a literary one) reveals that Melville, as usual, stole, embellished, and electrified. Porter's corresponding plate (of course, we can be sure Melville saw other illustrations of South-Sea islanders) shows what looks emphatically like a "cock" (that is, rooster) feather (Porter 310), but the use of the phrase "tropical bird" is just too close to the actual name of a candidate species to ignore. And Melville's description doesn't match Porter's illustration in a couple of other ways: Porter's feathers, for instance, don't droop.

The tropic-bird is a medium-sized pelagic bird (meaning that although it breeds ashore as all birds must, it spends most of its time foraging at sea and is most normally encountered out of sight of land). The central tail feathers are long and whip-like, drifting conspicuously behind the bird in flight, and in one species, the red-tailed tropic-bird, these are red, contrasting with the bird's primarily white plumage.We know that Melville knew this tropic-bird: in *Omoo*, after mentioning a gray "albatros" [sic], he writes, "Or flights of the tropic bird, known among seamen as the 'boatswain,' wheeled round and round us, whistling shrilly as they flew" (35). He named the tropic-birds again a decade later in "The Encantadas," where the tropic-bird is associated with his beloved chanticleer. Fortunately, bird species can be relied on to be more or less the same in aspect and behavior even at the separation of a century and a half, and the long-tailed, shrill-voiced tropic-bird you can see and hear today can be relied upon to be the same one Melville referenced and (at least for me, beyond doubt) actually saw. Murphy writes, "the tail plumes of the West Indian tropic-bird were formerly valued by the Caribs just as those of the Pacific Red-tailed species were by Polynesians" (802, and I can't imagine Murphy drew this conclusion from reading *Typee*). For non-birders, I'll include Murphy's note on the more musical of the two calls of the bird, although it is a commonplace: "The latter note, of course, is the 'boatswain's whistle' which has given the species its commonest name among sailors" (801).

There is a reference to "Aka's Voyage for Red Feathers," on the website of the Polynesian Voyaging Society although the feathers sought are apparently wing rather than tail feathers of the kula, which may be a mythical species or may be a kind of parrot. At least one description (again, depending on web sources for Polynesian folklore, which is really beyond my ken although it might not have been beyond Melville's) speaks of the kula bird's ulcerous face and describes it as lame—the former may imply an unfeathered head, while the latter would be a characteristic description of many seabirds on land. About the tropic-bird, for instance, Murphy reports, "they are nearly helpless on a level surface, and there capable of progressing only by crawling and bouncing along on flattened tarsi" (805). A similarly named and red-feathered bird, the Kura, existed in Rarotongan legend but was extirpated with the advent of firearms. The site also provides a detail Melville might have known: Captain Cook traded feathers from Tonga in the Society Islands (Tahiti). A web index to Cook's journal records four mentions of the red-tailed tropic-bird in 1769: 15 March, 20 March, 21 March, and 23 March (130-131). According to Bercaw and Sealts (*Sources* 1987; *Reading* 1988), plenty of commentators (including Melville himself) have suggested that Melville knew Cook, but Melville's own copies of the voyages (if he owned any) have not been identified.

Not to be confused with long drooping tail-feathers are the thousands of feathers from the Iiwi or red honeycreeper used to fashion Hawaiian cloaks such as the one associated with Sir Joseph Banks and Captain Cook. These feathers were short, were fashioned into a cloak (not a hat), and were not individually conspicuous. Nevertheless, the artifact shows the predilection for red feathers (Beasley and Braunholtz 1-2).

So, did the long drooping tail feathers of *Typee* belong to a tropic-bird and not a generic "tropical bird"? That would be my hunch, and that in turn would call for a conjectural emendation to the text of *Typee*: "The splendid long drooping tail-feathers of the tropic bird." In defense of the original wording, "tropical bird" would cover any species with a long tail. But what are the other candidates to be encountered in Melville's experience or reading? The long-tailed jaeger? This could be the "jay" of Rock Rodondo. And in "The Chase—First Day" Melville fuses a fairly obvious storm-petrel image ("the light toes of hundreds of gay fowl softly feathering the sea, alternate with their fitful flight") with a tropic-bird or long-tailed jaeger, "the long tail feathers streaming like pennons" (*Moby-Dick* 409; on the long-tailed jaeger: "With each wingstroke, their long central tail feathers would undulate up and down, seeming almost independent of the bird itself." Kaufman 232). The bird of paradise of *Mardi*? The bird of paradise was a New Guinea bird, and Melville would not have encountered it first-hand on his whaling voyage. In *Mardi*, the bird of paradise is used at first rather impressionistically (compared to the careful description of the headdress in *Typee*) to indicate the decoration of Yoomy's turban (197), then metonymically to indicate Yoomy himself (414, 433), and finally symbolically in Babbalanja's quasi-Emersonian sermon (575; Emerson's *Poems* came out in 1847, but Melville's copy [Sealts 206] was not given to him until 1859. There is no shortage of critics who discuss Melville's reaction to Emerson, but in light of Melville's thirty years as poet the relationship between the characters Yoomy and Babbalanja and the model of Emerson still deserves further scrutiny). Melville did not hesitate to spell out "bird of paradise" in *Mardi* when he wanted that particular image and its rich associations, and had that bird been on his mind during the composition of *Typee* he would have spelled it out there as well. It wasn't, and he didn't. He did have the tropic-bird on his mind throughout his career as a novelist, and I really suspect that the manuscript of *Typee* read, "The splendid long drooping tail-feathers of the tropic bird."

II

Melville's "Rock Rodondo," the third sketch of "The Encantadas" (collected in *The Piazza Tales*), is devoted to the description of a hierarchy of birds (above) and a "lowerarchy" of fish (below). From the Spenserian quotation which heads the chapter, one would expect a certain line of development of these "ravenous races" along the lines of the static symbol of the white noddy employed in "Benito Cereno" or the complexly developed image of the haglets in the poem so-named. But there is no such development, and the next chapter makes of Rodondo only a convenient viewing point for an imagined view of the entire Galapagos archipelago.

There is some question whether Melville ever ascended Rock Rodondo, fished in its shadows, or even saw it ascending like a sail in the distance. In a volcanic world where heights are measured in the thousands of feet, a two-hundred-fifty-foot rock would not seem the most towering of viewpoints (the word "tower" or its cognates occurs at least a half dozen times in the short sketch, almost suggesting a subconscious awareness of Tower Island, another in the Galapagos group frequently associated with breeding seafowl), although from the thwart of a whaleboat even a rock of that height would seem imposing. And later writers have asserted the difficulty of ascending even the most modest of Galapagan cinder cones (cf. Beebe, passim).

As for Rodondo's appearing like a sail, the tiny pictorial image of the rock in the Moll chart accompanying Cowley's account (reproduced in Porter) shows a perfect twin-summited tophamper on a flat trapezoid of base that is a perfect miniature of the diagram labeled "Fore & aft Schooner" in Richard Henry Dana, Jr.'s *Seaman's Friend* (Bercaw 188b). I wouldn't argue for any special significance for this vignette except that it is odd that an illustrator would fancifully engrave a "Round Rock" as jaggedly peaked.

The orderliness of the ledges on Rodondo may owe more to Dante (Sealts 174) or the systematic sub-antarctic rookeries described by, I think, Morrell (Bercaw 509; Sealts 372), than to Melville's first-hand observation (I haven't seen a photograph of the Rock). The birds Melville describes are pretty much in line with what other observers have recorded, but his use of sailors' names obscures some of the identifications (unlike the specificity Melville attains when he wants to develop a symbol): penguins, pelicans, albatross, boobies, shearwaters, jays (jaegers?), sea-hens (?), sperm-whale-birds (?), gulls of all varieties, storm petrels, and tropic birds. I don't think Melville is spinning this list out of his head—the way he differentiates the Galapagos albatross from other species shows some exercise in the field or study. But beyond associating the storm petrel with maritime folklore and the tropic bird with the barnyard cock, Melville does nothing with this list, and his ornithological ascent does nothing to prepare us for the rest of the sketches. This sketch, on the face of it, may do no more than twit Darwin on his natural history, as H. Bruce Franklin pointed out in "The Island Worlds of Darwin and Melville" (353-370). The deliberate absence of land birds in Melville's description need not be merely literary—Melville's "dead desert rock" may simply not have offered a micro-environment suitable to land species observed elsewhere in the archipelago.

I'm guessing that Melville didn't come to the writing of "The Encantadas" with any fixed plan. On the contrary, I suspect that he ran across this material while gathering "certain wild legends in the Southern Sperm Whale Fisheries" (*Correspondence* 163) of which "Town Ho's Story" made it into *Moby-Dick*, while "Benito Cereno" and the Galapagos material had to wait for separate publication. There is a kind of unity among all these wild tales which can be recognized in Reynolds's "Mocha-Dick" as well, but the unity of the Galapagos material strikes me as only geographical. Melville's usual sources show up, and I would suggest that any source hunting on his part after the publication of *Pierre* smacks of Melville's revisiting old friends rather than undertaking new projects. This is certainly true of Porter and Delano (Bercaw 200), whose own sources opened up as clear a bibliographical trail to the early exploration of those seas as the *Penny Cyclopaedia* did for the whaling sources of *Moby-Dick*.

If "The Encantadas" represents the leftovers of a project that began with *Moby-Dick* and continued through "Benito Cereno," what was the driving principle? I think a partial answer begins back in London in 1849 when Melville was gearing up to write what became *Israel Potter*. Not only are there verbal similarities between the latter work and "Rock Rodondo" ("craggy keep" and the Ailsa description [borrowed from *Penny Cyclopaedia*]; the "great full moon" and the Richard fight sequence [borrowed from Cooper]—you could probably find more), similarities we would expect given the closeness of publication dates—I'm struck also by the instances of "friar" imagery in both "Benito Cereno" and "Rock Rodondo": Grayfriars in the latter; Blackfriars in the former; unspecified but present in "Town Ho"—in all sounding like a tour of Elizabethan theatres.

In 1849, shortly before returning to America, Melville purchased a folio of the plays of Ben Jonson (Sealts 302). I would guess that most readings of "The Encantadas" have been powerfully influenced by the desolating sense of landscape that runs throughout the sketches and is reinforced by the Spenser snippets. Without the landscape, however, the tales resolve themselves primarily into unrelated sketches of character—a series that could easily include "Town-Ho's Story" and "Benito Cereno" as what we might almost call tragedies of humor—tragedies of "victimized confidence." Certainly "Benito Cereno" falls immediately into this category, nor do I think Steelkilt and Radney, Patrick, the Dog King, or Hunilla are far beyond being character types almost as unilateral as their forerunners in the bitter Jonsonian comedies of humors. I don't know whether to suggest a deliberate Melvillean experiment with Elizabethan drama in these stories, but I certainly couldn't dismiss it with an author who gave us Lear in *Moby-Dick*, Hamlet in *Pierre*, and all those Spenserian epigraphs in "The Encantadas"—or one who introduces the *Town Ho* narrative with the phrase "For my humor's sake."

The flat descriptions of the varieties of sea birds on Rodondo aren't meant, therefore, to be intricately developed parallels to complex characterization, but mere types contributing to the "dissonant din" which might characterize a Bartholomew's Fair as much as a Rock Rodondo. Melville did not need to wait till composing *The Confidence Man* before putting his Jonson to use.

Works Cited

Beasley, H. G., and H. J. Braunholtz. "Joseph Banks' Feather Cape from Hawaii," *MAN: A Monthly Record of Anthropological Science* 33 (January 1933).

Beebe, William. *Galapagos: World's End*. New York: Putnam, 1924.

Bercaw Edwards, Mary K. *Cannibal Old Me*. Kent, OH: Kent State Univ Press. In Press.

—. "The Infusion of Useful Knowledge: Melville and *The Penny Cyclopaedia*," *Melville Society Extracts* 70 (1987): 9-13.

—. *Melville's Sources*. Evanston: Northwestern University Press, 1987.

Cook, James. *Cook's Journals: Daily Entries*. March 2004. <http://southseas.nla.gov.au/journals/cook/index_r.html>.

Craighill, E. S. *Handy's Marquesan Legends*. Honolulu: Bishop Museum, 1930.

Foster, Elizabeth. "Another Note on Melville and Geology." *American Literature* 22 (1951): 479-487.

—. "Melville and Geology." *American Literature* 17 (1945): 50-65.

Franklin, H. Bruce. "The Island Worlds of Darwin and Melville." *Centennial Review*, 11 (1967): 353-70.

Hillway, Tyrus. "Melville as Amateur Zoologist." *Modern Language Quarterly* 12 (1951): 159-164.

—. "Melville's Geological Knowledge." *American Literature* 21 (1949): 232-37.

Kenn Kaufman. *Kingbird Highway*. Boston: Houghton Mifflin, 1997.

Madison, R. D. "Literature of Exploration and the Sea." *A Companion to Herman Melville*. Ed. Wyn Kelley. Malden, MA: Blackwell Publishing, 2006.

—. "Melville's Haglets," *Leviathan* 5 (2003): 79-84.

—. "The Strange Fowl of 'Benito Cereno,'" *Melville Society Extracts* 70 (1987): 15-16.

Melville, Herman. *Correspondence*. Ed. Harrison Hayford et al. Evanston and Chicago: Northwestern University Press and The Newberry Library, 1993.

—. *Moby-Dick*. Ed Hershel Parker and Harrison Hayford. New York, Norton, 2001.

—. *Omoo*. Ed. Harrison Hayford et al. Evanston and Chicago: Northwestern University Press and The Newberry Library, 1968.

—. *The Piazza Tales*. Ed. Harrison Hayford et al. Evanston and Chicago: Northwestern University Press and The Newberry Library, 1987.

—. *Typee*. Ed. Harrison Hayford et al. Evanston and Chicago: Northwestern University Press and The Newberry Library, 1968.

Polynesian Voyaging Society. <www.pvs.hawaii.org>

Porter, David. *Journal of a Cruise*. Ed. R. D. Madison and Karen Hamon. Annapolis: Naval Institute Press, 1986.

Sealts, Merton M., Jr. *Melville's Reading*. Columbia, University of South Carolina Press, 1988.

CHAPTER FIVE:

FROM REPRESENTATION TO REALITY

MARE MEMORIAE

JESSICA BEHM

> Water is the archê of all things.
> —Aristotle, *Metaphysics*
>
> Memory is the intersection of mind and matter.
> —Henri Bergson, *Matter and Memory*

The theory of the Aquatic Ape still circulates covertly in a number of biology departments.[1] There is little verifiable science for it but its hypotheses hold an odd allure, a hidden longing for the sea and its metaphors that has ensured it continues to wash up amidst sounder scientific theory.

Simply stated, the aquatic theory of evolution proposes that humans, already taxonomically advanced to a hominid stage, emerged from aquatic environments rather than strictly woodland or savannah habitats. More specifically, it suggests that many of the unique characteristics of the evolving *homo* genus cannot be explained without recourse to an aquatic or semi-aquatic developmental period. Cited evidence for our aquatic ancestry includes: a bipedal skeletal morphology hypothetically adapted for wading in water; a waterproof layer (*vernix caseosa*) covering all human infants at birth otherwise found only on neonate marine mammals; a comparatively naked body with minimal hair streamlined for sea currents; the capacity for conscious breath control absent in other land-dwelling organisms but present in all marine mammals; the prevalence of the ventro-ventral mating position (face-to-face) used by aquatic mammals

---

[1] This theory is occasionally entertained by researchers, perhaps under the influence of Alister Hardy, an Oxford-educated marine biologist who first explored an aquatic ape theory (AAT) as early as 1930 and published his findings in 1960. Hardy's work was later popularized by Elaine Morgan's book, *The Aquatic Ape Hypothesis,* in 1997 and further developed by Denis Montgomery in his *Seashore Hypothesis*, revised for print in 2007. An aquatic hominid origin was independently theorized by Max Westenhofer (*Der Eigenweg des Menschen (The Road to Man)* in 1942.

LIVERPOOL JOHN MOORES UNIVERSITY
LEARNING SERVICES

to copulate; the brain's unusually large requirement for omega-3 fatty acids which are difficult to procure in a terrestrial food chain but commonly found in marine environments; and the production of saline excretory fluids such as sweat and tears which are unique to human primates, but common to elephants also believed to have marine ancestry. Hominid littoral diaspora is frequently hypothesized to have occurred during the Pliocene-Pleistocene epoch, though fossil procurement is one of the many difficulties of the Aquatic Ape Theory (AAT) as these geologic areas of the African coasts are now mostly below sea level and aquatic marshes and swamps, lacking low-oxygen and high-acidity conditions, are not optimal for fossil-preservation.

The evidence for our aquatic ancestry is varied and often biologically imprecise—paleoanthropologists have offered alternate explanations for the physiological and physical traits that AAT attempts to theorize, but the exact conditions and environmental pressures that catalyzed the unique divergence of the *homo* genus, of which *homo sapiens* is the sole survivor, are continually contested.

In evolutionary biology and paleoanthropology the debate regarding hominid development has generated a number of contradictory hypotheses to explain our bipedal locomotion (rare in terrestrial mammals where quadrapedalism is the efficient norm) and our unusual saline and mating adaptations. The Savanna Theory, forwarded by South African paleo-anthropologist Raymond Dart in the 1920's, suggests that ancestral hominids gradually shifted from forested, arboreal habitats to open savannah edges and grasslands in search of prey. The Mosaic Theory propounds that organisms experienced varied rates of evolutionary change acting on individual anatomical structures, functions, and adaptations; in humans, it is thus hypothesized that bipedal locomotion evolved independent of skull or brain size, even though these changes might theoretically have accompanied the added complexity of adapting to bipedal modality.

While the fossil record continues to suggest alternate evolutionary taxonomies as well as multiple physical sites of origin, the varied evidentiary lacunae have allowed for the emergence of a theory of human aquatic ancestry that seems to speak more to our longing than to indisputable, laccolithic evidence. Perhaps those scientists who have interpreted paleontological and phylogenetic data to suggest that we came from an aquatic environ are haunted by other imaginings of the sea—the pull of primordial tides or the call of sirens swimming just beyond the horizon. One expects to find them peering Narcissus-like at their own reflection hoping it reveals not an image, but the truth of our evolution from Pliocene waters.

At some time it may be an irrefutably proved fact that humans diverged from their primate ancestors by struggling to stand, to see the horizon beyond their immediate vision. But even the poetics of this—our posture gradually adapted to our heightened sight—is eclipsed by a seemingly inescapable *mare memoriae*—though our hominid ancestors may not have evolved from water, we still live in continual memory of the sea.

I. The Memory of Matter

Traveling home from the coastal island of Öland to her village on Sweden's mainland, a young girl named Karolina Olsson nearly died from drowning in the winter of 1876. Her fate, one might feel, was far worse.

Some historical annals say she fell through the ice and was trapped below for some time before rescuers could pull her from the icy floes, others say she slipped on the ice and fell momentarily unconscious. Only thirteen years old at the time, the stories all concur on one unusual fact—Karolina Olsson slipped into a coma she would not wake up from until 1908, three decades later at the age of forty-five.[2] By the time she did open her eyes and was declared a medical phenomenon, her mother had died, two of her brothers had also drowned in the Atlantic ocean, and Sweden, dissolving the Kiel Treaty which conjoined its territory to Norway, had formed its own nation-state.

Karolina Olsson, a thirteen-year-old sleeping beauty of the sea, awoke three decades later as a middle-aged woman and declared that all she could remember was the image of the "blue men" submerged below the water, or submerged perhaps in her own unconscious for more than thirty years.

In the opening pages of *Matter and Memory,* Henri Bergson suggests that his work will affirm the existence of both spirit and matter via the possibility of memory. He defines matter, in philological response to the dual philosophical traditions of idealism and realism as an *image*: "Matter, in our view, is an aggregate of 'images.' And by 'image' we mean a certain existence which is more than that which the idealist calls a *representation*, but less than that which the realist calls a *thing*" (9).

---

[2] Monograph, documents, and informal interviews from the Kalmarlan Museum, Sweden. http://www.kalmarlansmuseum.se/

Bergson's articulation of the property of matter succinctly locates it, both practically and phenomenologically, partway between Cartesian mathematical extensity (matter as a "thing") and Berkeley's mental interiority (matter as a "representation")—that is, partway between the "imaginary" mind and "real" materiality. Bergson thus envisions matter more precisely as a "self-existing image": "For common sense, then, the object exists in itself, and, on the other hand, the object is, in itself, pictorial, as we perceive it: image it is, but a self-existing image" (10).

Bergson suggests that the Kantian criticism intervenes in this binary, recovering materiality from mere mathematical epiphenomena, as well as delivering it from imprisonment as a solipsist construct in the human mind; however, Bergson advises, a Kantian precept of matter yet limits both sense and understanding: "The human mind, in this direction at least, would not have been led to limit its own range; metaphysics would not have been sacrificed to physics, if philosophy had been content to leave matter halfway between the place to which Descartes had driven and that to which Berkeley drew it back—to leave it, in fact, where it is by common sense" (11).

The "common-sense" of matter, as elegantly pleasing as the notion seems, is, however, by no means common; it is necessarily predicated on a definition of "sense" which is, for Bergson defined in contradistinction to Kant—it is both of the perceptive senses *and* of cognitive sense. More rigorously, the definition of sensation—conceived of not as "pure" sensory input nor as "pure" mental phenomena but rather as the *educated* and thus necessarily *selective* acknowledgement of various sensory information (i.e. sight, touch, sound, etc.)—allows Bergson to theorize the category of perception, a necessity en route to his twin teleological destinations—the reconciliation of matter and spirit—in *Matter and Memory*.

A precise reexamination of sensation is necessary because it allows Bergson to discard the notion that an aggregation of sensory inputs simply coordinates to form a stable object, a "real" harmonious materiality which corresponds to the laws of nature. Or conversely, that sensation is the isolate purveyance of individual minds arbitrarily and abstractly acting at whim to create the illusion of laws of nature. Analogous to Bergson's suggestion that matter acts as self-existing image, sensation thus acts as self-existing interpretation—that is, matter and sensory interpretation are both kinds of images—co-extensive with objects in the exterior world *and* extant in one's interior world, moderated and modulated simultaneously. Bergson describes this recuperative act as an evolving *education* of the senses: "The diverse perception of the same object, given by my different senses, will not, then, when put together, reconstruct the complete image of the object; they will remain separated from each other by intervals which measure, so to speak, the gaps in my needs. It is to fill these intervals that an education of the senses is necessary" (49).

An understanding of sensation is prerequisite to Bergson's discussion of perception, which in turn informs his ontological definition of matter *in relation to memory.* When examining perception, Bergson avoids the Heiddegerian pursuit of Being, momentarily content to suggest it is possible that an image may *be* without *being perceived*—that is, though it is present (in space) it need not be represented (in consciousness). Perception is, for Bergson, the unique modulation of the *space* between the historical categories synchronically inscribed as matter and mind. Perception, he declares, "is master of space in the exact measure in which action is master of time. [...] We [can] infer the necessity of perception, that is to say, a *variable* relation between the living being and the more-or-less distant influence of the objects which interest it" (32-33).

Perception thus defined is not the awareness of all material conditions, but rather the discernment of those that will uniquely and *variably* influence our actions. More precisely, perception, rather than simply a material epiphenomenon that *affirms* objects already in the world (as posited by materialism) or a mental epiphenomenon that *creates* objects of the world (as posited by idealism) is a physically embodied act of understanding. Perception as such is a selective process, a choice, among extant objects that in turn prepares the body for action. Bergson states of perception:

> It is necessary to leave to perception its true office, which is to prepare actions. [...] Conscious perception has an entirely practical destination, simply indicating, in the aggregate of things, that which interests my possible action upon them: I can then understand that all the rest escapes me, and that, nevertheless, all the rest is of the same nature as what I perceive. Idealism cannot pass from the order manifested in perception to the order which is successful in science, that is to say, to reality. Inversely, realism fails to draw from reality the immediate consciousness we have of it. (229-230)

This slight ontological fissure, between *being* and *being perceived,* between matter which is *present* (an object in one's house) and matter which is *represented* (an object in one's mind) opens the space for Bergson's critical metaplasia—the transformative theorization of matter into the theorization of the *memory of matter.*

As Bergson's definition of perception is necessarily embodied—constitutive of present action—he diverges from philosophical thought that judges memory to be physiologically coterminous with perception, and thus simply a variation of storing sensory information in the brain. Uniquely, for Bergson, memory[3] is both a material and metaphysical affirmation of the nature of matter (and eventually, spirit).

Perception alone (a sensorial image of the present) cannot give rise to recollection (a synthesized image of the past) as memory inherently already requires a material past, and it is by definition an *absent* past. This exigency, while seemingly self-evident, forwards Bergson's claim that matter, continually and variably perceived, must also be continually remembered. In other words, if perception alone cannot conjure the past (since it is an action of selecting from among objects *in the present*), and if perception also cannot persist in the absence of recollection (since it requires previous recognition of objects *from the past* prior to their selection *in the present*) then it is memory that must intercede in our understanding of all matter.

Memory, rather than a neural process of physiological storage, constantly mediates both perception and understanding—fundamentally, *it allows for our recognition of matter as such.* Bergson concludes:

> The truth is that memory does not consist in a regression from the present to the past, but, on the contrary, in a progression from the past to the present. [...] Between the plane of action—the plane in which our body has condensed its past into motor habits—and the plane of pure memory, where our mind retains in all its details the picture of our past life, we believe that we can discover thousands of different planes of consciousness, a thousand integral and yet diverse repetitions of the whole of the experience through which we have lived. (239-241)

In this sense, we live continually *in memory of matter.* Of metaphysical consequence, Bergson also suggests that if, constantly distracted as we are by the demands of present action and living, we cannot understand the relationship between matter and memory, we might—and we are the only animal capable of doing so—experience it in a state of dreaming.

---

[3] Bergson distinguishes between perception, memory-image, and pure memory. Though related on a continuum, he suggests they are different in kind, not simply in degree, and relate to varied embodied as well as physiological processes, the variations are outside the scope to this paper for discussion, but provide pivotal theoretical substrate in *Matter and Memory*.

In a dream state, whether awake or asleep, Bergson suggests we can access the past, still always understood in relation to the present, without the interference of perception—the subterfuge of our day-to-day actions. More uniquely, this dream state, when not entered into deliberately, may also occur through trauma that inadvertently places us in a dream-like state of consciousness—for example, in the act of drowning.

> Memories, which we believed abolished, then reappear with striking completeness; we live over again, in all their detail, forgotten scenes of childhood; we speak languages which we no longer even remembered to have learned. There is nothing more instructive in this regard than what happens in the cases of sudden suffocation, as in men drowned. Such a man, when brought to life again, states that he saw, in a very short time, all the forgotten events of his life, with their smallest circumstance and in the very order in which they occurred. (154-155)

Thus while we may live in the memory of matter, our dreaming—or our drowning—allows us an alternate possibility for understanding how matter is continually imaged and imagined through acts of remembrance. If, following Bergson, our phenomenological understanding of matter appears to us as *image*—an entity which is neither "pure" materiality (*extant* without sense and understanding) nor "pure" interior mentality (*extinct* without sense and understanding)—and this image is inextricably linked to our memory of it, then we have arrived at a question which the next section will take up: if matter is an image continually modulated by memory, are there other phenomenological qualities to this image? That is, can we discern the material properties of this image beyond its fundamentally constitutive relation to memory: if we continually experience the memory of matter, what is the *matter of memory*?

II. The Matter of Memory

In the exhibit held at the New York American Craft Museum in November 1997, *Four Acts in Glass: Installations by Chihuly, Morris, Powers and Vallien,* Swedish glass artisan Bertil Vallien sculpts his vision of Karolina Olsson's story of drowning—trapped beneath the water for only moments but suspended within her own consciousness for more than three decades. His work explores the haunting image of her utterance that upon waking all she recalled was "a great darkness and blue men."[4]

---

[4] See Bertil Vallien, *Four Acts in Glass: Installations by Chihuly, Morris, Powers and Vallien.*

Displayed with stark simplicity, dozens of blue heads—sculpted in varied hues of opaque, frosted, and transparent glass—rest, but as if impaled, atop tall pipe-like stands (Figure 1). As one walks through the sea of faces perched at eye-level some are turned on their side, as if dreaming, while others stare into space or appear to gaze directly at you. The sculptures are an eerie counterpart to Vallien's other work, a series of two to twelve foot glass boats with tiny, inscrutable objects embedded inside of them (Figure 2); of this project Vallien declares—"I make ships that sink, but they sink through the depths of memories."

Figure 1: Head 18 ©Bertil Vallien, Artist[5]

Figure 2: Boat 1, ©Bertil Vallien, Artist

---

[5] The images of Bertil Vallien's work were reproduced for this publication with his permission. Additional images and information regarding his work may be found at http://www.bertilvallien.nu/gallery/index.html.

In Vallien's work we find one material incarnation of Bergson's metaphysical engagement of matter and memory. While Vallien's sea of blue faces captures Olsson's singular memory of her past—Vallien physically sculpts Bergson's notion that in the absence of memory there is little matter to recognize or reconstitute—it is Vallien's glass ships that speak to the darker silhouette of her words—the potential obscuration of memory and the opaque lacunae that shape memory's transference *from* past to present as well as its evocation *of* the past in the present. Whereas Bergson's theoretical work examines the *memory of matter*, Vallien's sculptural work explores the *matter of memory*—and it is haunted by the sea. Like water, his sculptures simultaneously appear dense and buoyant, opaque and luminous, made from a liquid but quickly cooled into icy glass, and like memory, they are in the present but of the past.

In experiences recounted by some revived drowning victims, they describe a feeling of serenity in the single inhalation before their descent into total darkness. As the body draws oxygen from deep, abandoned tributaries and their mind is flooded with thought, as water seeps into the crevices of their consciousness and their vision slowly disappears, they suggest a sense of calm remains.

Submerged and suspended at once did Karolina Olsson, like the others or Vallien's ships, also sink through the depths of memory; for the fleeting moment before she was plunged into irretrievable blackness was it possible to inhale her young past—stored in bone, muscle and gesture— and exhale her future as she surrendered to the present. And of the thirty years that followed, is it possible to understand her utterance upon waking, her memory of the blue faces at sea, metaphysically as well as neurologically?

While our dreaming and our drowning may reveal the collusion of matter and memory, these states also portend the darker spaces inherent to each condition. Perhaps heretofore submerged memories are revealed at the moment one wakes from dreaming or, more rarely, when one is revived from drowning. But if memories can be resuscitated during these fluid states, when the body and consciousness are momentarily suspended (or submerged), then it is the originary nature of their liquid materiality that must be examined: that is, the *matter* of memory.

Thales, crowned by Aristotle as the father of natural philosophy, is said to have declared that water is the *archê* of all things: an initiation of the philosophical problem of matter shaped in relation to the natural sciences.

Though there exists no written record of his work, in the *Metaphysics* Aristotle reports that "Thales says that it [the nature of things] is water" (*Metaphysics* 983 b20). Aristotle hypothesizes that Thales' theory of water as originary matter derived from his understanding "that the nurture of all creatures is moist, and that warmth itself is generated from moisture and lives by it; and that from which all things come to be is their first principle" (*Metaphysics* 983 b23-25).   Thales, it would seem, foreshadowed a long lineage of scientists pondering humanity's aquatic origins.

The force of water as an actant in many biological, geological, and meteorological processes would have been known to Thales at the time. Likewise, metallurgical techniques would have demonstrated the potential to "return" solid matter to a liquid state, and evapo-transpirative conditions the transformation of water to other, secondary or tertiary material states. Seemingly without recourse to God, and while nutritive theories of mist and spontaneous generation (abiogenesis) circulated, Thales nonetheless attributed the generative properties of the universe to water, theorizing that not only were we born of water, but that we would return to it as our final material state.

We now know that water as a material substance has particularly complex properties—even as ice it is always in flux. The molecular composition of water is such that when water coalesces, forming tessellating, geometrical configurations of ice, it yet remains fluid within its own molecular structure. Each hydrogen atom is in a constant state of exchange with those of adjacent water molecules. Chemists refer to this property as *vibration*; water is described to *bend* and may have symmetrical or asymmetrical *stretch*.   Though they are chemically dissimilar, the molecular exchange of water and that of the neurological, synaptic exchange influencing memory have some similarities in their fluid ability to transport (information or goods), submerge (the past or people), and transform states (of molecular condition or consciousness)—along swift currents. As Thales proposed, it is not difficult to imagine, metaphysically if not metabolically, the ways in which we are influenced by the matter and metaphors of water.

Aristotle also suggests that Thales' proximity to the sea of Lade and the river of Maeander may have influenced his reliance on water as an originary life source—Thales, too, it seemed lived in memory of the sea. His appointment of water as the *archê* of all matter necessarily implies that the matter of memory is inextricably linked to the matter of water—that is, in the physiology of its fluid synaptic firings as well as its fluid metaphysical state, our memory is *from* the sea, even if we do not have ancestral memories *of* the sea. While Bergson's metaphysics suggests that matter is always mediated by memory, Thales' metaphysics suggests that matter is always mediated by water—in relationship, it follows that the matter of memory, our past as *bourn by* the present and our present as *borne from* the past, may exist in fluid relation to the sea. We live in perpetual possibility of *mare memoriae*.

Works Cited

Aristotle. *Aristotle's Metaphysics*. Trans. Joe Sachs. 2nd ed. Santa Fe, N.M.: Green Lion, 2002.

Bergson, Henri. *Matter and Memory*. Eds. Nancy Margaret Paul and W. Scott Palmer. New York: Zone Books, 1991.

Ross, Barbara. *Four Acts in Glass: Installations by Chihuly, Morris, Powers and Vallien*. Exhibit Monograph. New York: American Craft Museum, 1997.

Vallien, Bertil. *Original Sculptures*. Copyright permission of Bertil Vallien. 12 February 2007 <http://www.bertilvallien.nu/gallery/index.html>.

SHIP GROUNDING IN THE CARIBBEAN: CONSIDERATIONS FOR CORAL REEF RECOVERY AFTER MARINE INCIDENTS

SEAN GRIFFIN AND MICHAEL NEMETH

Coral reefs are one of the most biologically productive and diverse ecosystems on the planet, similar to terrestrial tropical rain forests. Due to various natural and human factors, such as overfishing, pollution and disease, these valuable resources have been in a state of decline over the last few decades. Conservation of these fragile ecosystems is crucial because they are an important source of food for both humans and marine organisms, providing both habitat and sustenance in an otherwise nutrient deficient area. Coral reefs also protect islands and coastlines from erosion by storms and waves.

Coral reefs are threatened by an array of natural and anthropogenic stressors that may act together, through unfortuitous synergy, leading to a decline in their health. While the natural phenomena that threaten coral reefs include storms, disease outbreaks, and bleaching, the human factors are pollution, sedimentation, and overfishing, as well as direct physical impacts such as trampling, anchoring and—of special interest to us here—ship groundings.

About 95% of the world's commerce is transported by ships at one point or another, and the Caribbean Sea is a major thoroughfare for the traffic connecting the Atlantic Ocean to the Pacific via the Panama Canal. Apart from marine commerce, there is also a wide array of recreational boating that goes on in the Caribbean. Damages to coral reefs from ship groundings can range from minor injuries by small recreational vessels to extensive damages to the reef community and structure from large commercial vessels such as tankers and freighters. Natural resource agencies respond to ship groundings on coral reefs in order to assess damages, take emergency action to mitigate impacts and provide for restoration to avoid the loss of natural resources. These actions should be based on an understanding of how the ecological processes on a coral reef influence the recovery of the system to insure an effective restoration of the community.

It is impossible to completely compensate for the loss of a coral reef whose physical structure has been formed through thousands of years of growth. The goal of restoration activities by these agencies is to enhance recolonization and recreate to the extent possible, habitat that resembles the surrounding community. Two of the most common type of coral assemblages in the Caribbean are classified as "spur-and-groove"[1] and "hardground" communities. Spur-and-groove communities are typically characterized by high relief structures with dense coral cover and high diversity, while hardground communities typically have a low profile with low coral concentrations and diversity.

As William Precht et al. have noted, it is imperative to have a careful, systematic assessment and documentation of the injury along with a detailed restoration plan. A thorough assessment of the surrounding reefs will provide species composition and size distributions of each species. Using data from the assessment transects, growth estimates can be compared with size distributions to estimate the time required for recovery of the coral populations in the damaged area to resemble those found on undamaged reference habitats. Once a complete damage assessment is compiled, a detailed restoration plan should be drawn up. Emphasis should be placed upon flattened denuded reef areas where recovery will not occur without restoration activities.

When a vessel collides with another object like a coral reef, it can leave patches of anti-fouling paint from its hull on the reef. John Owens has aptly pointed out that these paints should be removed from the reef as soon as possible due to the harmful effect toxins in these paints can have on corals and other reef biota.

Complex coral reef ecosystems like spur-and-groove habitats seldom recover naturally. The damage caused by groundings in these areas can be devastating. The injured habitat will continue to degrade and may result in a shift in reef structure and function. As Precht, Lirman, Miller and other observers have noted, there could eventually be a phase-shift to an alternate community structure similar to natural hardground communities. Hardground communities typically have low topographic complexity,

---

[1] Spur-and-groove reefs typically have elevated reef areas ("Spurs") with dense coral cover and high species diversity that are separated by sand channels ("Grooves").

consisting of flat limestone pavements with crustose coralline algae, gorgonians and isolated coral colonies. Spur-and-groove habitats have more complex topography, higher species diversity and greater coral cover.

Various studies, such as those by the NOAA and by Baruch Rinkevich, have demonstrated that high relief areas that add 3 dimensional structure to the reef will not recover to their original community structure without a proactive restoration program to encourage reef development. Moreover, as Precht has shown, damaged spur-and-groove habitat will not recover rapidly to its former state and may not recover at all without substantial restorative engineering. When the reef structure and substrate is broken down into rubble and sand, the reef's ability to recover from natural processes of recruitment by the next cohort of hard corals is diminished. Loose broken substrate is dynamic and can be easily moved by storms and current. Young coral recruits that settle to the bottom as minute larvae may experience higher sedimentation and increased mortality from overturning and abrasion. In 2003, Fox et al. demonstrated that this type of habitat is favorable for soft coral aggregations that compete with new hard coral settlers. This loss of topographic complexity has serious implications for the recovery of the reef community, such as fish and sea urchin populations, in spur-and-groove habitats. Nevertheless, as Richard Aronson and Deborah Swanson show, restoration efforts must not only include reattachment of corals and stabilization of the substrate but also reestablishment of the topographic complexity to enhance recruitment and growth of coral species that naturally occur in spur-and-groove habitats.

Recovery Rates

Several studies, such as those by Precht and by J. Walter Milon and Richard Dodge, have demonstrated that the recovery time of the coral reef can be reduced by active restoration, substrate stabilization, and coral transplantation. Natural recruitment is the settlement of coral larvae onto the substrate, which then grow into adult corals providing the framework of the reef. Transplantation of coral colonies/ fragments onto denuded areas as well as rubble stabilization are best implemented when natural recruitment is unlikely or limited because of the existence of un-consolidated substrate or when a disturbed area has the potential to undergo a phase shift to a hardbottom community dominated by soft coral or macro algae. Because of the recent decline in coral reef health, once a reef undergoes a phase shift to a different type of community, it can be difficult for the reef to return to its original state.

Table 1 lists estimates for recovery rates of different types of coral reef communities when no active restoration programs have been implemented. In 2001, Becker and Mueller observed that many of the reefs in the Florida Keys are hardground communities which consist of substrate that is primarily cemented "live rock" overlaying unconsolidated loose reef material with crustose coralline algae, soft corals[2] and isolated hard coral colonies. These areas have a low concentration of corals and low species diversity and are typically very flat with little 3 dimensional relief. After a ship grounding, this type of community could take up to 10 years to recover naturally to where the affected area can no longer be distinguished from the surrounding reef. In some cases, it can take slightly more than half a decade. For example, as studies by Precht, Lirman, Miller and Barimo have shown, it took 6 years for the M/V Elpis grounding site which damaged an existing hardground community, to be statistically indistinguishable from adjacent hardground sites.

Table 1: Estimated recovery rates for different coral reef communities with no active restoration to offset interim losses and natural recovery rates to baseline conditions

Community Type	Recovery Time
Hardground Communities	10 years
Spur and Groove Habitat	At least 100 years, possibly never
Stony Corals	35 years
Gorgonian Corals	15 years
Algae/ Other Organisms	5 years

(Milon and Dodge, 2001; Precht et al., 2001).

Because of their low topographic relief, species diversity and coral density, these hardground communities are different from the coral rich, high diversity and complex relief of the spur-and-groove communities. Precht claims that these habitats would take at least a hundred years to recover, possibly never without restoration. Examples of the long-lasting effects of groundings include the 1984 grounding of the M/V Wellwood in the Florida Keys and two nineteenth-century groundings at Pickles Reef in

---

[2] The terms "soft corals" or "octocorals" refer to corals that do not significantly contribute to reef accretion but create 3 dimensional relief because of their vertical profiles. Their skeletons are more flexible than the hard corals, thus directly contributing to reef growth through secretion of calcium carbonate skeletons that provide physical structure to the reef. Crustose coralline algae has no vertical profile whatsoever but is important in cementing the framework of the reef.

the Florida Keys National Marine Sanctuary. Studies by Precht, Lirman, Miller and Barimo indicate that the former site now more closely resembles natural hardground communities rather than the spur-and-groove habitat that had been destroyed by the accident. In the case of the later site at Pickles Reef, the reefs never recovered to their original spur-and-groove community structure. This site, Precht shows, is presently characteristic of a hardground coral community.

Recruitment

Recruitment of corals onto the substrate is the first vital step to habitat recovery on coral reefs. The importance of recruitment on recovery rates of restored habitats suggests that restoration activities should emphasize providing appropriate recruitment substrate for coral recruits. A flattened reef with high sediment loads will not provide an adequate site for coral recruitment. In a recent report from NOAA (2002) on recovery of the M/V Wellwood grounding site, there has been little or no recovery in the areas where the reef was crushed. Moreover, Maida et al. pointed out in 1994 that coral recruitment does not occur on the surface of the substrate because of sedimentation; rather new recruits favor the sides of surfaces or within crevices. In 1998 Struan Smith et al. demonstrated that there was no increase in juvenile coral abundance and diversity within the M/V Wellwood site since 1989 and pointed out the relative absence of juveniles of hard corals (figure 1), which are the major frame builders of the reef because of the calcium carbonate skeletons that they produce. This indicates that there has been no recruitment of corals to restore the reef to its prior condition.

In Florida, W. J. Harrigan and Stephen Gittings reported (in 1984 and 1988 respectively) higher recruitment rates for the octocorals (Figure 2) *Pseudopterogorgia americana* than *Plexaura* spp. and *Gorgonia ventalina* (qtd. in NOAA 2-7). Yoshioka (1997) also reported higher rates of recruitment for *Pseudopterogorgia* (up to 34.7/ m^2) while the highest rate for *Pseudoplexaura* was only 8.1/ m^2. At the M/V Wellwood grounding site, Harrigan and Gittings point out, *P. americana* is now common while *Plexaura* and *G. ventalina*, once common, are now rare This suggests that transplantation of these latter species rather than *P. americana,* should be the focus of restoration activites. As with hard corals, the successful recruitment of octocorals is limited by movements in the sediment bedload. In general the faster-growing species (*Pseudopterogorgia*) will be able to recruit and reach a size where they will not be smothered by sediment.

Figure 1: An assemblage of several species of hard coral. Photo: Michael Nemeth

Figure 2: An assemblage of several species of soft coral (octocorals). Photo: Michael Nemeth

It is evident, then, that natural recovery of reef communities impacted by ship groundings is strongly dependent on recruitment of corals and octocorals. Since recruitment success is known to be influenced by substrate type (amount of sand, stability of rubble) monitoring of recruitment variability will aid in better determining the expected rates of recovery.

Coral Growth Rates

As suggested in Table 1 above, abundance and diversity of hard corals may return to an impact site within 10 years, but maximum coral size and original size distribution of the corals can take up to 35 years to return to baseline conditions. The slow growth rates of hard corals make recovery of these communities inherently slow. For example, Table 2 lists estimated growth rates for several common species of coral found in the Caribbean.

Table 2: Estimated growth rates for several common species of coral

Species	Rate (cm/yr)
Acropora cervicornis	10 – 20 cm/yr
Acropora palmata	Up to 10 cm/yr
Agaricia agaricites	0.16 cm cm/yr
Colpophyllia natans	0.41 cm/yr
Dendrogyra cylindrus	Vertical Growth - 1.8 cm / year average Lateral Growth - 75 cm^2 / year average
Diploria labyrinthiformis	0.33 – 0.46 cm/yr
Montastraea annularis	0.634 cm/yr 0.29 – 1.02 cm/yr at depths of 6 – 12 m
M. cavernosa	0.436 cm/yr 0.29 – 0.45 cm/yr
Porites astreoides	0.475 cm/yr 0.19 – 0.31 cm/yr
Siderastrea Siderca	0.15 – 0.3 cm/yr

(Highsmith et al., 1983; Hubbard and Scaturo, 1985; Huston, 1985; Hudson and Goodwin, 1997).

Dennis Hubbard and David Scaturo have shown that growth rates vary between species and decrease with depth. Previous restoration work with *Dendrogyra cylindrus* showed almost a 100% survival rate when toppled pillars were restabilized vertically on the reef by cementing their bases into the reef. As James Hudson and William Goodwin demonstrated, these colonies then grew vertically at an average of 1.8 cm / year. The plasticity of *D. cylindrus* to regrow from fallen pillars has been well documented, but if not replaced upright, it would take a fallen pillar or toppled colony about 50 years to reach a height of 1m at an average growth rate of 2 cm / yr. This species can help contribute to the vertical profile of the reef which is important for providing habitat and refuge for the marine organisms that live on the reef.

A. cervicornis and *A. palmata* are faster growing than the other stony corals listed in Table 2 and have the potential to rebuild the reef faster than the other species. Due to drastic population declines throughout the Caribbean in the last few decades, these two corals have recently been listed as threatened species under the Endangered Species Act of 1972. There has been a successful history of transplantation of *A. cervicornis*, as Austin Bowden-Kerby and Ricardo Muñoz-Chagín have demonstrated, while Andrew Bruckner and Robyn Bruckner have noted the same case with *A. palmate*. In Hawaii, for example, Evelyn Cox has shown that initial growth of fragments is lower compared to larger colonies, but these rates increase exponentially each year and can catch up in about 4 years Table 3 lists mean growth rates for several common species of octocorals. The maximum growth rates of individual colonies may be greater than those in the table, as the values presented here are averaged across multiple colonies. Paul Yoshioka and Beverly Yoshioka have observed that because of the variability in growth rates within individual species, colony height is a poor indicator of age. For example, a 100 cm colony of *P. americana* could be between 14 to 60 years old. However, by measuring the size distribution of colonies at an unimpacted site, it is possible to estimate recovery time by using the mean growth rates in Table 3.

Table 3: Mean growth rates for several common species of octocorals

Species	Rate (cm/yr)
Pseudopterogorgia americana	4.48 cm/yr
Gorgonia ventalina	2.34 cm/yr
Pseudoplexaura porosa	2.22 cm/yr
Plexaura homomalla	1.99 cm/yr

(Yoshioka and Yoshioka, 1991).

Long term monitoring

Imprecise references to previous anthropogenic impacts on coral reefs can quickly become controversial and hinder the search for appropriate replacement projects. Restoration activities and recovery rates on hardbottom communities in the Florida Keys cannot be accurately applied to damage and recovery of spur-and-groove reef habitats in other areas.

Given the slow growth rate of corals and coral reefs, Precht maintains that long term monitoring is required to evaluate the efficiency and effectiveness of a restoration program. The success of the restoration effort can be shown not only by recruitment and survivorship rates of corals on the restoration structures but by resemblance to the characteristics of the reference population as well. Yet it is only through long term monitoring that recruitment and survivorship can be measured.

Long term monitoring is necessary to establish meaningful estimates of natural and active recovery on damaged coral reef sites and make future predictions. Reef scientists can identify when restored reefs do not functionally match natural systems and, consequently, make appropriate recommendations. Monitoring will help evaluate whether or not the restoration design meets the desired objectives; if it does not then the restoration program should be modified.

As Milon and Dodge have warned, unless the government agencies responsible for coral reef damage assessment and restoration planning perform damage assessments and census of restoration activities, they will be viewed as arbitrary if they are conducted for legal proceedings. This approach will provide a statistically and ecologically defensible basis upon which to document the injury, set restoration goals, implement the appropriate restoration program, and gauge overall project success of coral reef recovery.

Works Cited

Aronson, Richard B. and Deborah W. Swanson. "Disturbance and recovery from ship groundings in the Florida Keys National Marine Sanctuary." *Dauphin Island Sea Lab Technical Report* (1997): 97-102.

Becker, Lillian C. and Erich Mueller. "The culture, transplantation and storage of *Montastraea faveolata, Acropora cervicornis* and *Acropora palmata*: what we have learned so far." *Bulletin of Marine Science* 69 (2001): 881-896.

Bowden-Kerby, Austin. "Coral Transplantation in sheltered habitats." *Proceedings of the 8ᵗʰ International Coral Reef Symposium* 2 (1998): 2063-2068.

Bruckner, Andrew W. and Robyn J. Bruckner. "Condition of restored *Acropora palmata* fragments off Mona Island, Puerto Rico, 2 years after the *Fortuna Reefer* ship grounding." *Coral Reefs* 20 (2001): 235-243.

—. "Survivorship of restored *Acropora palmata* over six years at the *M/V Fortuna Reefer* ship grounding site, Mona Island, Puerto Rico." 10ᵗʰ International Coral Reef Symposium, Okinwawa Convention Center. Okinawa, Japan. 28 Jun. 2004

Clark, Susan and Alasdair J. Edwards. "Use of artificial reef structures to rehabilitate reef flats degraded by coral mining in the Maldives." *Bulletin of Marine Science* 55 (1994): 867-877.

—. "Coral transplantation as an aid to reef rehabilitation: evaluation of a case study in the Maldive Islands." *Coral Reefs* 14 (1995): 201-213.

—. "An evaluation of artificial reef structures as tools for marine habitat rehabilitation in the Maldives." *Aquatic Conservation: Marine and Freshwater Ecosystems* 9 (1999): 5-21.

Cox, Evelyn F. "Fragmentation in the Hawaiian coral *Montipora verrucosa*." *Proceedings of the 7ᵗʰ International Coral Reef Symposium (Guam)* 1 (1999): 513-516.

Fox, Helen E., Jos S. Pet, Rokhmin Dahuri, and Roy L. Caldwell. "Recovery in rubble fields: long term impacts from blast fishing." *Marine Pollution Bulletin.* 46 (2003): 1024-1031.

Gittings, Stephen R., Thomas J. Bright, Akira Choi, and Richard R. Barnett. "The recovery process in a mechanically damaged coral reef community: Recruitment and growth." *Proceedings of the 6ᵗʰ Intl. Coral Reef Symposium* 2 (1988): 225-230.

Highsmith, Raymond C., Rebekka L. Lueptow, Sandra C. Shonberg. "Growth and bioerosion of three massive corals on the Belize barrier reef." *Marine Ecology and Progress Series* 13 (1983): 261-271.

Hubbard, Dennis K. and David Scaturo. "Growth rates of seven species of Scleractinian corals from Cane Bay and SALT River, St. Croix, USVI." *Bulletin of Marine Science* 36.2 (1985): 335-348.

Hudson, James H and William B. Goodwin. "Restoration and growth rate of hurricane damaged pillar coral (*Dendrogyra cylindrus*) in the Key Largo National Marine Sanctuary, Florida." *Proceedings of the 8th International Coral Reef Symposium* (1997).

Huston, Michael. "Variation in coral growth rates with depth at Discovery Bay, Jamaica." *Coral Reefs* 4.1 (1985): 19-25.

Kobayashi, Akira. "Regeneration and regrowth of fragmented colonies of the hermatypic corals *Acropora formosa* and *Acropora nasuta*." *Galaxea* 3 (1984): 13-23.

Lirman, Diego and Margaret V. Miller. "Modeling and monitoring tools to assess recovery status and convergence rates between restored and undisturbed coral reef habitats." *Restoration Ecology* 11.4 (2003): 448-456.

Maida, Mauro, John C. Coll, and Paul W. Sammarco. "Shedding new light on Scleractinian coral recruitment." *Journal of Experimental Marine Biology and Ecology* 180 (1994): 189-202.

Miller, Margaret W. and John Barimo. "Assessment of juvenile coral populations at two reef restoration sites in the FKNMS: indicators of success?" *Bulletin of Marine Science.* 69.2 (2001): 395-405.

Milon, J. Walter and Richard E. Dodge. "Applying habitat equivalency analysis for coral reef damage assessment and restoration." *Bulletin of Marine Science.* 69.2 (2001): 975-988.

Muñoz-Chagín, Ricardo F. "Coral transplantation program in the Paraiso coral reef, Cozumel Island, Mexico." *Proceedings of the 8th International Coral Reef Symposium* 2 (1998): 2075-2077.

NOAA – Marine Sanctuaries Division. "Environmental assessment: *M/V Wellwood* grounding site restoration. Florida Keys National Marine Sanctuary." Monroe County, Florida: 2002.

Owen, Richard, Anthony Knap, Megan Toaspern, and Kelly Carbery. "Inhibition of coral photosynthesis by the antifouling herbicide Irgarol 1051." *Marine Pollution Bulletin* 44 (2002): 623-632.

Precht, William F., Richard B. Aronson, and Dione W. Swanson. "Improving scientific decision-making in the restoration of ship-grounding sites on coral reefs." *Bulletin of Marine Science* 69.2 (2001): 1001-1012.

Rinkevich, Baruch. "Conservation of coral reefs through active restoration measures: recent approaches and last decade progress." *Environmental Science and Technology* 39 (2005): 4333-4342.

Smith, Struan R., Dan C. Hellin, Sheila A. McKenna. "Patterns of juvenile coral abundance, mortality, and recruitment at the M/V Wellwood and M/V Elpis grounding sites and their comparison to undisturbed reefs in the Florida Keys." *Final Report to NOAA Sanctuary and Reserves Division and the National Undersea Research Program.* University of North Carolina, Wilmington: (1998).

Yoshioka, Paul M. "Are variations in Gorgonian recruitment determined by "pre-settlement" or "post-settlement" factors?" *Proceedings of the 9th International Coral Reef Symposium* 2 (1997): 1175-1181.

Yoshioka, Paul M. and Beverly B. Yoshioka. "A comparison of the survivorship and growth of shallow-water gorgonian species of Puerto Rico." *Marine Ecology Progress Series* 69 (1991): 253-260.

SOMETIMES A GREAT NOTION: CREATING A MARINE RESERVE IN RINCÓN, PUERTO RICO

STEVE TAMAR

Much like a symphony, people's view of their relationship with the sea undergoes a constant process of theme and variation. In our very cellular arrangement is recorded the knowledge that this deeply mysterious place is where we came from, and on this primal and preconscious level we regard it as our "terrible mother" who is the source of sustenance and sudden, unforeseeable danger and death, whose limitless horizons served to underscore our own emerging sense of self.

Perhaps this was the underlying psychological framework of most coastal dwelling people as they began to slowly build a cultural context with which to manipulate the uncertain rewards and very real risks of their environment. Schools of deities, devas and demons were postulated to be swimming freely in the depths in our ancestral attempts to isolate and codify the numberless factors that influence a constantly changing element whose restless surface was a most dubious foundation on which to launch a livelihood. Hopes and fears sink equally like stones into uncertainty, to take on a life of their own. They become things to be worshiped or avoided according to our own desires, but always respected and propitiated according to our means. Offerings were scattered on the waves, songs chanted as the sight of land slips away, we clutch our culture's constructs as talismans when setting sail on the face of this mystery.

With the passage of time we begin to think we are actually getting somewhere. Reflecting our constant elaboration of social pathways we begin to see the elemental deities as linked through associations of family and tribe. We create "civilization" in the sense of nation-states and empires, and impose this level of organization on the unknown. Natural forces are given names and attributes far beyond their sensible aspects and we attempt to manipulate these hidden dimensions in the laboratory space of temples and priestly gestures. Along with claiming the ability to control—at least partially—the seas' restlessness, the empire traces its sigils of conflict and commerce on the face of the deep, attempting to tattoo trade routes and political territory on what is seen as a blank, blue slate. The ephemeral equivalents of walls, roads and bridges are constructed in the collective mind and made to float like an unseen dream somewhere in the waters. We feel our original mystery has been bent to our will, its awe-inspiring expanse now something to be gotten over, or defended, or otherwise claimed as 'ours.' Even if only in our minds, we begin to chart the trackless, the monsters and mermaids slowly being compressed to the margins (and marginalia) of our understanding.

It was inevitable that this ability to displace what we could not fully comprehend in our imagination also led to a further displacement of our relationship with the oceans. As our technology evolved and our abilities to travel, measure, and otherwise subdivide the planet increased, the hazy limits of our understanding seemed to recede beyond our concern. In fact, somewhere along the voyage they seemed to have dropped off the map completely. This confusion of the map with the territory, this loss of boundaries within which to locate our actions in anything but a human reality led us to declaring some pretty arbitrary spheres of influence as regards our original birthplace. We would no longer move upon it cautiously as hunter/gatherers but proudly stride like owners, mining it for our profit and using it as a dump for the inconvenient by-products of our civilization. We had moved so far from that cellular sense of connection that we began to claim some sort of 'right' to do so. And the results of our ignorance have begun to catch up with us, physically, mentally and spiritually.

And so once more our relationship with the ocean begins to change. In a restatement of our ancestral theme the new tools of post-Einsteinian understanding have simultaneously brought our limitations much closer while restoring their original mystery. Once more we regard the ocean (indeed, the entire planet) as a form of 'super-organism' whose processes and objectives do not necessarily coincide with our own. Once more we stand on the shore gazing over something we do not—and may never—fully comprehend. Once more we clutch talismans, and propitiate only barely understood powers with our words and gestures, not to seek our own personal survival but that of our entire species. Sometimes these gestures are attempted on a global scale—such as the Kyoto and G8 summits—which involve participation by heads of state and receive worldwide publicity. Other attempts are less grandiose but are no less important, and are sometimes more successful: they are a microcosmic gesture of our attempts to protect our planet and its species. One such gesture is the creation of the Reserva Marina Tres Palmas (RM3P).

An Encounter with Tres Palmas

Tres Palmas has inspired in residents of the area an arguably unprecedented grassroots movement to rescue it, but perhaps an imaginary walk through the beach will give a reader unfamiliar with it a sense of its beauty and the passions to save it that it has inspired.

Looking at a map of Puerto Rico the reader will see that it has a fairly rectangular shape except for a triangular piece of land that juts westward from the northwest coast. At the tip of that extension you will find the town of Rincón (approx. pop. 25,000). Most foreigners will probably say "Ahah! I know why they call it Rincón!" (which means 'corner' in Spanish), and are wrong: although Rincón does indeed mean 'corner,' the town is named after the family name of one of the holders of the original land grants bestowed by the Spanish crown.

Let us imagine you are standing on that westernmost tip of the point, facing the setting sun. On your right hand, to the north, is the open Atlantic Ocean. To your left is the Caribbean Sea. In front of you, slightly to the northwest, you'll see at a distance of 20 km. the small island of Desecheo (literally "the discarded"), an extinct volcanic cone, uninhabited but for passing smugglers and illegal immigrants due to its lack of fresh water sources. It is officially a wildlife sanctuary. Behind you is a decommissioned nuclear power plant, but that is another story, for another book.

You begin walking southward along the Caribbean coast. In a few minutes you pass a lighthouse, and another few will bring you to a sign that informs you that you're entering the RM3P. You continue walking along some of the world's best beaches, with tidal pools and coral reefs to one side and palm groves and (mostly) open pasture and scrub on the other. If it is winter you will likely also be seeing world-class surf somewhere along this walk (with waves reaching 20-30 ft. at times) or perhaps a pod of humpback whales passing by towards their local calving areas. Intrigued, you put on your facemask and flippers to swim out, and have a chance of encountering a hawksbill turtle or bottlenose dolphin, or even a visiting manatee if you're very lucky. Glancing down you'll be seeing hundreds of types of colorful corals and multi-hued tropical fish, maybe one of the few remaining lobsters, and the usual selection of sea urchins, snails, slugs and other more sessile shell-bearing species. The farther you swim you notice the bottom sloping down and you pass over a series of rock and coral outcrops separated by sandy trenches, looking very much as if a giant had reached down and run its fingers over the seafloor a long time ago. As the water gets deeper the ecology seems to get simpler and far more sparse. Eventually, around 60 ft. of depth, sunlight can no longer penetrate to the bottom and the reef system comes to an end, which also marks a boundary of the Reserve. You are now several hundred meters off the shore.

Figure 1: Reserva Marina Tres Palmas - Location

Swimming back you will perhaps observe a unique grouping of three palm trees—i.e. "Tres Palmas," which marks the easiest way to cross the reefs to shore, an important landmark for surfers and boats—which lends its name to this particular beach and the Reserve in general. At this point you're probably passing over some interesting reddish-brown coral formations with upward branching arms, looking a bit like elk horns. Remember this sight, because in one sense it's what the fuss is all about. Aiming just south of the three palms, you eventually reach the beach again.

Continuing your walk south for five or ten minutes, you start seeing signs of "civilization" in the shape of homes, guesthouses, and newly-constructed condos. In another ten minutes you reach the town's marina area and a sign that marks this boundary of the Reserve, and another couple minutes bring you to Rincón itself. This imaginary walk is, in this writer's view, the next best experience to recognizing the passion that the Tres Palmas Reserve project has inspired–other than the actual beach itself.

But to frame the picture of this imaginary walk more completely, in a geological/topographic sense you have passed over ground composed mostly of igneous bedrock of a volcanic and volcaniclastic nature, with some metamorphic outcrops, fractured with minor faultlines, whose bedding lie inclined at several planes due to some quite violent past geologic activity. Low but fairly steep hills begin to rise just a couple hundred meters from shore, and a chain of submerged mountains connects the point we originally started from to Desecheo Island.

In the oceanographic sense this is where two separate ocean systems meet, with differing patterns of wind and water currents, salinity, temperature, nutrients and biota. This very complex interaction often results in an offshore current running contrary to the nearshore direction. At times, a strong northerly running current meets the submerged mountains and deeper water on the Atlantic side to form an actual 'standing wall' of water several inches high. Waves striking from either direction tend to 'wrap' around the point, and if they meet another ocean's swells can develop a cross-hatched configuration of whitecaps, and these sorts of interference patterns have seasonal variations as well. This often results in the sand of the beaches and nearshore floor 'migrating' up and down the coast annually, but sometimes in the course of days. This process is by no means well understood, and there is much concern over the fact that within the last decade or so a lot of the sand seems to be leaving the area completely for unknown reasons.

The uniquely complicated interaction of all these factors has encouraged an equally fascinating biological system to form in an extremely small area (the Reserve itself is only a bit larger than a square kilometer), not easily matched for diversity anywhere else in the world.

The sociocultural framework is equally fascinating. At the time of Spanish contact there were at least two permanent settlements of the native Taíno culture in the Rincón area, though their sites have been lost or destroyed without study. Poorly documented sources suggest it was also the site of regularly held winter 'jubilees' or reunions every several years of tribes from the Greater Antilles chain, for uncertain purpose but likely including trade, intermarriage, council and ceremony. More clearly recorded is the fact that these villages attracted some of the earliest Spanish settlements in Puerto Rico, and the island's second sugar mill was constructed in the 1520s somewhere south of Rincón to take advantage of the fertile lowlands, convenient sea access to Santo Domingo, the largest Spanish settlement in the New World at the time, and, of course, slave labor of the indigenous population. Perhaps for this very reason the Rincón area seemed to be the central nexus of native resistance to Spanish oppression, beginning with the deliberate drowning of Diego de Salcedo in 1511 in the Rio Grande de Añasco just south of town (to prove he was not a god), and ending with the complete destruction of the last hostile village a decade later, just to the north. Rincón has thus been no stranger to conflict and the clash of competing cultural values. In spite of this bellicose beginning the majority of the area's history unfolds fairly tranquilly thereafter, as a primarily agricultural community whose major cash crops were sugarcane, rice, plantains, peanuts and, to a much lesser degree, tobacco, and truck farming for local consumption from small, individually owned farms. African slaves never formed much of a population anywhere in this area, and most immigrants came from southern Spain, the Extremadura region, and Corsica (whose most famous scion was the pirate Cofresí). So a history of poverty is noted as a direct importation. Despite the fairly rich fishing grounds close by a significant industry in this respect never developed, most likely due to the lack of secure anchorage and the often challenging local seas. Furniture appears to have been the only significant non-agricultural product. But certainly the Puerto Rican plantation culture was established here early, with a few families owning most of the land and the individual freeholders ("jibaros") working in the large fields ("campos") for money and raising most of their own food on their own small "fincas" which were either bought from or given by the landholding families. This social structure remained in place virtually unchanged well into the twentieth century, and echoes of it are still fairly strong.

The 'American invasion' of Rincón did not really begin until 1968 and the first World Surfing Competition, with thousands of non-Hispanic people suddenly flooding the town. Though they then left after the contest, some would return annually and eventually buy land and reside year round, while the fame of Rincón as a surf destination spread through the sport. Up until the mid 1980s this was a fairly stable situation with only a very small number of new residents each year, but this changed into a wholesale explosion soon after, to the point that now about half of Rincón's residents are non-natives. This very sudden demographic dislocation comes with its own array of associated problems, with which the town and the local environment struggle to come to terms.

Personal Involvement

My own personal involvement with the RM3P began in the usual mythopoetic spacetime dimension of long, long ago, in the manner of all such tales. To put a number to it, 1980. Having decided the previous year to permanently reside in Puerto Rico we (being myself, my wife Judith Anne and our daughter Serena) were in the process of visiting every beach on the island in our search for a place to settle down. Beginning in San Juan we had proceeded in a clockwise manner, investigating every stretch of sand accessible by vehicle or foot, often camping for days at a time in the most appealing areas, and in the fullness of time such leisurely questing brought us to Rincón—which in those days was a very small beach town indeed. Of all the excellent beaches in the area Tres Palmas soon became our favorite, and even after we'd bought land farther up into the hills on the south side of town we would frequently vacation by camping there and exploring the reefs and nearshore waters. I do not seek to exaggerate their beauty, but suffice it to say that in those days you had to wave—literally— all the fish out of your way to get a close look at the coral. Or as Serena put it in the wisdom of her seven years as she surfaced from her first snorkeling expedition, "It's just like swimming in Marine World!" This was certainly one immediate reason for our attraction to this spot, and yet another was its inexplicable sense of familiarity which, for lack of a more exact word, I must describe as its 'vibe.' It slowly dawned on me that this sense of tranquility and resonant timelessness went way beyond any comfortable beach lounging to re-mind (again, literally) me of other sacred spaces that I had been to during my life.

The Tres Palmas beach naturally suggested itself as a venue for the activities of a small group of local residents developed that were interested in studying ceremony, ritual and meditation. This place was perfectly suited to these purposes: an eternal but constantly changing intersection of earth, water and sky, with the addition of a small fire all the elements are present, which is the bare minimum needed for most ritual work or 'natural magic.'

In response to the spiritual teachings of dignitaries from the various schools of holistic thought, local gatherings began to include a prayer/meditation for the beach itself, and several of the regular participants were instrumental in forming the first environmentally activist group on the island that was not specifically focused on industrial pollution. The next ten years showed reasonable progress in the sphere of ecological awareness for the town, with the formation of the island's first recycling program, preservation of the tree-lined road into town during highway expansion, creation of the island's first 'whale watching' regulations and the initiation of Earth Day Fairs that eventually drew thousands of people from all over the island for a weekend of environmental and cultural activities.

The mid to late 1990s proved to be an inauspicious time both for meditation and the environment, here and elsewhere. Economic and social factors led to the disbanding of the ecological group, and Rincón was 'discovered' by the real estate vultures who were pretty blatantly aided by a less-than-honest municipal government which approved any sort of development anywhere, whatever the long term costs to the town as a whole. These factors, among others, also led to a thinning out of the Tres Palmas beach group as people left the island to try to make their living.

There was definitely a millennial end-of-the-world feel to the announcement of plans to build three large projects on the land adjacent to the beach in 2000. We'd already seen the damage to the reef resulting from the unregulated construction of a single McMansion further in the hills, and that September the first developer had bulldozed access roads into the pasture and survey stakes had their ribbons fluttering, like a parody of prayer-sticks. It was a very sad reunion of the few remaining members for the autumn equinox on a chilly, drizzling evening as we coaxed a small fire into life and said our prayers for the earth, sea, and sky. We admitted to ourselves that this would probably be the last ceremony held here, and apologized to the beach for not having done a better job defending it. As a final act of sympathetic magic we each picked up a stick off the sand and held it out, saying (in our personal ways) that we felt helpless in the face of the forces arrayed against this area and really didn't know what to do, and could only hope and pray that as we broke the stick the ambitions of those threatening forces would be broken and their desires would turn to ash, and we threw the pieces into the fire. A man who had been watching then asked me if I really thought this ceremony would do any good at all. I could only shrug and reply that it couldn't hurt, and was way better than doing nothing.

A few days later I was attending an ultimately futile protest gathering at the town hall of homeowners in the Tres Palmas area when this guy rushes up, clutching a bunch of papers. "Who wants to sign a petition to save Tres Palmas?" he asked. I sighed and inquired what issue the petition was based on, knowing full well we'd made no progress using the usual objections. "It's the elkhorn coral on the reef there, it's a federally protected threatened species protected under the Endangered Species Act." With those few words, like a lightning bolt of satori, a whole possible scenario of effective long-term protection flashed into my mind... and yes, it did rather feel like an answer to our prayers. "Lemme sign," I said, thus becoming (as I later found out) the first physical signature of a Rincón resident on the petition, and asked "Who's organizing this?" thus becoming involved with Surfrider.

Enter Surfrider

The Surfrider Foundation, as I soon discovered, is a non-profit environmental organization dedicated to "the protection and enjoyment of the world's waves, oceans and beaches, for all people, through conservation, activism, research and education," with its national office in San Clemente, California. It was founded in 1984 and now has about 35,000 members in 57 American chapters, with international affiliates or chapters in Australia, Brazil, Canada, Europe and Japan, and others currently forming in Central and South America.[1] There was already a chapter established in San Juan who were very helpful in the initial organizing in Rincón, but it soon became apparent that some sort of formative group needed to happen locally to spearhead the necessary petition drive and coordinate the information gathering to support any legislation. We Rincoeños eventually decided it was better to do so under the Surfrider banner rather than try to resurrect the ecology group (with its associated and unresolved issues) since the Foundation was amply demonstrating abilities to organize access to information and funds at the level that would be needed as soon as possible. Monthly meetings began to be held to successfully push for temporary injunctions against further construction on the beach, and a few months later we were ready to begin trying to collect signatures from half the registered voters in town in support of a 'marine protected area' for Tres Palmas. This objective we considered pretty ambitious, given the history of similar efforts in the past and the current economic environment, but a core team of dedicated volunteers (including members of the meditation group) hit the streets with petition blanks.

---

[1] See their website: www.surfrider.org and www.surfrider.org/rincon.

This effort went extremely well, better than we had anticipated, and shortly people were stopping team members and volunteering signatures. Obviously, residents felt very attached to the Tres Palmas area just as it was, and in the surveys we carried out in the next couple of years both residents and tourists consistently ranked Tres Palmas as their favorite beach. This is kind of odd, on the face of things, since the beach has very limited parking space, no nearby amenities such as restaurants or bars or shelter; it is certainly not the widest beach in the area, nor does it have a very sandy bottom, and is often subject to very strong currents or waves which make swimming fairly risky. And yet almost everyone feels it is "a good place." This definitely worked in our favor, and well before our target date of a year we had almost three quarters of the electoral list signed up, and thousands more from nearby towns and over the internet.

With this success the 'Save Tres Palmas' campaign moved from the grassroots to the political sphere and Surfrider de Rincón (as a chapter-in-formation) moved into an educational and coordinating role. Education began with the members of course, and we soon found out how little we knew about marine biology and the associated sciences. Fortunately, Surfrider Foundation has a very active intern program of sponsoring students, whom they happily cycled through Rincón as they pursued their degrees, and so we not only got one-on-one tutoring but also got help with collecting of data and became familiar with scientific methodology. Using this knowledge we set up a program of lower and intermediate grade school presentations on local marine life and began 'family beachwalks' to acquaint residents with the resources in the Tres Palmas area.[2] We also had to educate the municipality itself as to these same resources. In a typically Rincón situation you had a beach town highly dependent on tourism with neither a clear idea of the value of this business, nor of the natural attractions it already had, nor any policy in place to foster either. Surfrider had to sponsor our own socioeconomic survey (again, using interns provided by the Foundation) to prove to the town council that tourism generated about half of the town's economic activity rather than about half that amount the council was estimating. There was also the need to inform departments such as the Department of Public Works of the dangers of continuing to use outmoded standards when it came to bulldozing areas near the beaches, garbage collection scheduling, and related activities. This has turned out to be a very fruitful partnership and lately has been supporting us when we have problems with the town council, which may also be another first for the island. Surfrider de

---

[2] This program is fairly autonomous now, but still volunteer-driven.

Rincón has also developed some very good working relationships with most of the other governmental agencies involved in forming what would become the Marine Reserve, which comes in handy for other occasions, such as planting trees for erosion control or logistical support during beach cleanups, not to mention providing expert testimony during legal actions against irresponsible development. Having a 'stable' of scientific experts in the university system has also proven very valuable, and will no doubt prove even more so in the longer term monitoring of the Reserve area.

It would only be honest to mention some drawbacks of the Surfrider approach to environmental activism. The Foundation itself has a very 'corporate' structure compared to the much more laid-back attitude in Rincón, which raises questions such as 'why do we have to have a monthly meeting when there's nothing of substance to discuss?', or 'why should we formally organize as a chapter with a board of directors etc.?' and the minor matter of filing receipts and keeping records straight. So this turns a lot of prospective members off, though the Foundation itself continues to cut us a lot of slack in these regards. More distressing to potential members is the fact that, under the Surfrider charter, if a local grassroots group organizes and raises a minimal amount of money to challenge an environmental threat anywhere near the coast then we must do our best to help them, even if the chances of success are very slim. Plenty of time, energy and money are thus spent in actions that we're pretty sure are going to be useless, and that we then duly lose. This is pretty hard to justify to your average working-class person, and so we have not really penetrated the 30-45 year age group. And of course being called Surfrider implies you have to be a surfer to join, and environmental activism still remains tainted with the concept of being a 'gringo thing.' These are the questions and problems I tend to encounter on the street level, as well as people being upset that we don't function as an 'environmental 911' and deal with their problems, instead of telling them where and how to file their complaints. Once the Marine Reserve becomes established as a functioning entity our local group will have to find other ways of continuing to encourage environmental protection, whether under the Surfrider banner or not.

Reserva Marina Tres Palmas: A Retrospective

Naturally, the form of the Reserva Marina Tres Palmas is a result of the confluence of these many factors, as well as a conscious attempt to address some of the more significant issues arising from them. The primary goal is to conserve natural resources, but it is well understood that without an awareness of the pressures bearing on this area no such conservation will ultimately be possible. In the broadest sense the RM3P is a forum where the scientific, political, economic, civic and environmental organizations find a common voice. In a narrower sense, it is a place where the various social groups and communities of a town that are often divided because of their respective interests learn to work together for the common good. But in the most importance sense, it is an area where, however briefly entered, the human and non-human worlds can acknowledge the most fundamental of truths—the mutuality of their own existence.

The RM3P organization and the Surfider de Rincón association have been linked since their conception, as the local group formed initially to foster the creation of the Reserve. The events over the course of the last six years remind me, as I write this now, of nothing less than the process of cell division and specialization as once tightly interlinked chains of activity and information begin to unravel themselves and separate, and each begin to develop specific organs and functions as they take on independent existences. This version of mitosis is almost complete although, as in every natural system, they will likely remain interlinked in some form of symbiotic relationship.

Nobody, least of all me, had much of an idea of what we were getting into when the project began. Parenting is like that. We (both the people gathering signatures on the original petition and the people signing it) had a pretty clear vision of what we wanted for the Tres Palmas area but were extremely ignorant of how to fit that into the legal definition of a 'marine protected area.' On the other hand, we (as the people willing and able to do the actual work) had some fairly clear federal guidelines, some rather less clear outlines from the Dept. of Natural Resources, and only a vague idea of how to make them function in such a particular (or peculiar) place. Given the realities of Rincón it was felt by both parties that the option of co-management was the best way to unite these two, often contradictory, views into a sustainable degree of protection for what was to become the RM3P.[3]

The challenges to be faced were apparent from the start of the petition drive. By the book, any sort of 'marine protected area' designation

---

[3] This approach has only been used once in Puerto Rico in the case of Casa Pueblo in the town of Adjuntas, which is a land preserve administered by the Department of Natural Resources but run as coffee producing co-op by the town, as is also a 'butterfly garden' to promote tourism and species conservation.

severely limits human activity and carries a whole schedule of possible fines and penalties. As Rincoeños we knew the area already saw a lot of activity; since most of it was not damaging to the ecology, we were unwilling to further give up access to those recreational or commercial opportunities (which were already being limited by rampant condo development). As Surfrider members, we had the ambition not only to promote eco-tourism and environmental awareness but to demonstrate to the town that preserving and correctly managing this valuable resource would be of direct economic benefit, so that protecting it would become a matter of encouragement rather than enforcement. The long term, and very hopeful, goal would be to have town authorities and residents initiating other conservation efforts, and providing a role model for other municipalities in this regard. Further complicating factors were its urgency (from immanent construction within the area to be protected), the language/culture divide, the inherent Puerto Rican mistrust of governmental agencies (often justified), the economic/social schism (the rich as 'them,' who'll do what they want anyway), the constant pressure of party politics in the background, and the fact that by its very name Surfrider was assumed to be a bunch of gringo surfers whom you wouldn't take seriously.

The immediate success of the petition drive showed that this effort had a lot of popular support and was going to become an issue of consequence on the political agenda, so we quickly had to move into defining the project. We began with a standard model, delineating a core region containing the most endangered species (the elkhorn coral) that would be established as a no-take zone for fishing and closely monitored to prevent damaging activities (like anchoring and garbage dumping) surrounded by a larger region with only limited fishing and specific anchorage sites, and that whole area enclosed by a more loosely monitored region of allowed seasonal fishing and appropriately managed beachfront construction. This entire protected area was envisioned extending north of the municipal marina area completely around the point, for a total distance of about four kilometers. This plan met with the approval of most small fishermen (which I define as those using outboard engines) since they were the group most aware of the need for conservation efforts because of declining takes. They were also the most helpful in showing us where the usual fishing grounds were and coral structures they thought needed protecting, as well as explaining that the area usually didn't contain much in the way of food species anyway, which tend to school in deeper water. On the other hand there was very vocal opposition by many of the bigger operators, sports fishermen and tropical fish collectors, who objected to limits being placed on their access or their catch, as well as behind-the-scene opposition by developers. When we calculated the difficulty of effectively monitoring such a large area, and the much longer time it would take to implement any sort of protection for the elkhorn coral faced with constant objections, we reluctantly abandoned this vision and entered into a series of compromise negotiations. After several months an area only slightly larger than the core region was deemed acceptable by all parties, and well over half of the registered voters in Rincón had signed the petition, and even more were collected from nearby towns and through the internet. With these goals met, the initiative of forming what seems to be the world's smallest marine reserve was passed to the political process.

During this time the group was in the process of becoming Surfrider de Rincón, and the Surfrider Foundation was being very generous in providing needed funds, and furnishing organizational expertise as well as putting us in touch with people with more specialized skills and training regarding what a marine reserve would entail. Monthly meetings began to be held to keep everyone informed of the progress and the ponderous workload, and soon the meetings were held in the common room of the local senior citizens' center (thanks to the goodwill of the mayor's office) so that they could be open to the public. And as in any volunteer-driven organization a tiered structure of commitment developed, with a wide base of members who occasionally attend meetings or activities, a narrower level of those who regularly attend or volunteer for things they are interested in, and the inevitable core group who are willing to do whatever is needed. Native Spanish speakers seem to form about half the group at all levels and meetings are most often bilingual. Consensus is the governing policy, though members have voted a few times on strategic issues, for example consistently voting yearly against organizing as a chartered chapter with a board of directors (which is felt would only add to the workload of four people in the core group) or, when the San Juan Surfrider chapter closed, of becoming Surfrider de Puerto Rico and extending our field of operation to the entire island.

Once the Reserve proposal was submitted to the Puerto Rican congress and passed more into the hands of governmental and regulatory agencies, our local group began to diversify, with smaller groups performing the usual non-profit activities of running information tables at surf contests (or other such events), beach clean-ups and tree planting campaigns. More autonomous groups focused on environmental campaigns in the local schools, hosted eco-themed art projects in the area, or served as local guides for interns or other experts that the Surfrider Foundation sent down to Rincón to assist our efforts. So rather than thinking of Surfrider de Rincón as an organization it would be much more accurate to say it's a focus for a wide variety of continually changing special-interest groups with an environmental emphasis. The truth is, Rincón is not a very good place to try out hierarchical schemata. The native residents have a built-in mistrust of such structures unless provided by the church, school or state, and so an NGO such as Surfrider is unfamiliar territory (i.e. a gringo thing). The nature of Rincón is such that long-time non-native residents (such as myself) are generally not 'team players' in any sense, with little patience for meetings and so forth. And so it is that more recently arrived residents make up most of this half of the group, tending to be older, retired or more affluent or educated, making us a very disparate entity indeed. I'm continually surprised at how effective we have been, given the constantly changing membership, diverging interests, and shifting of roles.

Governor Sila Calderón's approval of the bill takes us to the end of the process which resulted in the legal existence of the Tres Palmas Marine Reserve. The interesting thing to note at this point is that the phrase 'marine reserve' does not have a formal, exact definition while we do have a formally exact delineation of its boundaries. So when I mention a management plan for the Reserve I must emphasize that this is very much an act of creation "ex nihilo" that is constantly redefining not only ways and means but also what it is talking about under the rubric of a marine reserve in the first place. Approaching the project, as I do, from a Buddhist viewpoint, I have found this to be a fascinating example of the 'inter-dependent co-creation' process that results in the existence of all things in this universe. This one just leaves a better paper trail, which will certainly have its own ramifications. For instance, the only other des-ignated 'marine protected area' in Puerto Rico is the submarine park off the island of Culebra, and it has been waiting to have a management plan implemented for 8 or 9 years now. It is quite likely that the one being created for RM3P will be used as a blueprint for this case. And in the other direction, we have learned some lessons from the Culebra project, principally in the benefit of keeping the working teams small. The steering committee in Culebra consists of more than a hundred people—no doubt accounting for their very slow progress—while the committee forming the management plan for RM3P is about a dozen.

Figure 2: Reserva Marina Tres Palmas – View facing west.

The Reserve itself has entered into a very similar phase with the management plan process. Once the RM3P was passed into law, there was only a very general outline provided by the Department of Natural Resources (DNR) as to what a marine reserve consists of, and how co-management works. The group in charge of drawing up the detailed description of how this will actually be implemented in Rincón has a fluctuating membership of experts added to the core group as necessary. Thus how the Reserve is defined constantly evolves under the influence of input of concerned agencies, private citizens, community groups and the town itself. One aspect of this redefinition deals with the Reserve's buffer zone, which is federally mandated to a mere 100-meter strip along its borders. But along with being so small, the Reserve is unique among similar Caribbean marine preserves because the hills extend so close to the beach with no intervening wetlands, and thus watershed protection of this drainage area becomes critically important. It may very well be that the development interests pressing for the most limited Reserve will ultimately lose access to a much larger area as a result, since the DNR seems sincere in their desire to impose the strictest erosion control measures for the watershed.

Another complicating factor in this phase of the RM3P formation is the issue of co-management. The easiest way to end up with a management plan would have been to simply allow the DNR to write it according to their quite restrictive guidelines, which would prohibit virtually all human activities in the area. This was not really a viable option for us, and directly contrary to the guiding philosophy with which people were approached for the petition signatures, since it was community members who were out in the streets collecting them. There was never any sense that the Reserve would be a "taking away" from the town, but rather a preserving (and hopeful embellishment) of an extremely valuable resource that was already threatened. This cooperative spirit of working towards a win/win situation had already been amply demonstrated during the first phase by a willingness of the various groups of participants to compromise on contested issues (including the very size of the Reserve) and by keeping as many as possible of the meetings open to the public and distributing pamphlets detailing the progress of negotiations. Although the DNR would be the regulatory agency ultimately responsible for the Reserve, it was determined that carrying this cooperative attitude into the management planning phase would be the best, if not only, way to ensure the success of the primary goal of conservation. If the town of Rincón as a whole was not completely supportive of this effort, it would fail—and the surest way to do that would be to make the community feel left out of the decision-making process.

This has led to further new roles for our local group, which has tended to segment as well. Issues of shoreline erosion, seawall construction, pollution and beach access have come up, along with the perennial problem of beachfront building. The group has been co-plaintiffs in several lawsuits, has given depositions in front of Senate investigating committees, and has done the necessary groundwork for the town to do its own planning and zoning, all with varying degrees of success. More importantly, the frustration level has increased as a consequence of all this. If, on one hand, you are working closely with the Parks and Preserves department of the DNR to conform to their rules, and on the other hand you are actively suing the permitting department for not having done their job properly, many otherwise enthusiastic volunteers don't bother to get involved. During the more lengthy lawsuits, even the most committed pro bono lawyers must get back to paying their bills and we end up doing our own paralegal work, with very few people wanting to get involved. While we have good turnouts for most physical activities, we are definitely having problems generating the needed amounts of administrative work

LIVERPOOL JOHN MOORES UNIVERSITY
LEARNING SERVICES

without totally exhausting the core group, and no clear strategy has yet developed in this regard.

In the next couple of months the penultimate version of the management plan will be drawn up and submitted to the Planning Board for verification. Following that approval a series of public hearings will be held to collect comments from any groups or individuals who have not yet made them through the internet or at the Surfrider general meetings. If necessary, a final revision will be made and then submitted to the various regulatory agencies for approval and confirmation. With luck this will bring a complete and comprehensive management plan to RM3P more or less on time and within budget.

It is reasonably safe to assume that once the management plan for the Reserve is approved and implemented it will force another modification of the way Surfrider de Rincón operates. The plan allows for future expansion of the protected area as various target goals are met, and modification of the operational flowchart to cover new responsibilities, and so, it is hoped, the Reserve itself will continue to evolve. The local group will have to evolve with it, taking roles in monitoring and enforcing the preservation of the area, collecting further data, and conducting a more comprehensive educational campaign to inform residents and tourists of the hows and whys of conservation. It is likely that more autonomous teams will emerge and handle these particular tasks, while the group as a whole goes on to deal with other pressing local issues such as seawall construction, beach access and pollution. The next few years promise to be very interesting ones for all entities involved.

This, of course, is where the holographic simile shows its aptness. From whatever viewpoint you choose to approach the formation of the RM3P you find a totality somehow enclosed, and focusing on the smallest detail only blurs the larger picture. And the picture is quite large. The geophysical boundaries—an arbitrary administrative area—reflect the entire history of this part of the coastline and project into the future, carrying with them all the forces shaping the island's current and potential well-being as well as illuminating global processes and challenges while being affected by them at the same time. A holographic cellular entity, if you will. Or a very ancient theme restated in modern terms. Or simply, the most current redefinition of humanity's eternal relationship with the sea.

Appendix: Timeline[4]

September 2000 - Puerto Rico was visited by a coalition group organized by the non-profit Surfers Environmental Alliance to study the island's "environmental hotspots." The threat to endangered elkhorn coral off *Tres Palmas* beach was identified and a "call to action" was then issued. Chad Nelson, the environmental director of Surfrider Foundation, begins on-site organizing; Azur Moulart of Environmental Defense begins the legal work at the commonwealth and federal levels.

December 2000 - Preliminary injunctions against any further construction in the Tres Palmas area was issued, pending further study of the reef's vulnerability to such activities.

October 2001 - Community organizing begins. A local chapter, Surfrider de Rincón, is instituted by Surfrider National to serve as one of the foci of the petition drive to get some form of legally effective conservation under the guidelines of a 'marine protected area.'

March 8, 2002 - The Puerto Rican Planning Board makes its first "vista ocular" or site inspection of the Tres Palmas area, in response to the petition drive.

April 12, 2002 - Puerto Rican Planning Board denies Villa Ikaria construction permits. Of the three projects planned for the land adjoining the Tres Palmas beach Villa Akaria was the one closest to being able to begin building.

October 10, 2002 - La Coalición Pro Calidad de Vida en Rincón, Surfrider Foundation and Environmental Defense were given an achievement award by the U. S. Coral Reef Task Force in recognition of the group's "... outstanding leadership and commitment in protecting Puerto Rico's valuable coral reefs by promoting designation of a Natural Reserve in Rincón."

November 6, 2002 - A bill was introduced into the Puerto Rican legislature to establish a Tres Palmas Marine Reserve.

---

[4] This is a very brief and highly edited timeline that follows the process of creating the Reserva Marina Tres Palmas, based mostly on activities that I attended, prepared for, or in which I had some degree of participation. For the full treatment you will need to contact: salvatrespalmas@yahoo.com, or www.surfrider.org/rincón.

December 2002 - March 2003 - A series of public hearings is held at the Capitol in San Juan. At these hearings the need for, and support of, a Marine Reserve was presented by many community, scientific and regulatory agencies and groups. Opposing opinions were also voiced by some commercial fishing interests, but by far, most of the presentations were supportive.

March 1, 2003 - A second "vista ocular" of the Tres Palmas area by the Puerto Rican Planning Board results in new (smaller) coordinates for the planned Reserve.

September 14, 2003 - The Puerto Rican House of Representatives unanimously approves the bill that designates the Tres Palmas Marine Protected Area.

January 8, 2004 - Both Houses sign the bill into effect, now known as Law 17, the Law of the RM3P in Rincón.

January 12, 2004 - Governor Sila Calderón approves the bill and signs it into law, also approving a budget of $100,000 for the creation, implementation and administration of a management plan for the Reserve.

March 1, 2005 - A community development workshop is held in Rincón to promote public participation in the various processes that will shape the town's future, including the formation of RM3P.

August 3, 2005 - The first meeting of the steering committee for the management plan of RM3P. The committee consists of a representative from: the DNR (who also represents other concerned agencies such as the Dept. of Fisheries, Corps of Engineers etc.); the Dept. of Marine Sciences, University of Puerto Rico; the municipality of Rincón; the Tourism Association of Rincón; the Captains Association of Rincón; and Surfrider de Rincón.

August 4, 2005 - The first of the interpretive signs go up at Tres Palmas beach, with pictures of the rare or endangered marine life and a listing of prohibited and permitted activities. (Four more signs are installed at other public access sites in the next few weeks by Surfrider and Rincón's Dept. of Public Works).

October 4, 2005 - The second meeting of the steering committee, when the composition of a Technical Advisory Group (TAG) is determined. This group will provide scientific, economic and sociocultural data, and include representatives from the National Atmospheric and Oceanographic

Administration, Dept. of Fisheries, the local fishermen's association and the municipality.

January 25, 2006 - The TAG meets with the steering committee to provided preliminary input and help determine what further data is needed

April 28, 2006 - Steering committee meets to incorporate the latest TAG reports

December 10, 2006 - The final TAG reports are given, and input gathered from various citizen's groups and community organizations is presented to the steering committee.

February 1, 2007 - Steering committee meets to chart out the final phases of the management plan. An overview is given at the Surfrider general meeting in Rincón, and an appeal made to get in touch with any local community groups who have not yet been contacted for their input, so this phase can be closed.

June 2007 - Fundación Surfrider (as the Rincón group is now known) aquires copies of the proposed Rincón Bike and Pedestrian Path construction documents. Among the many design flaws of the proposal, where the 'path' (actually a 14 foot wide paved surface built on a raised road bed) parallels the beach of the Marine Reserve it completely changes the drainage pattern of the area. In some places it is to be built on gabion reinforced retaining walls actually on the beach itself, and completely blocks public access at the principal entrance to Tres Palmas Beach. Needless to say, Surfrider initiates a wave of public opposition to the proposal as planned.

June-August 2007 - A comprehensive debris mapping and removal project is carried out on the RM3P sea floor. Each piece of garbage is registered by its GPS coordinates and, if possible, removed by divers or boat winch, and a 'trash map' is created to define areas where garbage tends to accumulate. The greatest volume of removed objects was automotive tires (251 in total); the most common garbage was plastic and aluminum cans.

Late August 2007 - SECORE, an international multi-institution cooperative program to preserve and propagate coral species, comes to the RM3P to collect elkhorn larvae during the spawning season. See "Spawning for a better life," *Science* 318 (Dec. 14 2007): 1712-1717.

October 8, 2007 - Fundación Surfrider resumes weekly testing of seawater at the most popular recreational beaches in the local area, using enterococcus bacteria as the indicator species of fecal contamination. This makes Rincón the first, and only, town on the island to do its own water quality testing. Since fecal bacteria contamination has been associated with white banding and other coral disease (to say nothing of public health issues) the beaches of the Marine Reserve get special attention, with Judith Anne and Steve Tamar usually doing the sampling and testing for this area. A history of the test results can be seen at: http://www.surfrider.org/bwtf/ BWTFoutput.asp

October 17-19, 2007 - The Puerto Rican DNR and NOAA install 3 permanent study sites in the RM3P, and precisely counted and measured coral colonies and size in a 150 square meter area for each marked site. Three other reef systems in other locations around the island are also part of this permanent monitoring study.

January 18, 2008 - RM3P steering committee meets to review final changes to the management plan.

April 12, 2008 - Version 8 of the RM3P management plan sent to TAG for final comments. The plan is to be presented to the DNR and Planning Board in June 2008.

March 19-22, 2008 - The 'Spring Break Swell' where the north and west coasts of the island experience unusually large waves of about 25 feet, causing much coastal erosion and damage to the reefs. Since the permanent study sites had already been mapped and measured in the Marine Reserve an accurate assessment of the damage done by this swell was possible, showing the RM3P elkhorn coral suffered the least of the four reefs undergoing long term monitoring. Survival and recovery rates of the broken coral fragments will be precisely measured as well.

April 20, 2008 - The Earth Day fair returns to Rincón, organized primarily by Judith Anne, Steve Tamar, and a member of the original meditation group. With very little promotion the one day event attracts 1000 visitors, and is a great success. Fundación Surfrider has its best outreach effort ever, as far as fundraising, new memberships, and information disseminating are concerned, with our work on the RM3P and the water testing program getting the most public approval and support.

April 20, 2008 - The Earth Day fair also marked the web publication of a comprehensive cataloging of all the marine life species to be found in the RM3P. This was a volunteer task undertaken by Wessley Merten, a marine biology graduate student of the Dept. of Marine Sciences UPR-Mayagüez, who took all the photographs, compiled the data and created the website—which is rapidly becoming the favorite teaching tool of anyone interested in the Reserve. Check it out at www.surfrider.org/ rincon/mlg

June-August 2008 - The second debris removal project at RM3P, where the primary focus will be tabulating and removing trash wrapped around the corals during the March swell, and expanding the 'trash map' to cover adjacent reef systems.

CONTRIBUTORS

Jeffner Allen is Professor of Philosophy, Interpretation, and Culture, of Philosophy, and of Women's Studies at SUNY Binghamton. She is the author of *r e v e r b e r a t i o n s across the shimmering CASCADAS*, of *SINUOSITIES: Lesbian Poetic Politics*, and of *Lesbian Philosophy: Explorations*, editor of *Lesbian Philosophies and Cultures*, and of *The Thinking Muse: Contemporary Feminist Thought*. At present, she is working on *Dear Voluptuous: Between Coral Reefs*, a book of experimental and creative writing and reflection on coral reef communities.

Pablo Bartholomew is an internationally acclaimed Indian photographer. Winning World Press awards for "Morphine Addicts in India" (Photo of the Year 1975) and "Bhopal Gas Tragedy" (Picture of the Year 1985), his work has been widely exhibited in museums and Photo Festivals, most recent shows including "Outside In: A Tale of 3 Cities" (Delhi, Mumbai and New York), Noorderlicht Photo Festival (Netherlands), ChobiMela (Bangladesh), Angkor Photo Festival (Cambodia), Month of Photography (Japan), Recontres d'Arles Photography Festival (France). His work has been published in magazines like *Newsweek*, *Time*, *National Geographic* and *Geo*, and has included features such as "They Stopped the Sea" (July 1987 *National Geographic*), "Guerre au Deluge" (October 1998 *Geo* France), and "Chennai: Water Story" (August 2006 *Geo* France).

Nandita Batra was born by the sea in Bombay but moved inland for her education at the University of Delhi and the University of Rochester (New York). She returned to live by the sea in Puerto Rico, and is Professor of English at the University of Puerto Rico-Mayagüez, where she is also editor of *Atenea*, the University's journal of humanities and social sciences. Her main areas of interest and publication have been in nineteenth-century British literature, especially in Anthrozoological Studies. She has co-edited two books with Vartan Messier: *Transgression and Taboo* (2005) and *Narrating the Past* (2007).

Jessica J. Behm graduated from Cornell University with a BFA in Neo-Tropical Biology and Dance, and worked in Brazil as a biologist over a span of four years. She holds a Masters from New York University in Interactive Telecommunications (ITP) and was on the faculty at NYU in the writing department from 2001-2005. She currently works as an interactive engineer in New York City. Her work explores the embodied intersections of wireless, virtual, and haptic-kinetic technologies in performance and installation, and has been shown in the United States, Europe, South America, and Australia.

Graham Benton received his Ph.D. from Rutgers University, The State University of New Jersey, and is an assistant professor in the Department of Global and Maritime Studies at the California State University, Maritime. His research interests include twentieth-century American literature, the cultures of globalization, and literature and cinema of the sea. Recently he has published on Thomas Pynchon, filmic adaptations of *Mutiny on the Bounty*, and American literary representations of post-soviet Eastern Europe. Prof. Benton has also written widely on issues pertaining to maritime education and training.

Ian Copestake lives and works in Frankfurt. He is editor of *American Postmodernity: Essays on the Recent Fiction of Thomas Pynchon* (2003), *Rigor of Beauty: Essays in Commemoration of William Carlos Williams* (2004), and *The Legacy of William Carlos Williams: Points of Contact* (2007). In 2008 he will assume the Presidency of the William Carlos Williams Society.

Kathryn Ferguson is an ARC Postdoctoral Fellow at the ARC Centre of Excellence for Coral Reef Studies, at James Cook University in Australia. Her research brings into play an unusually wide range of critical theories, intellectual models, and disciplinary approaches to investigate how places come to be known and narrativised in specific and oft-times contradictory ways. Refusing the false dichotomies of science/society and nature/culture, her scholarship has examined an eclectic set of controversial sites. Recently, she has come to question the changing place of the Great Barrier Reef in the Australian national landscape, and the constitution of the Reef as a national icon.

Mary Beth Gallagher is currently a Ph.D. student at Morgan State University in Baltimore, Maryland, having completed her course work, she has entered the dissertation phase of the degree, her topic being Hemingway's use of luck in his major works. She began her academic career when she completed her Master's degree at Hofstra

University in Long Island, New York. Before this, Ms. Gallagher taught grammar school and high school English and Literature at Colegio Villa Caritas in Lima, Peru for two years. Her area of specialty is Modern American writers, but her research interests include gender studies and Latin American writers. Ms. Gallagher is currently teaching at her alma mater, Immaculata University outside Philadelphia.

Sean P. Griffin received his Ph.D. in Biological Oceanography from the University of Puerto Rico. Currently, he is working for Lighthouse Technical Consultants, Inc. His work involves damage assessments, reef restoration and monitoring following ship groundings and oil spills. His research experience has covered a variety of areas in coral biology including pathology, bleaching, biomarkers, spawning, thermotolerance, and monitoring programs as well as other areas of ecology. He is an avid surfer by avocation.

Peggy Hinaekian is an Armenian/American artist born in Egypt. Her work is present in numerous public and private collections and has been exhibited worldwide. It is from Egypt that her two favorite colors emanate: the orange of the Sinai desert and the turquoise blue of the Mediterranean Sea. Her life path has taken her from Egypt to Canada, to New York, and then to Switzerland. In her paintings, colors and forms are guided by her emotions as she progresses. She is represented in the U.S. by Etra Fine Art Gallery in Miami. More samples of her work can be seen at www.peggyhinaekian.artspan.com

Tom Leskiw is a hydrologic/biologic technician for Six Rivers National Forest and an independent scholar and writer. He co-authored "A Study of Plant Materials Suitable for the Rehabilitation of Landslides and Riparian Areas in the Trinity River Watershed, California" and "A Guide to Birding in and Around Arcata [California]." His essays have appeared in *Birding*, *NILAS, Watershed*, *Pilgrimage*, and on-line at www.terrain.org, www.watershedjournal.org, www.lanternbooks.com, and elsewhere. A partial archive of his monthly column in the local Audubon chapter newsletter is available at www.RRAS.org. His book reviews appear at H-NET www.h-net.msu.edu/reviews.

Karen Lentz Madison is Assistant Professor of Writing and Associate Director of the Writing Center at Loyola College in Maryland in Baltimore. Her expertise is the nineteenth-century novel, and her scholarly interests are cross cultural and transatlantic. She is currently preparing a scholarly edition of Edward Everett Hale's *The Man without a Country* with Robert D. Madison.

Robert D. Madison is Professor of English at the U.S. Naval Academy in Annapolis, Maryland. He is a Textual Editor of *The Writings of James Fenimore Cooper* and an Editorial Associate of The Northwestern-Newberry edition of *The Writings of Herman Melville*. He has edited many works of land- and sea-literature and is currently preparing a scholarly edition of Edward Everett Hale's *The Man without a Country* with Karen Lentz Madison.

Vartan P. Messier, an ardent surfer, is a Doctoral candidate in Comparative Literature at the University of California at Riverside. His research focuses on the critical discourses on modernity, modernism, and postmodernism in literature and the visual arts. In addition to having co-edited *Transgression and Taboo* (2005) and *Narrating the Past* (2007) with Nandita Batra, he has also recently published articles on cinematic adaptation and intertextuality, consumerism and globalization, and the transgressive properties of the gothic novel.

Michael Nemeth began working in Marine Sciences during his Master's degree in Biological Oceanography at the Department of Marine Sciences, University of Puerto Rico. He was later employed by the Puerto Rico Department of Natural and Environmental Resources to conduct coral reef monitoring. He is currently working on a Doctoral Degree on Reef Fish Ecology at the University of Puerto Rico. His research interests include the spatial ecology of reef fish and the use of marine fishery reserves for conservation.

Mark P. Ott teaches at Deerfield Academy in Massachusetts. He is the author of *Ernest Hemingway and the Gulf Stream: A Contextual Biography* (Kent State University Press, 2007). Ott has presented academic papers at international Hemingway conferences in Spain, Cuba, Oak Park, Bimini, Italy, and Key West, and his scholarship has been published in The Hemingway Review. He has been awarded grants from The Ernest Hemingway Society, The Ernest Hemingway Collection at the John F. Kennedy Library, and the Arts and Sciences Advisory Council of the University of Hawaii-Manoa. He lives in Deerfield and Kailua, Hawaii.

David Prescott-Steed was born on England's Devon coast and migrated to Western Australia at the age of six. Having exhibited artwork since 1993, David continues to pursue a creative praxis and, in 2006, completed his PhD on representations of the abyss. He currently lectures in Cultural History and Theory in the Faculty of Education and Arts at Edith Cowan University and also works within the Faculty of Architecture, Landscape, and Visual Arts at the University of Western Australia. His research interests include deep-sea imagery and concepts, historical representations of the unknown, and the role of indeterminacy in everyday thinking.

Bruce Robinson is a coordinator within the policy unit of the Office of Teaching Initiatives of New York's State Education Department. But he has discussed various aspects of the works of Marcel Pagnol both in the U.S. and in Fiji. A graduate of Kenyon College and the Johns Hopkins University, his poems have appeared in journals in the U.S. and Australia. He feels at sea, but he feels at home at sea.

Steve Tamar moved to the beach town of Rincón, Puerto Rico from Florida 30 years ago. He has been an ecological activist for just as long, with a particular focus on beach activism. His special project is the creation of the Reserva Marina Tres Palmas as an educational, scientific and economic resource for his home town.

Maeve Tynan is an Assistant Lecturer in Mary Immaculate College, University of Limerick, Ireland. Her research interests are Caribbean literature (particularly Anglophone Caribbean poetry), creolization, adaptation and black British writing. She has published articles on the poetry of Derek Walcott and the novels of Zadie Smith and is currently working on a book to be entitled *Encircling Reversible Worlds: Derek Walcott's Voyages of Homecoming*.

INDEX